W9-BCE-871

THAILAND AND THE UNITED STATES

By FRANK C. DARLING

PUBLIC AFFAIRS PRESS, WASHINGTON, D. C.

TO MY WIFE ANN

419 New Jersey Avenue, S.E., Washington 3, D.C.

Printed in the United States of America
Library of Congress Catalog Card No. 65-16717

INTRODUCTION

In foreign policy, many propositions which we have come to consider as dogma—that is, as being in the nature of things—are nothing more than the perpetuation of historic accidents or pragmatic arrangements, and we consider them as immutable only because we have forgotten their accidental or pragmatic origins. Thus in 1914 Germany regarded its alliance with Austria-Hungary as the unquestionable foundation of its foreign policy. This in turn led to the unqualified support of the Austrian-Hungarian policies towards Serbia, in which the First World War originated. Yet when Bismarck concluded that alliance in 1879, he did so for strictly pragmatic reasons, and years later he looked back upon the alliance with unrelieved skepticism when he remarked that he thought he had made an alliance with the powerful Emporer of Austria while in actuality he had made it with the Hungarian parliament.

Of this general rule of accidental or pragmatic innovations being erected into a dogma to provide a seemingly immutable rule for conduct, the foreign policy of the United States presents two outstanding examples: the dogma of unqualified isolationism and the dogma of unqualified intervention. Both isolationist and interventionist policies were born of certain pragmatic needs of the hour, and continuous usage tends to make us forget their pragmatic origins. Scholarship, then, must perform the function of a collective memory. It must remind statesmen and public of the historic roots of contemporary propositions and alignments. By doing this, it serves not only historic truth but also the political interests of the nation.

It is the great merit of this book that it performs this function for the relations between Thailand and the United States. The question which concerns this book is not primarily whether or not the contemporary relations between the United States and Thailand serve American interests, but what the true nature of these relations is. Only after this question has been answered can one proceed to answering the practical question as to whether contemporary policies are sound and, if not, what policies should take their place.

This book traces the history of American-Thai relations to their beginnings in the early nineteenth century. The main bulk of the book, however, naturally deals with the period since the end of the Second World War. The value of its analysis is greatly enhanced by the author's intimate knowledge of Thailand and of the personalities, both Thai and American, which have shaped the relations between the two countries. But its special value lies in the combination of historic research with political analysis, oriented toward the foreign policies of the United States.

HANS J. MORGENTHAU

Center for the Study of American Foreign and Military Policy, University of Chicago.

FOREWORD

Thailand (Siam) has long aroused interest in the United States. From the early nineteenth century Americans have viewed this small Buddhist kingdom as a fertile field for missionary activity, a source of lucrative trade, and a valiant defender of national self-determination during the era of aggressive European colonialism in Asia. Since World War II Thailand has become increasingly important to the United States as an ally in the defense of Southeast Asia from Communist aggression.

During the past few decades the Thai government and people have attempted to adjust their foreign and domestic policies to protect their national interest and advance the economic and social progress of their country. They have sought to alter their political system to cope with changing times and circumstances. These efforts have met with successes and failures. They have received both praise and criticism at home and abroad.

Many recent studies of Thailand and other underdeveloped countries have been oriented toward the indigenous sociology, psychology, cosmology, ecology, and culture in attempting to assess the process of political modernization. While some of these works have contributed to an understanding of the complex social forces in the transitional nations, few studies have endeavored to analyze the important external influences acting on these emerging political systems. Even fewer books have tried to appraise the impact of the foreign aid programs which have been established in these countries since World War II.

This study is based on the premise that the evolution of the Thai political system since 1945 has been influenced in some degree by international forces acting and reacting on the country, especially the impact exerted by American foreign policy and American foreign aid. The primary purpose of this book is to assess the interaction of American foreign policy on the domestic politics of Thailand during this period. It is hoped that this work will contribute to a better understanding of the effect of American foreign policy on the political affairs of small underdeveloped countries such as Thailand and to a more effective use of American foreign aid.

The study is based on extensive research in pertinent literature, first-hand interviews, and personal experience. I lived in Thailand for three years (1953-1956) and traveled in other countries in Southeast Asia. Some of my information was obtained while I served as a lecturer in the Faculty of Political Science at Chulalongkorn University in Bangkok. I also benefitted by a limited but usually adequate facility with the Thai language. From 1957 until 1960 I worked as a research assistant for the United States government in Washington, D.C. where I had the opportunity to observe from the "inside" some aspects of the process of making American foreign policy. During part of this time I conducted research on Thailand and other Asian countries.

I make no claim that this book is a definitive study of a topic as complex as American foreign policy in Southeast Asia and the political development of Thailand. Much more research is required on the continuing foreign impact on the political systems in the non-Western world. Yet I sincerely believe that this study is a step in the right direction in the difficult task of assessing the modernization of the underdeveloped nations.

The use of the terms "Thailand" and "Siam" to denote the country and "Thai" and "Siamese" to describe the people considered in this work may be somewhat puzzling to the reader unfamiliar with the background of this unique country. Actually the Thai people have always called themselves the "Thai" and their country "Muang Thai" or "Land of the Thai." The terms "Siam" and "Siamese" have been used during recent Thai history largely by foreigners. After 1939 when the name of the country was first officially changed to Thailand, foreign spokesmen have increasingly used the terms "Thai" and "Thailand," although many writers, especially British writers, still adhere to the traditional terms "Siam" and "Siamese." Thoughout this book the terms "Thai" and "Siamese" will refer to the same ethnic stock of people and the names "Thailand" and "Siam" will allude to the same geographical and political entity. When references are made to the Thai-speaking people living outside the present borders of Thailand they will be specifically described.

I would like to express my appreciation to the persons who have assisted me in this study. Professor Hans J. Morgenthau of the Department of Political Science at the University of Chicago and Professor Myron Weiner of the Center for International Studies at the Massachusetts Institute of Technology have been helpful both as informants and critics. Similar contributions have been made by the following professors from the School of Government and Public Administration at The American University in Washington, D.C.: Professor Robert E.

Goostree, Professor Edgar Robinson, and Professorial Lecturer Toshio G. Tsukahira.

Personal interviews with officials of the United States government have also been a valuable source of information. Special appreciation is given to Dr. Kenneth P. Landon, former Chief of the Thai and Malayan Desk in the Department of State and former Adviser on Southeast Asian Affairs to the Operations Coordinating Board in the Executive Office of the President.

Other Americans who have been helpful are the following: Dr. Francis B. Sayre, former adviser to the Thai government and former Governor-General in the Philippine Islands; Mr. Don Garden, former editor of the *Bangkok Daily Mail;* Dr. Joseph F. Gould, former economic adviser to the Thai government; Professor John Mitchell, Fulbright scholar at Thammasat University in Bangkok, 1962-1963.

Interviews with officials of the Thai government have likewise provided useful information and insights. To some extent these sources have compensated for the dearth of reliable political literature in either the English or Thai languages. These officials include the following: M. R. Seni Pramoj, former Prime Minister of Thailand and Thai Minister to the United States; Prince Wan Waithayakon, former Minister of Foreign Affairs and present Deputy Prime Minister; Kharb Kunjara, former Director-General of the Department of Public Relations; Ananta Chintakananda, former Third Secretary in the Thai Legation in the United States; Thep Jotinuchit, former leader of the Economist Party and assemblyman from Srisaket province; Klaew Norapati, former deputy leader of the Economist Party and assemblyman from Khonkaen province; Luang Bhadravadi, Director of SEATO Affairs, Ministry of Foreign Affairs; Luang Sithsayamakam, former Under-Secretary, Ministry of Foreign Affairs; Prayad Buranasiri, Adviser to the Under-Secretary, Ministry of Finance; Somchai Anuman Rajadhon, former Director of Asia-Africa Affairs, Ministry of Foreign Affairs.

I am grateful to the Council on Research and Creative Work at the University of Colorado for assistance in publishing this study.

Finally, I would like to acknowledge the invaluable services of my wife, Ann, whose help as a typist, reader, and grammarian have done much to make this work possible.

I am, of course, solely responsible for the information and opinions contained in this book. Any errors of fact or judgment are entirely my own.

Frank C. Darling

Boulder, Colorado

ABOUT THE AUTHOR

Frank C. Darling graduated from the Principia College, and holds a Master's degree in Political Science from the University of Chicago and a Doctor of Philosophy in the same field from American University in Washington, D.C.

He served for three years as a lecturer in the Faculty of Political Science at Chulalongkorn University and as an instructor at Thammasat University in Bangkok, Thailand. For eight years he worked for the Central Intelligence Agency as a research assistant on Asian affairs and an instructor in the Intelligence School. Since 1960 he has been an Assistant Professor of Political Science at the University of Colorado.

Dr. Darling has written articles on Thailand and Southeast Asian Affairs for such scholarly journals as *Pacific Affairs, The Western Political Quarterly, The Review of Politics, United Asia,* and *The Journal of Southeast Asian History.*

CONTENTS

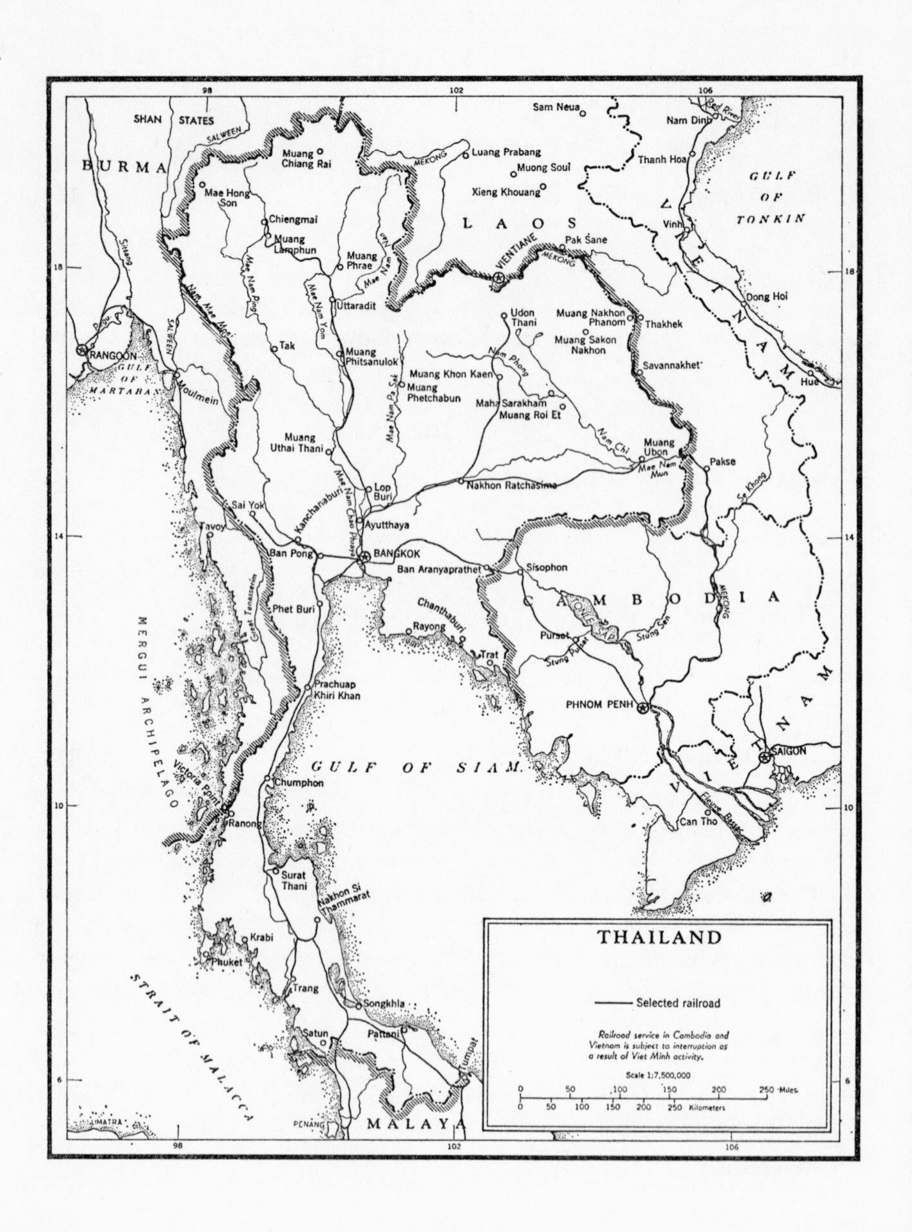
THAILAND
Selected railroad
Railroad service in Cambodia and Vietnam is subject to interruption as a result of Viet Minh activity.
Scale 1:7,500,000
Miles
Kilometers
BURMA
SHAN STATES
LAOS
CAMBODIA
VIETNAM
MALAYA
GULF OF SIAM
GULF OF TONKIN
GULF OF MARTABAN
MERGUI ARCHIPELAGO
STRAIT OF MALACCA
BANGKOK
RANGOON
VIENTIANE
PHNOM PENH
SAIGON

CHAPTER I

EARLY AMERICAN-THAI RELATIONS

When Americans and Europeans made contact with Siam early in the nineteenth century the Thai people had been governed for more than five centuries by an absolute monarch whose authority extended to all civil, military, and religious affairs.[1]

The monarch assumed the title "Lord of Life" (Chaw Chiwit) and he held the complete power of life and death over his subjects. He was also the "Lord of the Land" (Chaw Phaendin) and theoretically owned all the land in the kingdom. He ruled at the apex of a rigidly stratified and hierarchical social structure in which the rank of his subjects determined the size of their allotment of land and their status in society. Below the official hierarchy was a large body of free peasants who were required to render three months corvee labor for the king each year. At the bottom of society was a class of slaves which by the nineteenth century included approximately one-third of the population.[2]

In spite of the absolute authority theoretically vested in the monarch, his actual exercise of political power was moderated by several traditional and practical limitations. One restriction was imposed by the moral code embodied in the "Thammasat" which upheld the obligation to rule by "the ten kingly virtures" including liberality, rectitude, and gentleness. Another restraining force was the influence of Theravada Buddhism which often encouraged the king to exercise a benevolent rule. His authority was further limited by the lack of a unified bureaucracy embracing a common ideology, recruitment system, and cultural tradition as in Imperial China. At times the fear of a palace revolt likewise restrained his power and forced him to compromise with important factions at the royal court. Another limitation was the primitive transportation and communication system which usually restricted effective royal authority to the territory immediately surrounding the capital city.

The only contact between Siam and the West prior to the nineteenth century occurred when European maritime nations began their incursions into Asia for trade, religious converts, and power. The

Portuguese arrived at the royal court in Ayudhya in 1511, the Dutch in 1608, the British in 1612, and the French in 1662. When the Europeans discovered Siam as a flourishing and strategically located kingdom in the middle of the Indochina peninsula they sought the favor of the monarch. An intense rivalry for commercial privileges ensued and the king was forced to pit one group of Europeans against another to prevent the subversion of his country. In 1688 the French devised an ambitious plot to convert the ruler to Roman Catholicism and bring Siam under their control. This move sparked a brief rebellion which drove most of the Europeans from the country. Thereafter the Thai isolated themselves from the West much as the Japanese had done some fifty years before. Later attempts by European trading vessels to open commercial relations were viewed by the king as a threat to his absolute rule and a danger to the security of his kingdom.

American Influence on the Absolute Monarchy. The first contact between the United States and Siam occurred as a by-product of the expanding American trade with China and the East Indies early in the nineteenth century. There is little information on the first Americans to set foot in Siam, but in all probability the early trading vessels plying the waters of the Orient first learned of this remote kingdom through their trade at Hong Kong and Singapore, and some of the more adventurous Yankee sea captains sailed to Bangkok to see what trade they could obtain. Somchai Anuman Rajadhon has stated that trade relations with Americans were established in 1818 during the reign of King Phra Lertla, the second ruler of the Chakkri dynasty, who appeared somewhat less suspicious of Western traders than his predecessors.[3] This trade consisted largely of the exchange of firearms for sugar, rice, and other produce of the country. In spite of these early profitable contacts, commercial relations between the two countries were hampered after the accession of King Nang Klao in 1824 who retained a strong suspicion of Western nations and restored the traditional policy of isolation.

Trade relations flourished briefly after 1851 when King Mongkut ascended the throne and opened his country to extensive contact with the West. For several years prior to the Civil War trade between the United States and Siam expanded rapidly and in the peak year of 1858 American commerce was greater than that of any other country except Great Britain which was about the same. The Thai imported large numbers of steam engines from the United States that were used in rice mills and a new fleet of merchant vessels. Increasing competition from Great Britain and Germany caused American trade to decline rapidly after the Civil War, and it did not again assume a significant role until after World War II.

American relations with Siam were expanded when Protestant missionaries began arriving in the 1830's.[4] Their evangelical efforts had little success but throughout the nineteenth century they did much to acquaint the rulers and people with modern technological and social innovations. In 1835 Reverend Dan B. Bradley opened the first medical dispensary in the country and won the respect of the king for his efforts to curb the spread of cholera and small-pox. Bradley also brought in the first printing press and in 1844 he began to publish the *Bangkok Calendar,* Siam's first newspaper. Other missionaries taught the people better methods of hygiene and sanitation, and in 1848 they established a small informal primary school in an attempt to inaugurate a program of modern education.

One of the most important channels of American influence in Siam during the nineteenth century was the intimate personal relationship that developed between the missionaries and Prince Mongkut who eventually became king and opened the country to the West. While serving as a Buddhist monk Mongkut was tutored by Reverend Jesse Caswell in the study of English and science. With other missionaries he studied mathematics and astronomy. This experience gave Mongkut an intense interest in the advances of the Western world. It was undoubtedly instrumental in causing him to reverse the traditional policy of isolation and open his country to increasing intercourse with the West. Anna Leonowens, the English governess whom Mongkut later employed to tutor his children and serve as his private secretary, once commented: "He [Mongkut] had been a familiar visitor at the houses of the American missionaries, two of whom (Dr. House and Mr. Mattoon) were, throughout his reign and life, gratefully revered by him for that pleasant and profitable converse which helped to unlock to him the secrets of European vigour and advancement, and to make straight and easy the paths of knowledge he had started upon."[5]

During the reign of King Chulalongkorn the missionaries extended their efforts to the northern provinces where they initially encountered the hostility of the local rulers. On one occasion the Prince of Chiengmai executed two Thai Christians and threatened to exact similar punishment on other Christian converts in his province. The missionaries appealed to Chulalongkorn to uphold the provisions for religious freedom contained in the treaty negotiated in 1856 between Siam and the United States. The king thereby issued his famous "Edict of Religious Toleration," a portion of which stated: "That whoever wishes to embrace any religion after seeing that it is true and proper to be embraced, is allowed to do so without any restriction . . . That there is nothing in the laws and customs of Siam, nor in its foreign treaties, to throw any restriction on the religious worship and service of any one."[6] This act was the first attempt by a Thai ruler to define a civil right for his people. With few exceptions the freedom of religion has been enjoyed by all persons residing in Siam in spite of the fact that the overwhelming majority of the people are Buddhists.

In addition to these activities the missionaries became increasingly active in the fields of education and public health where they aroused a greater understanding of the need to improve the living conditions of the people. Chulalongkorn was greatly impressed with the educational work of the missionaries and in 1878 he requested Reverend and Mrs. S. G. McFarland to become the superintendents of a new government school. Their son, Reverend George B. McFarland, organized the Royal Medical College and served as a dean and lecturer from 1892 until 1926. Another son, Edwin McFarland, invented the first typewriter suitable for the Thai language. The missionaries also published additional newspapers in Bangkok which eventually encouraged the development of a local press.

The influence of the missionaries declined rapidly in the twentieth century as the government assumed an increasing role in the field of social welfare, and nationalism became a powerful political force. In spite of their declining role on governmental affairs the missionaries have continued their excellent work in Siam; they have likewise continued to enjoy the respect of the government and the people.

As increasing numbers of American traders and missionaries entered Siam they eventually voiced a demand for the establishment of diplomatic relations. During the administration of President Andrew Jackson the United States government sent Edmund Roberts, a former shipowner from Portsmouth, New Hampshire, to obtain official protection for Americans residing in Cochin-China, Siam, and Muscat. Roberts arrived in Bangkok in February 1833 and within a few weeks he negotiated a commercial treaty with the king similar to a treaty concluded with the British in 1826. He succeeded in adding a provision that protected American debtors from the harsh penalties a creditor could impose according to local law. The treaty negotiated by Roberts actually had little effect in improving trade relations between the two countries and few American vessels came to Bangkok until after Mongkut's reign began in 1851. Until this time the king and his officials circumvented many provisions of the treaty and they continued to manage foreign trade in an arbitrary manner.

The United States established permanent diplomatic relations with Siam in 1856 when Townsend Harris negotiated a new commercial treaty before taking his post as the first United States Consul-General in Japan.[7] Harris, like Roberts, was following in the wake of a diplomatic breakthrough achieved by the British during the previous year when they had concluded a favorable treaty. This treaty had contained the provisions for extraterritoriality and fixed tariffs so urgently desired by the British and other European nations. The American diplomat encountered some reluctance by Mongkut to deal with the representative of a republic as the florid correspondence exchanged between the king and Queen Victoria had intensified his desire to deal only with other royal heads of state. Harris tactfully upheld his position as the representative of a sovereign nation enjoying an equal status with Great Britain and he insisted that the Americans receive the same privileges as the British. He succeeded in obtaining a treaty similar to that negotiated by Great Britain, and the United States was also granted the privileges of extraterritoriality and fixed tariffs. Harris added a provision upholding the freedom of religion for Americans residing in the country. Implied in this provision was the recognition of freedom of religion for Thai subjects who were employed by Americans, and it was on this basis that the Protestant missionaries had encouraged King Chulalongkorn to issue his "Edict of Religious Toleration."

A unique opportunity to establish more cordial relations between the United States and Siam occurred in April 1879 when ex-President Ulysses S. Grant visited Bangkok briefly while making a world tour. Although the famous general was no longer an official of the United States, he was received with great honor by Chulalongkorn and treated as a state guest. During his visit the former president stressed the need for more intimate relations between the two countries. He specifically encouraged the king to send Thai students to the United States for higher education. "I hope," Grant declared in an informal speech, "that in America we shall see more of the Siamese, that we shall have embassies and diplomatic relations, that our commerce and manufactures will increase with Siam, and that your young men will visit our country and attend our colleges as they now go to colleges in Germany and England. I can assure them all a kind reception, and I feel that the visits would be interesting and advantageous . . . I trust that your reign will be happy and prosperous, and that Siam will continue to advance in the arts of civilization."[8]

In responding, Chulalongkorn pointed out that he desired to send more of his subjects to the United States. In an address before the former president, the Thai monarch stated: "Siam has for many years past derived great advantages from America, whose citizens have introduced to my kingdom many arts and science, much medical knowledge and many valuable books, to the great advantage of the country. Even before our countries were joined in treaty alliance, citizens of America came here and benefited us. Since then our relations have greatly improved, and to the great advantage of Siam; and recently the improvement has been still more marked".[9]

General Grant's visit symbolized a growing interest by some Americans in the impact of Western civilization on the nations of Asia. The visit also greatly increased respect for the United States in Siam and it added new international stature to this small Southeast Asian kingdom.

The ensuing era of good feelings between the two countries caused the United States in October 1882 to elevate its diplomatic mission in Bangkok from a Consulate to a Legation. The United States thereby became the first nation to raise its diplomatic representative to the level of a Minister which further added to Siam's international prestige. Two years later Chulalongkorn sent a diplomatic mission to the United States to obtain a treaty revision giving his government greater control over liquor and opium traffic in the country. The Thai envoys arrived in New York in May 1884 as the first officials from their country to set foot in the United States. Shortly thereafter they were received with great honor by President Chester Arthur. When presenting his credentials to the chief executive, the leader of the mission, Prince Krom Nares Waraviddhi, praised the scientific and educational work of the American missionaries in Siam, the recent visit of General Grant, and the elevation of the United States diplomatic mission to a Legation. On May 14, 1884, a treaty revision was concluded which gave the Thai government virtually complete control over liquor and opium traffic.

In spite of this growing intimacy between the two countries, diplomatic relations became intermittently strained during the following thirty years as the United States and other Western nations refused the request of the Thai government to abrogate their special treaty privileges. Chulalongkorn and his ministers continually insisted that Siam had made sufficient progress in improving its judicial system to warrant the abolition of extraterritoriality. They also claimed that the provisions for fixed tariffs were depriving the kingdom of urgently needed income. They employed a team of European jurists to rewrite the legal codes of the country and sent students abroad to study law. In 1903 Chulalongkorn also employed two American advisers to assist in improving the court system. Just prior to World War I the government again requested the United States to negotiate a new treaty which would give Siam complete judicial and fiscal autonomy. The Department of State postponed any move in this direction as the United States Legation in Bangkok continued to report that local judges were inexperienced and the courts still lacked efficiency.

This attitude on the part of the United States was altered when Siam entered World War I in July 1917 on the side of the Allies. Although the Thai did little to assist the Allied war effort in Europe they did gain additional respect from the Western nations. They also obtained a seat at the Versailles peace conference as one of the victorious powers. Throughout this conference the Thai delegation appealed to the Western statesmen for the restoration of complete judicial and fiscal autonomy.[10] The only Western leader to heed this appeal was President Wilson who agreed to relinquish the unequal privileges enjoyed by the United States. Negotiations between American and Thai officials began immediately in Paris and were later transferred to Washington. On December 16, 1920 a new Treaty of Friendship, Commerce, and Navigation between the two countries was signed.

In negotiating this treaty the United States was again the first Western nation to take a new step in promoting Siam's advancement toward international equality. The American government surrendered all rights of extraterritoriality and granted fiscal autonomy to Siam. Complete equality of treatment was given to the citizens of both countries. A unique provision stipulated that the treaty would become valid and Siam could raise its tariffs only on the condition "that all other nations entitled to claim special tariff treatment in Siam assent to such increases freely and without the requirement of any compensatory benefit or privileges." This provision placed a great moral obligation on other Western nations to follow the example of the United States. Further American support to Siam's quest for judicial equality was granted in a Treaty of Extradition in December 1922.

An additional contact between the two countries was established in 1903 when Chulalongkorn employed Edward H. Strobel, a former Bemis Professor of International Law at Harvard University, as a top-level foreign adviser to his government.[11] In this position Strobel was assisted by Jens I. Westengard, an Assistant Professor on the same faculty. These appointments began a precedent of filling this post with a professor from the Harvard Law School which lasted until 1940. The selection of an American for this high advisory position revealed the desire of the Thai government to obtain the support of a friendly and powerful non-European nation in its endeavor to gain freedom from unequal treaty restrictions and to oppose the territorial encroachments of the British and the French. A government publication has stated this attitude as follows: "It was felt in view of the special position occupied by the United States of America in the sphere of International politics, that the appointment of an American would remove from the minds of Foreign Governments all apprehension of partiality and at the same time would help Siam to avoid being involved in European controversies." [12]

In addition to their role as adviser in foreign affairs, the Americans who filled this high position were charged with the responsibility of assisting the courts since their improvement in organization and efficiency was directly tied to the move to abolish the unequal treaties with Western nations.

Strobel and Westengard took their advisory roles very seriously and continually impressed upon Chulalongkorn and his officials the need for a more efficient judicial system and a deeper respect for law. The two American advisers assisted in the revision of the legal codes and played an active role in the negotiations with the British and the French which restored considerable judicial authority to Siam. At international conferences both Strobel and Westengard stressed Siam's status as a free and equal nation and they appealed to the Western nations to relinquish their special treaty privileges.

Other Americans likewise rendered important service as advisers in foreign affairs. Wolcott H. Pitkins had considerable influence in bringing Siam into World War I on the side of the Allies. Eldon R. James was active at the Versailles peace conference and at the subsequent treaty negotiations in persuading the United States to abolish its special treaty privileges. Perhaps most renowned among the Americans to fill this post was Francis B. Sayre, son-in-law of President Woodrow Wilson, who was employed by the government in 1925 to head a diplomatic mission to Europe and obtain the highly-desired equal treaties according to the provisions set forth in the 1920 treaty with the United States. Using this treaty as a model, Sayre succeeded in this mission and by March 1927 Siam was finally granted complete judicial and fiscal autonomy by all Western nations.[13] In honor of his services he was granted the title of "Phya Kalyan Maitri" (True Friendship) by the government.

Early in the twentieth century additional channels were opened between the two countries that further strengthened the amicable relations of almost a century's standing. From 1916 until 1929 the Rockefeller Foundation launched a public health program which brought additional medical knowledge and services to Siam.[14] The Foundation provided both financial and advisory assistance to the Royal Medical College in 1917 when it was combined with the Civil Service College and established as Chulalongkorn University. American doctors sponsored by the Foundation taught at the University for many years and gradually raised its standards so that by 1923 it began awarding medical degrees.

In 1927 an American journalist, Andrew A. Freeman, was employed by Prince Svasti, the father-in-law of King Prajadhipok, as the editor of the English-language newspaper, the *Daily Mail*.[15] This newspaper was subsequently edited by two other Americans, Don Garden and St. Clair McKelway. Under their editorship the *Daily Mail* criticized the inefficiency of the government and urged administrative and social reforms. The newspaper also encouraged the Thai people to exercise more self-sufficiency and rely less on European tutelage and advice.[16] The progressive policies of the *Daily Mail* enabled it to win increasing respect from the local press which frequently repeated its criticisms in the Thai and Chinese languages.

Following World War I relations between the two countries became closer as increasing numbers of Thai officials and students came to the United States for observation and study. In 1920 the Prince of Kambaeng Bejra observed the railroad system in his efforts to apply the latest technical improvements to the railroads in Siam. Forty students entered American universities to pursue advanced training in the field of agriculture and public health.[17] In 1927 Prince Mahidol, the father of the present king, began his medical training at the Harvard Medical School where he received an M.D. degree. The most renowned visitor during the absolute monarchy was King Prajadhipok himself. The king came to the United States in May 1931 for medical treatment but he also made numerous observations of the American political system.[18] He seemed greatly impressed throughout his journey and he told a group of American news correspondents that he personally favored the granting of a constitution to his people. To illustrate his alleged democratic sympathies Prapadhipok shook hands with a group of Thai students who were attending universities in the United States. This was the first time in history that the king had touched the hand of one of his subjects.

The influence of the United States in the modernization of Siam during the absolute monarchy is difficult to assess. Other Western nations, especially Great Britain and France, played a very important role in this process. In some activities such as diplomacy the influence of the United States largely imitated that of Great Britain and the European nations. Yet in other areas the influence of the Americans was unique. Unlike Great Britain and France, the United States had no desire for territorial expansion in Southeast Asia. After the Civil War it had little trade with Siam. This situation enabled most of the Americans to promote activities which were generally more altruistic and humanitarian than those of the Europeans. The Protestant missionaries were perhaps the most exemplary in this endeavor. As European colonialism engulfed all of South and Southeast Asia except Siam, the Americans exhibited an unconcealed admiration for the people of this small kingdom and praised their ability to retain much of their national independence and sovereignty. This feeling was strengthened by the traditional anti-colonial sentiments in the United States. The Thai early recognized this sympathetic attitude and to promote their national objectives they often sought close relations with the United States. Thus by example, cooperation, and persuasion the Americans assisted in some degree in orienting this long isolated kingdom toward the values and institutions of the Western world.

The impact of Western technology, administrative techniques, and social advances throughout the absolute monarchy made significant changes in the role of the government and in the lives of many people. The extent of this influence is relatively easy to measure since most of these changes took place in tangible forms. Mongkut began the trend toward modernization by constructing roads and canals, establishing an official printing office and mint, and publishing a government newspaper. He also encouraged his subjects to learn European languages, especially English, and he began the practice of employing foreign advisers to assist in the administration of the country.

Chulalongkorn expanded this effort and began the construction of railroads, irrigation projects, and modern roads. In 1892 he made a sweeping reorganization of his government in which he completely abolished the semifeudal rule in many provinces and installed a centralized system of administration.[19] A Cabinet was formed under the king in which each minister was required to submit periodic reports on the work and expenses of his ministry. Chulalongkorn retained sufficient personal control over this rapidly expanding administrative structure by appointing members of the royal family as heads of the major ministries and as commanders of the military services. These innovations were made primarily to enhance the unity and power of the central government. Relatively little consideration was given to improvements in education and social welfare.

The first major social reforms were made during the reign of King Vajiravudh who promoted the expansion of public schools and enacted a compulsory education law. The king contributed to the improvement of public health, switched to the Gregorian calendar, and ordered his subjects to adopt surnames. His government made additional advancements in railroad construction, irrigation, and communications. Siam even began to develop a small airline service. Further progress was made in revising the legal codes of the country and in 1925 the first modern Civil and Commercial Codes were promulgated. Vajiravudh began a Boy Scout movement and made it compulsory for all school children. Few of these reforms were made for purely altruistic reasons. Instead they were initiated by the king to make Siam appear as a modern country in the eyes of Western nations. They were used to promote the quest for international equality and the abolition of the unequal treaties.

As the last king to reign under the absolute monarchy, Prajadhipok continued many of the reforms launched by his predecessors. Further improvements were made in transportation and communications and by 1930 Bangkok was becoming a leading airline center in Asia. Additional health laws were passed and in 1928 a civil service law was promulgated which required administrative appointments to be made on the basis of competitive examinations. The king began to impose modest regulations on the national economy and sought to expand the government's role in exploiting natural resources.[20]

The impact of Western political concepts throughout the absolute monarchy is much more difficult to assess than the influence of Western technology and social reforms. This is because the influence of these political values entered Siam largely through the absolute monarchy instead of from the hands of Western colonial rulers as in the surrounding countries in South and Southeast Asia. These concepts were applied by the Thai monarchs primarily to advance the interests of the nation as a whole, but not until the twentieth century did they gain modest acceptance in protecting the rights of individuals. The absolute tradition consequently remained intact. Although many Americans and Europeans criticized the arbitrary exercise of unlimited political power, the Thai officials upheld the absolute monarchy as a useful and desirable institution which was bringing rapid progress to a backward country. The adoption of modern technology and administrative methods actually enhanced the effective authority of the absolute monarchy, but at the same time these innovations provided opponents of the king with the means to challenge his traditional power.

Yet progress was made throughout this period in implanting some understanding of Western political ideas. The concept of equality was increasingly stressed through the channels of American diplomacy. In each official encounter between the two countries, beginning with the treaty negotiated by Edmund Roberts in 1833 and culminating in the treaty of extradition in 1922, the Americans emphasized the vital importance of equality under law. The United States assisted in conveying this concept to the rulers and people by its cooperation in Siam's struggle for international equality. The American advisers who aided in the modernization of the court system likewise stressed the nation's right to equal treatment under international law. They also helped to instill a wider recognition of the equality of individuals in the operation of domestic law.

The Western concept of the rule of law was also disseminated in some degree through the influence of American diplomatic officials and advisers. The great concern of the diplomats in drafting the various treaties and the continual emphasis of the advisers on higher standards in the court system gradually aroused a more widespread respect for law. As the Thai rulers increasingly realized the rights their nation enjoyed under international law, they became more willing to extend some rights to their subjects under domestic law. Evidence that some officials were obtaining an understanding of the rule of law was revealed in an interview between Townsend Harris and one of Mongkut's ministers during the negotiations for the 1856 treaty. "The accidental disposition and intelligence of the Monarch", the Thai minister stated, "controlled everything and kings in a few generations forgot that they sprang from the people, and lost all sympathy with them. It is essential to the prosperity of a nation that it should have fixed laws, and that nobles should be restrained from oppressing the people, otherwise the latter were like chickens, who instead of being kept for their eggs, were killed off." [21]

A growing respect for law was also revealed in the adherence of the Thai government to the unequal restrictions contained in the treaties with the Western nations in spite of the heavy burden they imposed on the finances of the kingdom. Less than forty years before the king had arbitrarily violated the treaty with the United States and other Western nations. By the end of the nineteenth century the government sought to obtain a revision of the treaty restrictions rather than defy them.

The concept of individual freedom was gradually implanted in the numerous treaty provisions designed to protect Americans residing in Siam from arbitrary treatment by the local authorities. The advisers succeeded in some degree in removing many arbitrary practices from the judicial proceedings of the country and in expanding an understanding of the rights and freedom of the individual under law. The missionaries were also effective in gaining a wider recognition of the freedom of each individual to choose and practice his own religion.

The idea of popular sovereignty was first introduced to Siam during the diplomatic mission headed by Townsend Harris. In subsequent contacts between the two countries the Thai rulers became increasingly aware that the government of the United States derived its powers from and was responsible to the American people. While the Thai have never entertained the idea of deposing the monarchy and establishing a republic, their leaders have increasingly administered the government for the welfare of the people. By the 1890's Chulalongkorn was publicly stating that the revenues collected by his government would thereafter be used for the defense of the country and the progress of the people, not for the aggrandizement of the monarchy. A similar attitude was voiced by his successors.

The essence of Western civilization based on the dignity of the individual was introduced primarily in the form of humanitarianism. This value was perhaps most effectively exemplified by the unselfish labors of the missionaries in providing medical and social services for the people. The diplomatic officials also stressed human dignity in their efforts to protect the lives and property of Americans residing in Siam. The desire of the Thai rulers to abolish the unpopular treaty provisions upholding extraterritoriality for over sixty years forced them to remove many inhumane practices from the local legal system. The Rockefeller Foundation, the American editors of the *Daily Mail*, and the many Thai returning from observation and study in the United States likewise encouraged more humanitarian measures in the government of the country.

Finally the concept of progress has had a profound impact on the modern development of Siam and every channel of intercourse between the two countries has continually widened the effect of this value among the people. The early American traders were among the first to introduce the modern technological progress of the West. This trend was expanded by the Protestant missionaries who introduced many social improvements. Through the channels of American diplomacy the Thai were continually prodded to make more progress in elevating their legal and administrative standards. The imposition of extraterritoriality was increasingly galling to the Thai rulers, but it served as a reminder that their court system was inferior to that in the West and many internal improvements would be required before these treaty restrictions could be removed. In Bangkok, General Grant voiced his hope that Siam would "continue to advance in the arts of civilization," and the American advisers consistently stressed the need for progress so Siam could achieve its rights as an equal sovereign nation. The experiences of Thai officials and students in the United States likewise caused them to promote more progressive measures on their return to the country.

The impact of Western political concepts in Siam had no effect on the structural basis of the absolute monarchy. Yet the influence of these values caused it to become more moderate and benevolent. Mongkut began this trend by removing some of the traditional isolation of the king and restoring the ancient custom of hearing petitions directly from his subjects.[22] He mitigated some of the more inhumane features of the local legal system which was still based on the Hindu Code of Manu. He altered the law to facilitate the payment of redemption money by debt slaves and restricted the right of parents to sell their children into slavery. He also made an attempt to control the practice of gambling, opium-smoking, and drinking spirituous liquors.

Chulalongkorn increased the humanitarian and benevolent role of the absolute monarchy. In his coronation ceremony he abolished the custom of prostration in the presence of the king. Throughout his reign he frequently appeared in the streets of Bangkok and often showed a sincere concern for the welfare of his people. In 1874 he decreed that no one could any longer be born a slave or sell himself into slavery. He also ended the use of corvee labor and in 1905 completely abolished the practice of slavery. As mentioned previously, one of Chulalongkorns' most humanitarian acts was to issue the "Edict of Religious Toleration" which established the freedom of religion.

The reforms inaugurated by Mongkut and Chulalongkorn to increase the benevolent role of the absolute monarchy served to reduce the traditional elevated status of the king. Consequently with the death of Chulalongkorn in 1910 and the accession to the throne by Vajiravudh less prestige was attached to the absolute monarchy and the king was no longer without internal opposition. During the early years of Vajiravudh's reign much of this opposition was directed at his extravagance and lack of leadership ability, but by the 1920's increasing numbers of Thai were questioning the validity of the absolute monarchy as a suitable political institution. In 1912 a group of military officers made an abortive attempt to overthrow the king and a similar plot by a group of army officers was uncovered in 1917. The local press occasionally published articles criticizing the absolute monarchy and in 1919 Vajiravudh retorted with a harsh censorship law. Criticism of the king also spread among Western-influenced civil servants. This opposition was scattered and unorganized at the time, but it revealed that the day of unquestioned loyalty to the absolute monarchy was drawing to an end.

Prajadhipok ascended to the throne in 1925 with the reputation that he favored the establishment of a constitutional form of government. The following year an official publication stated that "the power of the Monarchy depends more upon public approval than upon ancient prestige or mere political theory."[23] However, any moves Prajadhipok may have contemplated toward a more liberal form of government were blocked by the influential and conservative princes surrounding the king. These men stressed the rapid progress Siam had made under the absolute monarchy and they saw no reason to change the existing form of government. Prajadhipok's poor health and retiring nature also prevented him from making any serious attempt to liberalize the traditional political system.

The failure of Prajadhipok to grant any democratic reforms aroused widespread discontent among the small but growing middle class which by the 1920's included an increasing number of commoners who had become heavily imbued with democratic ideas during their studies in the West. Upon their return they were disappointed with their positions in the civil service which provided them with a meager income and little opportunity to make changes in a government they felt was in urgent need of reform. Western-educated Thai were especially irked by the traditional autocratic practices of the conservative princes who exerted a dominant influence in the government. "Can one be surprised," one observer commented, "that students from Oxford and Harvard were sickened at the sight of Siamese servants groveling on their bellies before their masters, a practice which though abolished in public, was still rigidly adhered to in princely households? It did not escape them either that the rural masses were denied anything but the rudiments of monastic education and were regarded by the government mainly as the necessary machinery for getting in the rice crop."[24]

Another writer noted: "That the autocracy was benevolent made it no less an autocracy and did nothing to reduce the ambitions of the liberal group for a more modern form of government."[25] As the worldwide economic depression struck Siam in 1931 and the budget cuts ordered by Prajadhipok caused many of these Western-educated liberals to lose their jobs, their opposition to the absolute monarchy became more intense.

The growing opposition to the absolute monarchy was also promoted by an emerging form of nationalism which the Thai adopted from their long and intimate contact with the West. This new force was first aroused by King Vajiravudh as he sought to transform the latent patriotism among his people into an articulate nationalism in his attempt to reduce European and Chinese influence. To achieve this objective he wrote numerous essays extolling the "Thai country, the Thai nation, the Thai people, the Thai virtues, etc."[26] The king placed many barriers on European commerce to gain bargaining power in his quest for complete judicial and fiscal freedom. The Chinese were likewise restricted in their economic activities and labeled as "the Jews of the Orient."

With the abolition of the treaty restrictions in 1927 the force of nationalism abated within the ruling class but it became more intense among the progressive-minded liberals returning from their education in the West. As these returnees sought a more influential role in the government for themselves and a more respected place in international society for Siam, the absolute monarchy was viewed as an intolerable obstacle in the path of national and individual progress. By 1932 the force of nationalism combined with the growing discontent caused by the depression aroused a small group of Western-educated civilian and military officials to overthrow the traditional system and seek the establishment of a more modern form of government.[27]

The First Constitutional Regime. The revolutionary group which staged the successful coup d'etat on June 24, 1932 was lead by a thirty-two year old intellectual named Pridi Phanomyong who had studied law and economics at the University of Paris. The major military leader was Colonel Phya Bahol Phonphayuhasena, a commoner who had received his military training in Denmark and Germany. The revolutionary leaders and their aides called themselves the "Promoters" or the "People's Party", and while seizing the ruling princes of the realm they proclaimed that the time had arrived for Siam to have a government "of the people, by the people, and for the people."[28] The coup leaders issued a provisional constitution that reduced the king to a virtual figurehead. A "Committee of the People's Party" inherited the broad powers formerly exercised by the absolute monarchy and it became the leading executive authority in the new government. The People's Senate was given broad legislative powers and it was organized in a manner that assured control by the People's Party for at least ten years. The legislature was to have two categories of representatives: the first category consisted of seventy representatives elected by the people; the second category consisted of seventy members appointed by the People's Party.

The provisional constitution envisaged a transitional period consisting of three stages during which the people would be prepared for full democratic representation in the legislature. The first stage consisted of the short period of complete party control while the new government was being established. The second stage included the introduction of elected representatives into the legislature as first category members. Whenever one-half of the people in any province had received a primary education the province would then be represented entirely by elected members. In the third stage complete democracy would be established and all representatives would be elected by the people. In no case would appointed representatives continue in the legislature after ten years from the date of issuing the provisional constitution.

On December 10, 1932 a permanent constitution was promulgated which restored some of the prerogatives of the king. However, these augmented powers were shared with the newly-created Cabinet and legislature, and any official act of the king required the counter-signature of a minister. The members of the Cabinet were responsible individually and collectively to the legislature and they could be removed by a vote of no-confidence. The legislature was named the "Assembly of People's Representatives." It was organized into two categories as outlined in the provisional constitution and was to proceed toward full democratic representation in the same three stages.

This new political system was similar in many respects to the constitutional monarchies of Western Europe and Meiji Japan. The dynastic sovereign was theoretically granted broad powers, but the provision that his acts required the approval of a responsible minister made him little more than a figurehead. In practice the royal prerogatives could be exercised with little restraint by the ruling regime using the aegis of the reigning monarch as the basis for broad grants of political authority. Unless this reservoir of vast potential power were checked by mature political parties and an enlightened public opinion as in

Great Britain and the countries of Scandinavia, it could be used by the new elite to impose an authoritarian rule. In effect the new constitutional system offered little restraint on the exercise of political power; the practical limitations were to come from within the emerging struggle for power among the three major groups; the royalist-conservatives, the liberals, and the military.

These three political groups were not formally organized nor were they unified in their struggles with opposing factions. They formed into loose, shifting, and complex coalitions in which the leaders and followers often disagreed among themselves as well as with other competing groups. The major forces which held these factions together were strong personalities and the fruits of power. Their membership became increasingly heterogeneous as members moved from one group to another in accord with changing circumstances and opportunities. There were commoners among the royalist-conservatives, royalty and military officers among the liberals, and civilians and conservatives among the military. All three factions were dedicated to the pursuit or maintenance of wealth. All three groups adhered to the traditional authoritarian system, although the liberal faction which had provided the ideological motivation for the 1932 coup was the group most likely to advance the nation toward some form of constitutional democracy.

The royalist-conservatives continued as an active political force for about two years after the overthrow of the absolute monarchy. Members of the royal family were "above politics" according to the new constitution and they were prohibited from holding public office.[29] Due to their inexperience in administration, the coup leaders established a government headed by Phya Manopakorn, the former Chief Justice of the Dika (Supreme) Court. Yet after one year a controversy over a radical economic plan proposed by Pridi combined with a fear of the restoration of the absolute monarchy caused Colonel Bahol to stage a second coup and take over as Premier. The royalist-conservatives declined rapidly when a royalist counter-revolt was crushed on the outskirts of Bangkok a few months later by government troops under the command of a young rising army officer, Lt. Colonel Phibun Songkhram.[30]

During the following year King Prajadhipok left for Europe allegedly for medical treatment. Pridi was cleared of communist charges and the Assembly passed three laws which further reduced the power of the monarch. In March 1935 Prajadhipok formally announced his abdication in Great Britain and denounced the new regime because it "did not give full democracy to the nation." The Bahol government selected Prince Ananda Mahidol, a nephew of Prajadhipok, as the new monarch. Since the prince was still a youth studying in Switzerland a three-man Regency was established until the king could take up residence in the country.

The liberals emerged as a significant political force during the first few years of the constitutional regime. This faction was led by Pridi whose courage and ability in planning the 1932 coup continued to inspire widespread support from liberal and military officials alike and enabled him to exert considerable influence on the government. While the liberals faced increasing competition from the military group in the formulation of public policy, they sponsored many of the measures intended to modernize the political system.

The first general election in Thai history was held in November 1933 for the elected seats in the Assembly. The vote was light throughout the country and in some provinces less than 1 per cent of the eligible voters went to the polls. The elected representatives included retired civil servants, lawyers, ex-revolutionaries, and school teachers. The Bahol government appointed an equal number of second-category representatives, most of whom were military officers.

In the general election held in 1937 the percentage of people who exercised their right to vote increased and the calibre of elected members improved. Many of the liberal representatives took their role very seriously and in spite of numerous obstacles they made some progress with parliamentary government. On three occasions between 1934 and 1938 the Assembly asserted its constitutional authority and gave the government a vote of no-confidence which caused the removal of several ministers from the Cabinet.

The liberals also promoted the establishment of local government. In January 1934 the Local Government Act was passed which created provincial and municipal assemblies designed to develop toward complete democracy in the same three stages as the national legislature.[31] Yet the forces of tradition and the lack of adequate guidance from Bangkok caused local government to develop slowly.

The liberal faction was a major force behind the efforts of the new regime to accelerate the economic progress of the country. When the absolute monarchy was overthrown approximately 95 per cent of the national economy was controlled by European and Chinese interests. The Bahol government promptly sought to reduce this vast foreign control and provide more opportunity for Thai commerce and industry. Heavier restrictions were imposed on European and Chinese commerce and larger taxes were levied on foreign residents. Although Pridi's economic plan had been earlier rejected, some of his proposals were adopted in promoting economic progress. The new regime provided cooperative credit societies for the peasants and established several nationalized industries producing sugar, paper, textiles, and cement. Further improvements were made in the transportation and communication systems of the country.

Among the most notable achievements of the liberal faction was the rapid expansion of education. This group upheld the view that greater educational opportunities among the broad masses of people were vital to the strengthening of the constitutional system. To achieve this goal the liberals promoted the construction of more schools throughout the country. Despite the growing influence of the military faction and the increasing expenditures for the armed forces, the Bahol government increased the educational program at a faster rate than any other government activity. By 1938 the thirst for education among the youth of Siam was growing rapidly.

The influence of the liberal faction gradually declined as an intensified form of nationalism emerged in the late 1930's. The forces of nationalism were strengthened as the government extended its control over alien commerce and removed foreign advisers from high-level positions in the administration. This trend gave renewed vigor to the traditional collective consciousness of the Thai people. It discouraged further development of individualism and pluralism which might have strengthened the new constitutional system. Perhaps most significant in this new nationalistic era was the rise of the military leaders to a dominant position in the political life of the nation which further jeopardized individual freedom and the evolution of democracy.

The political influence of the military leaders grew rapidly after Pridi requested the cooperation of Colonel Bahol and other military officers in staging the 1932 coup. The role of the military in political affairs continued to expand as the colonel forcibly ousted the reactionary regime headed by Premier Manopakorn, and Lt. Colonel Phibun Songkhram suppressed the royalist counter-revolt. In effect the psychological vacuum created by the sudden overthrow of the absolute monarchy and the absence of any alternative political force made it necessary for the new regime to fill this void with military power. Within a short time the military officers in the revolutionary group relied increasingly on their control of the armed forces as a means of keeping themselves in power. The traditional respect to the absolute monarchy was replaced by a coerced respect for military arms.

The influence of the military leaders was further enhanced by the absence and eventual abdication of Prajadhipok and the demise of the royalist-conservatives as an effective political force. Thereafter the military leaders were confronted only by Pridi and the small liberal group as they sought a greater role in national affairs.

The military faction gradually became the dominant political group under the leadership of Lt. Colonel Phibun Songkhram who gained much prestige following his skillful suppression of the royalist counter-revolt. Phibun became the major rival to Pridi and the liberals who were forced to rely on Siam's infinitesimal public opinion as a source of political support. These contending groups were kept in balance during the first few years of the constitutional regime by the mediating efforts of Colonel Bahol. Although the Premier was an army officer himself he was moderate in temperament and gifted with a common sense that won widespread admiration from both the military and liberal groups within the new regime. He had much respect for Pridi and the new constitution, and he sought to restrain the expanding influence of Phibun and the military faction in political affairs.[32]

The military group assumed virtually unlimited power in December 1938 when Bahol retired due to poor health. Phibun became the new Premier and the role of the military in government affairs rapidly increased. Pridi and other liberal leaders were retained by the new regime but their influence on public policy continued to decline. The trend thereafter was away from the modicum of constitutional government which had slowly evolved since 1932, and Phibun gradually established an authoritarian rule much like that exercised by the absolute monarchy. By 1939 the military leaders were well aware of the decisive political power they derived from their control of the armed forces and the corresponding weakness of the liberal faction which received little effective support from public opinion. "Young military officers led by Phibun," Vella declared, "had become increasingly aware of the fact that the indispensable factor in the success of the coups d'etat of 1932 and 1933 was support of the military. The very ease with which the coups were carried out and the absence of popular support for the civilian leaders and their programs made the civilian contribution to the change in government seem small as compared to their own."[33]

Phibun and his aides were also influenced by the emerging military dictatorships in other parts of the world, especially in Japan. To them the totalitarian nations appeared virile and strong whereas the Western democracies seemed docile and weak.

The Phibun regime promoted a militant form of nationalism which reached unprecedented fervor just prior to World War II. The role of the military in national affairs was widely publicized and glorified. The government launched new propaganda programs stressing military virtues and it created youth organizations (yuwachon) patterned after the Hitler Youth movement in Nazi Germany.[34] Phibun became recognized as the "leader" of the nation and his authority quickly expanded to virtually every phase of national life. When propaganda did not suffice the militarists resorted to the use of terror to enforce obedience to the new regime. Only one month after Phibun came to power, his government announced that a pro-monarchist plot had been uncovered, and for the first time since the 1932 coup twenty political prisoners were executed without a trial.[35] The military regime supplemented these efforts by programs promoting economic and cultural nationalism.

Phibun also initiated an irredentist movement that gained momentum in June 1939 when the name of the country was officially changed to "Thailand."[36] The new concept of the "land of the Thai" was construed by the military leaders as an expanding region which would eventually include all of the Thai-speaking people living in Southeast Asia. The fall of France in June 1940 before Nazi aggression weakened the position of the French military forces in Indochina and gave the Phibun regime its first opportunity to acquire additional territory. The Thai government promptly demanded the return of the "lost provinces" in Cambodia which the French had acquired from Siam at the turn of the century. This controversy eventually aroused the Japanese who were eager to expand their influence into Southeast Asia, and their mediation of this conflict enabled Thailand to gain control of a portion of the disputed territory. Much to Phibun's surprise, Japanese troops occupied Indochina in July 1941, an event which quickly ended his irredentist ambitions and caused him to turn to the vital task of preserving the nation's independence.

The influence of the United States in Siam was minor from the time of the overthrow of the absolute monarchy until World War II. American trade continued at a low level, although the outbreak of the war in Europe caused the Thai to turn increasingly to the United States as a supplier of manufactured goods. These imports included machinery and airplanes which contributed to the technological progress and military power of the nation. Yet trade relations between the two countries became plainly strained as tension mounted in the region. One American corporation, the Standard-Vacuum Company, became a victim of the government's program of economic nationalism, and by 1941 it had been forced to end most of its operations. An executive order by President Roosevelt to withhold the delivery of twelve airplanes to the Thai government as it attempted to regain territory in French Indochina did much to lower American prestige among the military leaders.

The influence of the missionaries declined further after 1932. The increase in the educational facilities provided by the government combined with rising nationalism made the mission schools less attractive and in many areas their enrollment decreased. The depression in the United States also reduced the number of missionaries sent to Siam, a trend which forced the Thai Christian movement to look increasingly to indigenous leadership. In 1933 the Church of Christ in Siam was established with the avowed purpose of uniting all Protestant Christians into an autonomous church. Medical and educational work continued until the missionaries were interned or fled the country at the beginning of World War II. Some of their welfare work was carried on by Thai Christians.

American advisers had no significant influence on the political system after 1932 and the number of Western advisers in the administration was rapidly reduced.[37] In 1935 Dr. James Andrews of Harvard University made a rural economic survey of the country in which he informed the government that the alleged profiteering role of the Chinese middlemen had been greatly exaggerated. Andrews' report drew a negative response from the new regime which continued to hold the Chinese responsible for the indebtedness and poverty of the peasants. Frederick R. Dolbeare of Harvard University replaced Raymond Stevens as the Adviser in Foreign Affairs in 1935. Mr. Dolbeare held this position until July 1940 when the outburst of irredentist sentiment and the inroads of Japanese influence made his position in the administration untenable. With his retirement the tradition of appointing an American as the leading adviser in foreign affairs came to an end.

The major contact between the two countries during this period occurred in 1937 when the United States agreed to negotiate a new treaty on the basis of complete equality. The 1920 treaty had included several minor provisions which obligated the Thai government to make further improvements in its legal codes. The Bahol regime completed this task in 1936 and the stirrings of nationalist sentiment caused it to press for the removal of these remaining infringements on the nation's sovereignty. The new treaty was signed on November 13, 1937, and with the exception that the Panama Canal Zone was excluded from its jurisdiction, it applied equally to both countries.

The Impact of World War II. On December 8, 1941 the Japanese armies in Indochina quickly occupied Thailand as they launched their lightning thrusts against the British in Burma and Malaya. The sudden occupation of Thailand caused Phibun to accede to a Japanese ultimatum and within a few weeks he signed a military alliance with Japan. Some members of the liberal faction within the Thai government opposed this acquiescence to the Japanese, and Pridi advocated a policy of token resistance.[38] However the failure of the British and the Americans to provide military assistance and the overwhelming power of the Japanese armies convinced Phibun and his aides that they had taken the only realistic course of action. Yet on January 25, 1942 Phibun took the drastic and unexpected step of declaring war on Great Britain and the United States, a move probably made to placate Japan even more and gain maximum autonomy for his regime under the Japanese occupation.

While the government in Bangkok struggled throughout the war to mitigate the impact of Japanese military rule, the Thai diplomatic mission in the United States opened one of the most important contacts ever made between the two countries. The Thai Minister in Washington, M. R. Seni Pramoj, announced that his Legation was independent of Phibun's government.[39] Seni further proclaimed that the real sympathy of the Thai people was with the Western Allies and not with the Japanese. At the same time he appealed for the formation of an underground resistance movement inside his country, and he announced that a "Free Thai" organization was being established by Thai nationals then residing in the United States.

A Free Thai group was promptly organized under the leadership of Seni, Luang Dithyakar Bhakdi, the Second Secretary of the Legation, and Colonel Kharb Kunjara, the military attache.[40] The Legation sent announcements of the new organization to Thai students studying throughout the United States and requested their active cooperation. Within a short time many volunteers came forward and at a meeting in Washington the new group drew up the following statement:[41]

"1. The Seri [Free] Thai is not a political party. It is merely a Thai organization whose main objective is to restore Thailand's independence.

"2. The Japanese army is the enemy of the Thais because the Japanese armed forces invaded Thailand.

"3. The Bangkok government is a puppet government because it has played ball [sic] with the enemy against the will of the people.

"4. The Seri Thai regards itself as the representative agency working for the will of the Thai people everywhere.

"5. The Seri Thai will not interfere with the law of succession of the king.

"6. A constitutional government and democracy will be restored to Thailand after the country's freedom is restored. The Seri Thai will release all political prisoners and will organize a people's court to investigate those who have cooperated with the enemy."

When Phibun's declaration of war was received by Seni he personally informed President Roosevelt and Secretary of State Hull that it did not represent the will of the Thai people and he requested American assistance to liberate his country. The United States government agreed to this request and refused to recognize the declaration of war.[42] American officials were generally impressed with Seni's sincerity and his appeal for an underground resistance movement inside occupied Thailand. After the entire region of Southeast Asia had been conquered by the Japanese the possibility of a clandestine organization in a strategically located country like Thailand offered a unique and unexpected opportunity to American military and intelligence services. Early in 1942 the United States government accordingly offered to assist the Free Thai organization. A group of seventy Free Thai volunteers was trained near Washington, D.C. under the direction of Dr. Kenneth Landon of the Department of State and Colonel Preston Goodfellow of the Office of Strategic Services (O.S.S.).[43] In the summer of 1943 a small detachment was sent to southern China to infiltrate occupied Thailand.

Just as this operation was about to begin two Thai agents arrived in southern China who had escaped from their country. They informed the American military officials that an extensive underground movement had been organized inside Thailand under the leadership of Pridi who was still serving as Regent and overtly cooperating with Phibun and the Japanese.[44] Within a few months American-trained Free Thai agents had successfully infiltrated the country and established contact with Pridi's underground headquarters in Bangkok. They soon provided the Allies with valuable intelligence on Japanese troop movements and political activities in Southeast Asia. By the end of the war many O.S.S. officers had been parachuted into Thailand and large quantities of arms and supplies had been provided to the Free Thai underground movement. They were able to liberate some

Allied prisoners of war. The Americans were especially heartened when news was received that half of the crew of the missing cruiser "U.S.S. Houston" was alive in a prison camp. Pridi continually pressed the Allies for permission to begin open resistance against the beleaguered Japanese, but this request was delayed long enough so that the surrender of Japan made overt military action unnecessary.[45]

Throughout the war the Phibun regime was able to maintain control over the administration of the country with the exception of the air fields, highways, and railroads. However, the Thai government was required to provide large quantities of food for the Japanese army and in November 1943 Phibun was persuaded to sign the Greater East Asia Joint Declaration which formally aligned his regime with the Japanese puppet governments in Asia. In return for these cooperative gestures the Japanese transferred four states in northern Malaya and two states in eastern Burma to Thai jurisdiction. Under this thin veneer of cordiality, however, the Thai gave little cooperation to Japan's war effort, and the Japanese occupation aroused increasing hostility from Phibun and his people.

By early 1944 the Thai dictator realized that Japan was not going to win the war, and he became aware that Pridi was maintaining an underground movement in cooperation with the Allies. In an attempt to exemplify his independence from the Japanese, Phibun sought at this late date to move the national capital from Bangkok to Petchaboon, a small remote town in northern Thailand. This project met with increasing opposition due to the prevalence of malaria in the region, and the army leader himself was forced to present his proposal to the legislature for the compulsory conscription of workers. To his surprise this unpopular plan was overwhelmingly defeated in the Assembly and he was forced to resign. By this time the Japanese were aware that their position in Southeast Asia was rapidly deteriorating and their growing suspicion of Phibun caused them to permit this change in the leadership of the government. Phibun himself probably felt that it was an appropriate time to retire from public life so that Thailand might receive more sympathetic treatment from the Allies and he might escape charges of collaborating with the enemy. With his overthrow the military faction in the government was completely eclipsed by the liberal group led by Pridi. The position of Premier was given to a civilian, Khuang Aphaiwongse, whose main task during the last year of the war was to placate the increasingly nervous Japanese.

When Japan announced its surrender in August 1945 the Thai government took immediate action to regain the favor of the Western

Allies. Pridi declared that the territory in Burma and Malaya which Thailand had received from the Japanese would be promptly returned to the British. He further stated that Phibun's declaration of war on the United States and Great Britain and the military alliance with Japan were illegal since they had never been constitutionally ratified by the Assembly nor signed by the Regency. The government was also prepared to show that no Allied assistance had been provided during the crucial early days of the war, and the Thai armed forces were in no position to oppose the advancing Japanese armies. To have offered resistance, they claimed, would have caused needless bloodshed and suffering. As they prepared for the difficult peace negotiations with the Allies, the Thai leaders knew their major challenge would come from their former mentors, the British and the French. And to gain moral and diplomatic support they looked hopefully to the more sympathetic Americans.

The intimate contacts between the O.S.S. and the Free Thai movement did much to win the cooperation of the United States at the end of the war. The sacrifices and courage of the Free Thai volunteers and their determination to liberate their country convinced many Americans that the Thai people were giving little aid to the Japanese and were basically sympathetic to the Allied cause. "The Siamese," one O.S.S. official declared, "were universally popular with the OSS men who worked with them. Like the people of many small independent countries, there is a sturdiness and simple patriotism without arrière pensée about the Siamese which endeared them to the many Americans in OSS who knew them." [46]

The Americans also admired Pridi's heroic role in the 1932 coup as well as his courage as the leader of the Free Thai underground movement inside occupied Thailand. "For the past ten years", another O.S.S. official stated, "Luang Pradist's [Pridi's] career had been an inspiration and a model for all young democratic and revolutionary-minded Siamese . . . What particularly excited the boys was that 'Ruth' [Pridi's pseudonym] . . . had been largely responsible for the success of the great Siamese revolution of a dozen years before. He had planned the steps to be taken, formed the People's Party, and led them in seizing power from the absolute monarchy. The virtually bloodless coup d'etat of June 24, 1932, overnight changed the history of the country and brought peace and order, freedom and equality, and democracy to the people of Siam. Luang Pradist's principles were no vague hopes of an idealist. Standing for universal education and remunerative work for everyone, he stamped out special privileges enjoyed by any group at the expense of other citizens."[47]

Although this sympathetic attitude led to an exaggerated view in the minds of many Americans regarding Pridi's accomplishments in reforming the political and social system, it brought United States diplomatic support behind the liberal leader and his followers and opened the way for Americans to exercise a greater influence in Thailand in the post-war era.

The impact of World War II brought about a complete realignment of the internal political groups. The militarists were discredited due to their wartime alliance with the Japanese and they were removed from important posts in the government. Phibun's military faction disintegrated as an active political force. Yet the military leaders continued to enjoy considerable popular support in spite of the hardships which had befallen the country. Some people still admired the progress which the militarists had achieved prior to the war and many Thai sympathized with Phibun's difficult position during the Japanese occupation. And the military leaders themselves did not forget their important political role before the trend in international affairs had led them into an ill-fated alliance with Imperial Japan. In effect, the legacy of militarism remained one of the greatest internal threats to political progress in Thailand. "Perhaps the most lasting effect of Phibun's wartime regime," according to Vella, "was to convince politically minded elements in the armed forces that they could control the government without allying themselves with civilian leaders or adhering to the spirit of constitutionalism."[48]

Many royalist-conservatives had regained considerable prestige prior to the war due to their known abilities and experience which were urgently needed by the new regime. By 1940 all but a few of the most die-hard royalists were cooperating with the government and many were able to render valuable service to the nation. During the war many royalists and conservatives assisted in the effort to end Japanese rule and restore the nation's independence. While they did not regain sufficient strength to make them a dominant political force, their new position made it inevitable that they would exercise some influence in politics in the post-war era.

The liberals emerged at the end of the war as the dominant political group. Pridi's heroic role as the leader of the Free Thai underground movement combined with his prestige as the prime mover of the 1932 coup made him the major political figure in the country. Other liberal leaders profited from their close association with Pridi. The wartime cooperation between the Free Thai movement and the Western dem-cracies also enhanced the position of the liberal group. As the war came to an end many people looked to Pridi and his aides to revive the democratic goals of the 1932 revolution and establish a constitutional government. Many Thai also hoped that the United States and Great Britain would assist in this endeavor.

Another force beginning to exercise more influence on Thai politics at the end of the war was that exerted by the dominant powers in international society which favored Thai national interests. To some extent the prevailing political attitude in Thailand had served for many years as a barometer of the shifting forces in international politics, and foreign relations had influenced Thai domestic affairs for almost a century. Mongkut and Chulalongkorn maintained cordial relations with the major Western powers in an era of aggressive European colonialism while at the same time they adopted Western technology and administrative techniques as rapidly as possible to preserve Thailand's independence. During the world-wide quest for national self-determination before and after World War I Vajiravudh espoused an ardent brand of Thai nationalism. During the 1920's when constitutional democracy was in vogue in many countries of the world Prajadhipok voiced some sympathy for the estabishment of a democratic government. Phibun likewise imitated certain aspects of the totalitarian Axis regimes when they appeared as the emerging trend in international society in the 1930's.

By the end of World War II foreign influence in Thailand had become much more extensive. The war proved that the shifting forces in the realm of international politics would inevitably have some effect on the Thai political system. Thus, Pridi and the liberals were able to remove the Phibun regime and assume control of the government, not because of widespread respect for constitutionalism or limitations imposed by internal political forces, but because of the defeat of Japan with whom the militarists were allied. In spite of the removal of the military leaders and the revival of the liberals, the future of Thai politics by 1945 was inextricably interlinked to the vagaries and uncertainties of the international political arena.

Chapter II

AMERICAN INFLUENCE ON THE LIBERAL GOVERNMENT

While the United States and Great Britain had played a unified role in the defeat of the Axis powers in Europe, their policies in the early post-war period in Asia revealed a sharp cleavage in their political and economic objectives. In few countries was this split between the major Western Allies more immediately apparent than in Thailand. The British had extensive commercial interests that had suffered serious damage, and they were certain to demand sufficient compensation. They were still piqued at Thailand's sudden acquiescence to the Japanese that had caused their armies in Burma and Malaya to suffer humiliating defeats.

Since they had recognized Phibun's declaration of war, they were in an advantageous position to impose certain conditions on the Thai government in the negotiation of a peace treaty. Their general position was outlined by Sir Josiah Crosby who had served as the British Minister in Bangkok prior to the war. "The case of Siam is exceptional in that she alone among the countries of Southeast Asia is at the same time an independent State and an enemy of Great Britain and the United States, upon whom she has formally declared war. When the terms of peace are dictated she will thus of necessity be liable to punishment, though if the provisions of the Atlantic Charter are observed, her sovereign status and her territorial integrity will remain unimpaired." [1]

Crosby did not specify the exact nature of the sanctions to be imposed on Thailand, but he advocated that some kind of "quasi-tutelary authority" be established in the country which would implement the recommendations of a group of foreign advisers chosen by the United Nations. He implied that Thailand would require a major foreign power to support its interests in the post-war era, and he indicated that this foreign power most likely would be Great Britain.

On one important point Crosby appealed for a joint effort by the Western democracies in Thailand. He requested that the Americans and the British give their wholehearted support to the democratic ideals for which World War II was fought by assisting the "liberal statesmen, who, if permitted, would address themselves with ardour to the work of carrying on the administration in accordance with constitutional principles."[2] He declared that the Allies must reduce the power of the Thai armed forces at the end of the war just as they were planning to do in Germany and Japan. He warned that if this action were not taken the establishment of a constitutional government would be doomed and the return of a military dictatorship would be inevitable. Regarding this matter he stated: "If the failure of constitutional government in Siam has proved one thing, it is that a relatively powerful army must represent a standing menace to the liberties of the people of any country in which the traditional form of government has been weakened or destroyed without the creation of an effective public opinion to supplement or replace it . . . Not until this impediment has been removed will there be a prospect for the application of democratic principles in Siam."[3]

Thus the policy of Great Britain toward Thailand at the end of World War II was to exert a moderately punitive sanction while at the same time to assist the liberal government which favored some form of constitutional democracy. The British recognized that the Thai government should not be unduly hampered in its attempt to regain its favorable pre-war economic status. They also realized Thailand's strategic importance to the security of Southeast Asia. Some spokesmen advocated that the country be required to join a Southeast Asia Federation which would be gradually merged with the British Commonwealth. This proposal was not seriously considered by the Attlee government.

The British position was mitigated by the courageous achievements of the Free Thai underground movement, the prompt repudiation of Phibun's declaration of war, and the promise to return the territories in Burma and Malaya. However, the British did not intend to be as lenient on the Thai as did the Americans. The refusal of the United States to recognize the declaration of war because it did not represent the will of the Thai people was criticized by many British observers. They pointed out that the Phibun regime had been in power since 1938 and had received much popular support for its ultra-nationalist programs. The American policy to treat Thailand as a friendly ally instead of an enemy nation was described by one British writer as a "curious anomaly."[4]

The contrasting policy of the United States toward Thailand at the end of the war was part of an all-embracing sympathy with the countries in Asia which had been ruled for many years by European colonial powers. The traditional anti-imperialist sentiments of the Americans demanded that the Europeans grant national independence to their colonies in Asia and bring an end to the exploitation of these backward people. Although the Americans were sympathetic to the enormous post-war difficulties confronting the British, the French, and the Dutch in Europe, they became increasingly critical of the attempts of their European allies to restore their former colonial empires. Many Americans were irked by Churchill's famous remark: "I have not become the King's First Minister in order to preside over the liquidation of the British Empire." From the moment of the Japanese surrender the United States advocated the early liberation of these former colonies as it was doing in the Philippines. Although Thailand had never been a colony, the Americans were suspicious of any attempt by the Europeans, especially the British, to tamper with Thai national sovereignty or to restore their former dominant influence in the country. Dr. Kenneth Landon, the leading American adviser on Thai affairs, declared: "Any appraisal of Thailand looking forward to a post-war settlement must take into consideration the fact that the Thai are an old nation with a distinct culture . . . Above everything else, the Thai want their freedom, their continued national existence. They would resist any forced coalition of the countries of Southeast Asia. An attempt to put them under the domination of an outside power would merely result in the creation of an Asiatic Ireland."[5]

The Americans hoped that the absence of a colonial background in Thailand would enable it to serve as a model to the former European colonies as they achieved their national independence. A *New York Times* correspondent foresaw a completely independent Thailand as "the forerunner of the new political order for Asia, freed of colonialism."[6] Some Americans predicted that the long tradition of national freedom would somehow help the newly-independent nations in Asia toward the goal of constitutional democracy. When receiving Prince Wan Waithayakon as the first Thai Ambassador in the United States, President Truman declared that "a democratic and stable Siam can make a great contribution to the peaceful progress of mankind, especially in Southeast Asia."[7] The general assumption was that a strong tradition of national independence automatically promoted a strong sense of individual freedom and the corresponding democratic institutions.

This sympathetic American attitude was due largely to the opinion that the policies and acts of the Phibun government during the war did not represent the real sentiment of the Thai people. The United States, unlike Great Britain, had suffered very little from Thailand's alliance with Japan. Any sense of hurt pride over the declaration of war was quickly salved by the belief that the people were actually sympathetic to the Allied cause. This feeling was strengthened by the long history of cordial relations between the two countries and the absence of any significant American commercial interests in Thailand. The close wartime collaboration between the United States and the Free Thai underground movement also convinced most Americans that the country had never been a loyal ally of Japan. In accepting the repudiation of Phibun's declaration of war, Secretary of State Byrnes declared that the United States regarded Thailand "not as an enemy but as a country to be liberated from the enemy." [8]

In preparing for the difficult post-war negotiations, the Thai quickly became aware of this friendly attitude, and they made a concerted effort to use American support to mitigate any heavy demands made by the British. Shortly after the Japanese surrender Pridi appointed Seni Pramoj, the Thai Minister in Washington, as Premier in an attempt to use Seni's popularity with the Americans to strengthen Thailand's position. This was a shrewd diplomatic move and it served its purpose very well. At first the British presented the Thai government with a proposal that would give them full compensation for their property losses, a monopoly of foreign trade, the right to station military forces in the country, the right to reorganize the armed forces, and a monopoly of the commercial airlines operating in Bangkok. When these proposals were revealed to the Americans they promptly intervened in the negotiations and forced the British to reduce most of these demands. At one point this pressure included threats from United States Congressmen to hold up a proposed multi-billion dollar loan to Great Britain. American intervention finally caused the British to accept a peace treaty in which they settled for the compensation for their property losses, moderate Allied control of Thai exports until September, 1947, the grant of 1½ million tons of free rice (which was never obtained), and other minor privileges. The British withdrew their demand to reorganize the armed forces and the Thai were given the authority to prosecute their own war criminals.

The most serious weakness of American intervention in these negotiations was the failure to support the British proposal to reduce the power and prestige of the Thai armed forces as previously recommended by Sir Josiah Crosby. This move was to have profound repercussions in post-war politics in Thailand. A unique opportunity for the

Western democracies to weaken the authoritarian political tradition by reorganizing the armed forces and discouraging military interference in politics was thereby neglected. What the Americans were doing in Germany and Japan to destroy militarism and promote democracy they would not allow the British to do in Thailand. Other than the removal of Phibun and his wartime military aides, the armed forces remained essentially the same. The new liberal government was consequently confronted at the outset with the possible resurgence of military interference in the political life of the nation. Regarding this failure John Coast declared: "Siam was no longer required to receive a military mission; in other words no precaution from abroad was to be taken against future attempts by the army to interfere in politics. The path to democracy would still have an Army road-block across it. This was regrettable, for the whole constitutional movement had been thwarted by a politico-military tradition kept alive by both Phya Bahol and Phibun."[9]

In retrospect, the policy of Great Britain toward Thailand at the end of the war was more realistic and far-sighted than that of the United States. While some of the initial British demands were extreme, many of their proposals were intended to assist the country in the long run, especially the proposal to reduce the power of the military. The good intentions of the Americans and their traditional sympathy for the "underdog" prevented an objective consideration of these measures. Actually the British were much better informed on the political and economic problems in Thailand than were the Americans, and their advisers were much more experienced in diplomatic and government affairs. The major American advisers were former missionaries who were unduly critical of the British and oversentimentalized the virtues of the Thai. American diplomatic officials who had served in the country prior to the war were not used by the United States government.

The Americans who suspected a restoration of British colonialism in Asia and excessive British interference in Thai internal affairs overlooked the important political and administrative reforms which Great Britain had already made in its Asian colonies, especially in India, and the significant progress it had achieved in preparing these people for self-government. The Americans also neglected the fact that the British government in July 1945 was taken over by the Labor Party, a party which for many decades had advocated the liquidation of the empire and the liberation of the colonies. A careful assessment by the United States of the long-run goals pursued by the British in Asia could have reduced this suspicion, and at least in Thailand a unified and enlightened policy by the two Western democracies might have achieved more lasting benefits for the Thai people.

The reasons for this unfortunate split between the United States and Great Britain were due primarily to their different experiences in dealing with the Thai government and people. The British had been involved with Thailand for almost a century largely in the fields of trade and diplomacy. Until World War II the Americans had been interested in the country mainly as a field of missionary activity. The experience of the British consequently tended toward the pragmatic and concrete; the experience of the Americans tended toward the humanitarian and altruistic. The Americans also suffered from the sentimental feeling that the Thai were an unusual and gifted people since they had retained their status as an independent nation during the nineteenth century when the neighboring countries in Southeast Asia were overrun by European colonial powers. Stewart Alsop voiced this opinion: "Muang Thai means Land of Free People; a not inappropriate name, since Siam was the only independent nation in Southeast Asia . . . Another result of this independent spirit is that the Siamese have never knuckled under to anybody. They had, in fact, before the war, established in their country the nearest approach to real freedom and democracy in any Oriental nation." [10]

Actually the Thai had been able to maintain their national sovereignty by a fortunate combination of several factors: their clever and opportunistic diplomacy, their relative isolation from the major centers of European penetration in Southeast Asia, and the mutual agreement by the British and the French to set up Siam as a buffer state between their colonies in Burma and Indochina. The latter factor was the most important. Contrary to American opinion, the Thai did not have any unique virtues which by themselves had prevented foreign domination. The British were aware of this and their more extensive experience in international politics made their policies in Thailand more realistic than those of the Americans.

One final advantage enjoyed by the British was their ability to understand the pluralistic nature of Thai society. Their attempt to reduce the power of the military leaders indicated a recognition of the need to permit other groups in the country to emerge and gain political influence and prestige. The Americans on the other hand considered Thailand largely in the collective sense as a tightly-knit nation. An understanding of the various groups within the society and their relative importance in domestic politics was lacking. To some extent this attitude was also due to the experience of the Americans during the previous century. The Protestant missionaries were prone to think of Thailand as the only small independent nation in an area dominated by European colonialism. The American diplomats were primarily concerned with the rights and obligations of Thailand as a sovereign nation. The American advisers were motivated largely by the attempt to remove the restrictions of extraterritoriality on Thai national sovereignty and gain for it an equal status in international society. In the early post-war era this emphasis on the nation, rather than on the individuals or groups within the society, was maintained by the United States. This attitude overlooked the fact that the preservation of Thai national independence by itself was no guarantee that the people would enjoy individual freedom and have the benefits of political and social justice.

In spite of these deficiencies, the Americans did much to assist the post-war recovery of the country. With the signing of the Anglo-Thai peace treaty on January 1, 1946 the United States promptly reestablished diplomatic relations with Thailand and supported its application for membership in the United Nations. The Americans provided a loan of $10,000,000 for the purchase of railroad equipment and the rehabilitation of the transportation system. They joined the British in several agreements to purchase Thai rice, rubber, and tin in an attempt to increase the foreign exchange reserves in the national treasury.[11] In addition to financial and economic aid, the Americans provided diplomatic support to the Thai government as it sought to restore normal relations with other major powers. The United States provided its good offices which enabled Thailand to reconcile its disputes with France; it played a mediating role in the negotiation of the first treaty ever signed between Thailand and China; and it supported the Thai leaders in the difficult task of establishing diplomatic relations with the Soviet Union which opened the way for their country to gain admission in the United Nations.

The Second Attempt at Constitutional Government. The victory of the Western democracies in World War II added great prestige to the liberals in Thailand as they again sought to establish a constitutional system. This time, however, they were not compelled to rely on the military leaders whose position had been temporarily subordinated in the aftermath of the war. With the major diplomatic crisis out of the way, the liberal government held the first general election in almost nine years. All wartime restrictions on political activities were abolished, and a former decree banning political parties was ignored.

The removal of the military from politics and the renewed enthusiasm for a democratic government enabled Pridi to emerge as the dominant political figure. Two political parties campaigned on his behalf: the Cooperative Party composed largely of Free Thai politicians from the poverty-stricken northeastern provinces, and the Constitutional Front consisting of the liberal faction in the People's Party which had overthrown the absolute monarchy in 1932. In opposition to these parties was the Democrat Party led by the former Premier, Khuang Aphaiwongse, and the Progressive Party led by Kukrit Pramoj, the younger brother of Seni Pramoj. Khuang represented the conservative interests who were suspicious of Pridi's radicalism in economic affairs. Kukrit represented the younger traditionalist groups close to the royal family who had never forgotten Pridi's role in overthrowing the absolute monarchy. In spite of this opposition Pridi's political position remained unshaken. His courageous role as the leader of the Free Thai underground movement and his close cooperation with the Western Allies gave him popularity and prestige unrivaled since the days of the absolute monarchy. In spite of his widespread appeal, however, Pridi hoped to remain aloof from politics and direct his followers from behind the scenes in his position as Regent for the young king.

The inchoate political parties which emerged in the early post-war period consisted of loose associations of aspiring party workers who were attracted to strong personal leaders such as Pridi and Khuang. None of these parties had a formulated program, a national organization, or grass-roots support. The majority of their followers consisted of the small educated elite centered in Bangkok, many of whom were close personal friends of the members in the other contending groups. Shifting loyalities of friendship, promises of appointment to public office, and money again encouraged many of these aspirants to shift their support from one party to another as opportunity dictated. Personalities more than party programs served as the dominant cohesive force. These emerging parties did little to enhance the prospects for the establishment of a constitutional system.

Despite this unpromising beginning, popular enthusiasm in the general election in January 1946 brought democratic aspirations to an all-time high. About 30 per cent of the electorate went to the polls.[12] The two parties supporting Pridi won a large majority in the Assembly. However, when he proposed one of his own aides as Premier, the legislature by a small majority elected Khuang, the leader of the Democrat Party. Upon assuming office Khuang found himself in bitter opposition to Pridi and two months later he resigned. Pridi was unable to find a suitable candidate for the office of Premier and he reluctantly stepped down as Regent and took the post himself. The Democrat and Progressive parties promptly joined ranks and formed an opposition to the liberal government.

In an attempt to strengthen the position of his political following, Pridi headed a special committee established by the Assembly to draft a new constitution. During these deliberations he requested Mr. Charles Yost and Dr. Kenneth Landon at the American Legation to provide him with copies of foreign constitutions and pertinent literature on democratic government.[13] Although no Americans took part in drafting the new constitution, the provision of this material by the American Legation had some influence in introducing certain features of the United States constitution into the Thai political system. The strong feeling of amity between the two countries and a sense of gratitude for American moral support in the post-war negotiations may also have encouraged the Thai leaders to imitate American institutions and practices. Many characteristics of British and French parliamentarianism incorporated into the former constitution were retained.

The major change made in the 1946 constitution was the establishment of a bicameral legislature. The new legislative body, now called a Parliament, was composed of a Senate and a House of Representatives. The Senate consisted of eighty members who could not be permanent officials of the government and who were elected by the lower house using a "method of indirect and secret voting." The qualifications for Senators were quite high and limited candidates to those persons over forty years of age who held a bachelor's degree, had high-level administrative experience, or had previously served in the Assembly of People's Representatives. The term for the office of Senator was six years with one-half of the Senate retiring every three years.

The House of Representatives was composed of members elected directly by the people. The term of office for members of the lower house was four years and they could not be permanent officials of the government. The king was given the prerogative to dissolve the House of Representatives although new elections had to be held within ninety days. The dissolution of the lower house could be ordered only once "for the same circumstances."

The powers of the king and Cabinet remained essentially the same as in the 1932 constitution. The Cabinet was renamed the "Council of Ministers" and it continued to be responsible, individually and collectively, to the Parliament.

A modest and unique attempt was made in the new constitution to establish some provision for judicial review. A Judicial Committee for the Constitution was created which consisted of fifteen "competent persons" appointed by Parliament who were to make the final decision on questions of law presented by the Dika Court regarding the constitutionality of legislation passed by Parliament. On other questions the absolute right to interpret the constitution was vested in Parliament. In effect these provisions did little to strengthen the role of the courts in judging legislation. The legislature remained supreme in resolving constitutional and legal disputes.

An important change in the new constitution was the absence of any restriction on members of the royal family from participating in politics. Thus some of the most competent and experienced men in the kingdom were able to participate in political affairs for the first time in fourteen years.

The most important American influence on the new constitution was the attempt to imitate certain bicameral features of the United States Congress. The creation of a Senate consisting of educated and experienced members to serve as a check on the more democratic House of Representatives indicated that Pridi and his aides wanted a more stable approach to the legislative process. American influence was seen in the adoption of an indirect method of electing Senators as practiced in the United States prior to 1913, although the Thai constitution provided for this election in the lower house of the national legislature and not in units of local government. The lengthy term of six years for Senators also indicated an attempt to imitate the practice used in the United States including the retirement of one-half of the Senators every three years, although the method of rotation in the upper house was slightly different in the United States.

Another American influence was seen in the modest attempt to introduce some provision for judicial review by authorizing the Judicial Committee for the Constitution to pass final judgment on the constitutionality of the law in cases pending before the Dika Court. The Thai may have intended to incorporate this distinctive American institution in their constitution by imitating in some degree the role of the United States Supreme Court. This attempt was greatly limited, however, by vesting this power in a special judicial committee instead of the Dika Court, and by the appointment of the members on this committee by Parliament and not by the executive as in the United States. This provision retained the primacy of political rather than judicial considerations in deciding the constitutionality of legislation passed by Parliament. In effect the legislature remained supreme in the interpretation of the constitution. The judicial system in Thailand continued to be more like that in Great Britain than in the United States.

The constitution was promulgated on May 9, 1946, and two weeks later the House of Representatives elected the members of the new Senate. Since the two parties supporting Pridi held a majority of the seats in the lower house, this election consisted largely of a wholesale packing of the upper house with more of his followers.[14] The result was a bicameral legislature whose membership was much like the previous Assembly of People's Representatives with its two categories of elective and appointive members. Under the new constitution, however, these representatives were meeting in two separate legislative bodies instead of one as before. Another difference was that the number of indirectly elected Senators was only one-half the number of elected members in the House of Representatives, and the power of the Senate was not as large as that of the lower house. This meant that the ability of the government to get legislation passed by Parliament was not as certain as before when the number of elective and appointive members was the same and each category of members had equal power. Yet the new legislative system was a decided asset to the liberal leaders, and it assured their control of the government for at least four years.

The drafting of the 1946 constitution by Pridi and his aides revealed an important custom which had become fairly well established in the development of the Thai political system, i.e., the essential purpose of establishing a new constitutional framework was to preserve a recent change in the domestic struggle for power and to provide an element of legality to the party which had emerged triumphant in this struggle. This consideration had been dominant in drafting both the 1932 and 1946 constitutions. Admittedly the new constitution was somewhat more democratic than its predecessor and it assured control of the government by the party in power for only four years instead of ten years as before. The liberals were undoubtedly aware that the formation of the new bicameral legislature had compromised their democratic ideals, and their methods were similar to those formerly used by the military leaders. However, with the constant threat of military interference in politics and in a country with little articulate public opinion, they probably felt they had no alternative in their endeavor to provide a stable government and keep themselves in power.

A final factor which favored the liberal government in the early months after the war was the return of King Ananda to Thailand in

December 1945. The family background and education of the young monarch encouraged a sympathetic attitude toward the establishment of a constitutional system. The king's father, Prince Mahidol, had received his medical training at Harvard University, and had worked earnestly to alleviate disease and suffering among his people until his untimely death in 1929. Ananda's mother was a commoner who had raised him to appreciate the advantages of a democratic society and the problems of the common people. The king had spent most of his life in Western Europe and had received a Western-style education in Switzerland. Upon his arrival in Thailand he took a sincere interest in the problems of his people and appeared sympathetic to the new liberal regime. Pridi and other members of the government were extremely pleased with Ananda's conduct and they felt his presence had helped to stabilize the country at a difficult time. The combination of a young democratic monarch and a liberal government caused many observers to predict that the opportunity for establishing constitutional democracy had reached an all-time high. "There seems little reason," one writer declared, "to doubt that full-fledged democracy will be attained in Siam. The king, brought up by democratic parents, is a genuine supporter of democracy and will defend it. Luang Pradit [Pridi], the ex-Regent, recognized as Siam's flaming liberal and an unswerving son of democracy, has blazed the trail for it." [15]

The Decline of the Liberal Government. At the very moment when conditions seemed most favorable for the achievement of constitutional democracy, the liberal government began to suffer in rapid succession a series of reverses which led to its downfall. The first of these setbacks occurred in April 1946 when the Dika Court held final judgment on the prosecution of Phibun and his wartime aides. Earlier in the year Pridi and Seni Pramoj had pushed a War Crimes Act through the Assembly, and at first they sought heavy punishment for the former military leaders. This attempt became increasingly unpopular as many Thai voiced their sympathy with Phibun's difficult position as Premier during the Japanese occupation. Many people forgot the excesses of his authoritarian rule, and the teachings of the Buddhist religion made them reluctant to inflict severe punishment. Some observers also recalled the "blood oath" made by the leaders of the 1932 coup that they would not shed each other's blood in future struggles for power. As the founder of the People's Party, Pridi possibly felt bound to this oath and was reluctant to cause the death of Phibun and the members of his wartime regime who had earlier helped in the overthrow of the absolute monarchy. A few persons claimed that Pridi never really intended to punish the former dictator but merely took this action to satisfy the punitive sentiment of the British and the Americans. This confusion was finally resolved when the Dika Court ruled that the War Crimes Act could not be made retroactive and hence was unconstitutional. Phibun and his aides were released and retired quietly to their Bangkok homes. The reasons for this unprecedented decision by the Dika Court were never fully explained. In all probability the judgment was the result of increasing public pressure and possible collusion by the leaders of the liberal government.

Actually the Dika Court did not have the authority under the 1932 constitution to declare a law passed by the Assembly unconstitutional as it did in the case of the War Crimes Act which enabled Phibun to go free. Nor did the constitution contain any prohibition of ex post facto laws. The draftsmen of the 1946 constitution were considering some form of judicial review at the time of this decision, but this power was to be exercised by the Judicial Committee for the Constitution and by Parliament, not by the Dika Court. The release of Phibun and his wartime aides was consequently an unconstitutional usurpation of powers by the high court. In the highly emotional atmosphere at the time in which almost all Thai regardless of political orientation desired the acquittal of the former military leaders, the intricacies of constitutional procedure were readily overlooked. Personal considerations took precedence over legal technicalities.

This incident revealed that Phibun had actually enjoyed much widespread popularity among the people. Many Thai had been willing to follow his leadership prior to the war, and they were willing to support him in his hour of need. This situation to a large extent showed the naivete of the American rejection of his declaration of war on the questionable grounds that it did not represent the real sentiment of the people. It illustrated once again that the British were much more sophisticated in their assessment of Thai politics during and after the war. The release of Phibun and his wartime aides likewise revealed that the Thai liberals were much more lenient toward their political opponents than the military leaders when they had controlled the government. On his rise to power in 1939 Phibun had many of his opponents executed. No "blood oath" or Buddhist scruples deterred the action of the military. However, when the liberals were in power they exhibited some sense of humanitarianism and a willingness to extend to their opponents the constitutional rights of Thai citizens. While this action was in keeping with Western legal practices, it had dangerous implications at the time for the future of constitutional government in Thailand. In a country with a weak democratic tradition, the liberated military leaders could at almost any time regain their control over the armed forces and seize power. In this action the liberals were unduly lenient and naive. They had unknowingly suffered a setback which was soon to bring about their own downfall.

The United States was partially responsible for this reversal suffered by the liberal government due to its failure to support the British demand to punish the members of the Phibun regime. Although the Western democracies would have confronted numerous problems in this undertaking, they could have meted out some punishment to the former wartime leaders. A sizeable minority in Thailand actually hoped the Americans and the British would undertake this unpleasant task. It is doubtful that the wartime actions of Phibun and his aides warranted death sentences or long terms in prison. Sentences of four or five years would have sufficed. They could have served these sentences in a British prison in Hong Kong, Penang, or Singapore. Or more symbolically, they could have served these brief terms with their former allies in the Sugamo Prison in Tokyo. While many people in Thailand would have opposed this action, the United States and Great Britain might have taken some measures to prevent the early release of Phibun and the members of his wartime regime. This action would have illustrated to the Thai people the strong opposition of the Western democracies to military interference in politics. It might have increased respect for civilian supremacy. In any case the highly emotional and sentimental Thai were themselves incapable of taking such action which could have benefited the future of the liberal government. The United States contributed to this failure, not by an act of commission, but by one of omission.

A second reverse came to the liberal regime with the tragic death of King Ananda who was found in his bed on the morning of June 9, shot in the forehead with a pistol. The inept handling of this incident by the liberal leaders reduced their former prestige and power. When announcing Ananda's death, the government first stated that he had been killed by an accident. Shortly thereafter it established an investigation commission, including American and British physicians, which was to determine the cause of the king's death.[16] The uncertainty aroused by this action was intensified when the commission issued a report that the young monarch had probably been murdered. Pridi's political opponents seized the unique opportunity offered by this incident to denounce the liberal regime with unprecedented vigor.

Within a few days Pridi was personally charged with implication in the death of the king.[17] As criticism mounted the liberal government reimposed many wartime restrictions on civil liberties. The press was censored, several houses were searched, and a member of the House of Representatives was arrested. These suppressive measures only served to incite greater bitterness toward the government, and within a short time rumors emerged that a conspiracy was being organized to overthrow the liberal regime. Pridi's popularity among the public continually declined, and in August 1946 he resigned as Premier. One of his wartime aides, Rear Admiral Thamrong Nawasawat, was appointed to take his place.

During the following year Pridi made two trips abroad which included a good-will tour of the United States and Great Britain. To the Western Allies he was still Thailand's "Elder Statesman" and the courageous wartime leader of the Free Thai underground movement. His excellent impression abroad did much to acquaint the West with Thailand as a friendly and progressive nation. After these successful foreign tours he returned home and tried to support the struggling Thamrong government. Although future investigations were made of the circumstances surrounding the death of the young king, this tragedy remained an unsolved mystery and it continued to weaken the position of the liberal regime.

The hostility aroused by Ananda's death crippled Pridi's political stature and he never again recovered the power and prestige he had previously enjoyed. His opponents continued to stress his allegedly anti-royalist sentiments in leading the 1932 coup, and he was frequently charged with attempting to establish a republic. Many conservatives recalled Pridi's radical economic plan and the animosity of King Prajadhipok toward the young liberal who had led the overthrow of the absolute monarchy. Few persons remembered that Pridi had never revealed any undue hostility toward the person of the king, and he had been opposed to the absolute monarchy only as an outmoded political institution. For almost five years he had served as Regent for the absent king and he could have conceivably used his position and his widespread popularity at the end of the war to abolish the monarchy and establish a republic. Instead, he had been instrumental in persuading the young king to return from Switzerland to help stabilize the country in the uncertain post-war era. Also, any attempt to displace Ananda and install himself at the head of the state would have required the removal of the king's younger brother and scores of other pretenders within the royal family.

There was little the United States could have done to alleviate the impact of this unfortunate incident. Americans have always shown much respect to the Thai royal family, and in an attempt to extend additional moral support to this small Southeast Asian country President Truman had invited King Ananda to visit the United States just prior to his return to Switzerland.[18] All the United States could do in this situation was to assist the struggling liberal regime as much as possible.

A third setback suffered by the liberal government was its failure to resolve the serious economic problems which confronted the country after four years of Japanese occupation.[19] The shortage of consumers goods caused a post-war inflation which raised retail prices to eight times their pre-war level. The damaged transportation system and extensive smuggling operations deprived the treasury of desperately needed foreign exchange. The low salaries of civil servants accompanied by high living costs encouraged widespread corruption, and the few attempts by the government to impose price controls were easily evaded. These unfavorable conditions did much to embarrass the liberal leaders and lower public morale.

Unfortunately corruption and profiteering were not confined to dishonest merchants and civil servants but extended to the Cabinet and Parliament as well. After Pridi resigned as Premier the discipline within his two political parties markedly decreased, and the desire of many members in the government and the legislature to enhance their personal fortunes became virtually uncontrolled. Scandals of the misuse of public funds rocked Bangkok almost every week but no effective official action was taken. One observer mentioned that the only persons enjoying any post-war prosperity were "the Chinese rice merchants, the smugglers, and the politicians."[20] Ironically, many of the corrupt officials were close friends of Pridi who did not become involved in these nefarious practices himself. Yet he refused to take any action against his followers and he continued to support the Thamrong government as best he could from within the quiet confines of his home. In the meantime public confidence in the liberal regime was rapidly deteriorating.

The serious economic problems confronting the government at the end of the war were due to the ravages of the Japanese occupation and the post-war shortage of manufactured goods. In a small agricultural country such as Thailand where the national income depended largely on the export of raw materials these problems were especially severe and they would have plagued the progress of any government. The corruption and profiteering after the war was also a legacy from the Japanese occupation in which the evasion of official regulations had been regarded as patriotic. These unfavorable conditions accompanied by the post-war freedom to criticize the government made the liberal leaders appear much more inefficient and corrupt than their predecessors.

In the early post-war period the United States sought to bolster the economy by providing the liberal regime with modest amounts of financial and economic aid. Also, private American trade expanded rapidly for the first time in almost a century. These conditions helped to improve the economy in some degree, but the recovery of the country continued to be halting and slow. The United States could have provided more economic assistance to the liberal government, but Americans generally felt that more time and effort would eventually restore pre-war prosperity. The highly publicized corruption of the liberal regime may also have discouraged the United States from extending additional economic aid, and most Americans saw no urgent need at the time to provide Thailand with large-scale economic or financial assistance.

A final factor which contributed to the decline of the liberal government was its inexperience with a constitutional political system. The Cabinet appointed by Thamrong in August 1946 lacked a strong personal following and it relied almost entirely on the two political parties which had supported Pridi. These parties, however, began to disintegrate because of his withdrawal from the government and long absences from the country. In the by-elections the same month in which the unsolved mystery surrounding Ananda's death had served as the major issue, Pridi's two parties had to fight for their political lives. They barely managed to hold a slim 54 per cent majority in the House of Representatives. These results encouraged the opposition Democrat Party to mount bitter and repeated attacks against the inefficiency and corruption of the liberal regime. Equally ominous was the announcement in March 1947 that Phibun had emerged from retirement and was reentering politics. On this occasion the former dictator proclaimed that thereafter he was "dedicated to democratic principles."[21] At the same time he formed a new political party, the Tharmathipat (Right is Might) Party, around a nucleus of his former wartime aides. Phibun and his followers promptly joined with the Democrat Party in opposing the Thamrong government.

During 1947 the political scene became increasingly fluid and complex. The organization of the leading political parties weakened as many members in Parliament were willing to leave one party and join another if they could obtain a sufficient price. In May 1947 a general debate forced the first Thamrong government to resign, although the liberal leaders managed to gain a vote of confidence by a narrow margin and establish a new Cabinet. At the same time the Democrat Party suffered a split within its ranks when one faction formed a new People's Party (Prachachon) and aligned its members with Pridi's Cooperative Party and Constitutional Front. The remaining members of the Democrat Party charged that this move had been engineered and financed by Pridi, and they allied their group more closely with Phibun's growing Tharmathipat Party. In addition to these factional disputes, the political atmosphere became charged with tension as several members of the Democrat Party were murdered and other major political figures narrowly escaped death in abortive assassination attempts.

By the autumn of 1947 the deterioration of political and economic conditions threatened the entire constitutional system which the liberal leaders had established after the war. Many Thai were becoming disillusioned with the second attempt at democratic government. Some persons looked back nostalgically on the more stable times of Phibun's military rule. A few observers expected the former dictator to make a political comeback and restore order to the administration of the country. At the same time rumors emerged that Thamrong wanted to resign as Premier. More persons predicted that he might be replaced by someone in the military services.[22]

On November 8, 1947 army troops suddenly seized strategic positions and major government buildings throughout Bangkok. Like the two previous coups this seizure of power was a bloodless affair. Thamrong and many members of his Cabinet had been forewarned and they escaped from the country. Pridi narrowly avoided capture and went into hiding at a naval installation for several days. With the assistance of the American and British naval attaches he succeeded in making his way to Singapore. The following day the Coup Group (Rataprahan) which had seized power announced that during the present emergency Field Marshal Phibun Songkhram would be in charge of the government and he would rule from the Ministry of Defense. The army leaders stated that they had overthrown the liberal regime because of its failure to cope with the corruption and inflation which were hindering the progress of the country and "causing unprecedented moral deterioration of the people."[23] Thailand's international reputation, they claimed, had also been jeopardized by the previous regime "which if allowed to continue unchecked, will lead to unending disaster for the nation and ultimately even to the loss of her independence."[24] The 1946 constitution was abolished and a new provisional constitution was promulgated.

The 1947 coup was actually planned and executed by two relatively unknown army officers, Colonel Luang Kach Songkhram and Lieutenant General Phin Chunawan. Two minor figures in the plot were Colonel Phao Sriyanon, who was General Phin's son-in-law and a rising and ambitious police officer, and Colonel Sarit Thanarat, who commanded the strategic First Army stationed in Bangkok. This new group of army leaders was vastly different from the military faction of the People's Party which had overthrown the absolute monarchy in 1932. The earlier military group consisted of many officers who had received their training in Europe and had been partially exposed to the practices of Western democracy. They were thus willing to go along with the attempt of the liberals to establish a constitutional form of government. A few officers such as Colonel Bahol had been especially devoted to upholding the 1932 constitution. All the leaders of the 1947 Coup Group, however, had received their military training in Thailand and none of them had been exposed to the democratic tradition of Western societies. These officers were consequently devoted to the authoritarian political tradition in which they had been trained.

Yet the new coup leaders were continuing the tradition of military interference in the political life of the nation. And there was an indication that they had acted for economic reasons as had their predecessors. Just as Prajadhipok's retrenchment measures in 1931 had partially contributed to the overthrow of the absolute monarchy, so did the economic policies of the liberal government in 1946-1947 lead to its eventual downfall. Prior to the 1947 coup the Thamrong regime was considering a cut in the armed forces in an attempt to lower the cost of the government and assist the economic recovery of the country. Rather than face possible unemployment or a reduction in salary, the military leaders decided to take immediate action and seize power. The Coup Group took advantage of the rising discontent toward the liberal leaders, and they justified their seizure of power with the familiar claim that only the military could provide for the order and security of the country. Like the spokesmen of the absolute monarchy and the former People's Party, the new military group declared that it was acting only in the interests of the people.

Phibun undoubtedly knew of the plan for the 1947 coup but he did not take a direct part in it as many observers suspected. The leaders of the Coup Group realized that their members were unknown either inside or outside the country, and they selected Phibun to lead the new regime to give it both national and international "prestige." He refused to head a new government but he agreed to serve as Commander-in-Chief of the Thai Military Forces and to countersign the provisional constitution.[25] The former dictator realized that he was still unpopular with the United States and Great Britain, and he undoubtedly counseled the politically naive leaders of the Coup Group to exercise restraint to prevent undue hostility or possible interference from the two Western powers.

The major effect of the 1947 coup was the removal of the liberals as an active political force. This incident also ended the first attempt to establish constitutional democracy in post-war Thailand. Thereafter the new military leaders were confronted only by the royalist-conservatives in their quest for dominant power. The prophetic admonition of the former British Minister, Sir Josiah Crosby, that one of the major obstacles to constitutional government in Thailand would be the leaders of the armed forces had been fulfilled.

An important reason for the failure of the liberals to establish a constitutional system was their own political inexperience and personal weaknesses. Perhaps most serious was their lack of discipline and their inability to develop themselves into a cohesive political force. Unlike the military leaders who relied on the highly-disciplined armed forces, the liberals failed to build a national party organization on which they could gain popular support. In spite of lip service to the democratic ideals of the 1932 revolution, they often used their official positions to enhance their personal fortunes instead of working for the interests of the people. This failure aroused much discontent even among the generally apathetic public, and it gave the military an excuse to interfere again in politics. The position of the liberals was also weakened because they did not resort to the extreme measures used by the military leaders in eliminating their political opponents.

However, these failures of the liberal leaders were not the only factors which contributed to the end of the first post-war attempt to establish constitutional government. Many of the reverses were beyond their control. The unsolved death of the king, the unfavorable economic conditions caused by the war, and the lack of a mature public opinion did much to hinder the progress toward a stable democratic system. Yet these were circumstances over which the liberals could have exerted little influence during the two brief years they were in power. With more time, patience, and experience it is possible that these conditions could have been significantly improved. However, the desire of the militarists for political and economic power prevented the liberals from pursuing this goal.

Also the domination of the economy by Western and Chinese enterprise continued to discourage most Thai from entering a business or professional career. Ambitious young people still sought a career within the already oversized governmental bureaucracy. The gradually expanding middle class from which opposition to authoritarian rule has come in many Western nations was thereby shunted away from economic and social activities that could eventually arouse a demand for some form of limited government. Chinese and Western commercial interests became involved in the corruption engendered by this system since they were important sources of income and were forced to buy the cooperation of the government to continue their business operations. The Thai who entered the ranks of the bureaucracy in most cases became obedient administrators for the party in power.

The Interim Before Military Rule. The provisional constitution promulgated by the coup leaders indicated that they were temporarily seeking the support of the Democrat Party in their quest for more political power. Certain provisions favored by the royalist-conservatives were included, such as additional powers for the king and the Senate. Many sections were loosely worded, however, and the new constitution could easily become the legal basis for an authoritarian rule. Yet the military leaders did not completely subvert the letter or the spirit of the previous constitution which had been influenced by the American and British political systems. Nor did they push their newly-won role in the government too far. They retained free elections, parliamentary responsibility, civil rights, and other democratic features. Their desire to maintain good relations with the United States and Great Britain undoubtedly encouraged them to remain temporarily in the background. They were also limited in political experience and they were aware that some popular support for democratic government still remained among the people. They consequently avoided the impression of a hasty return to a military rule.

The initial restraint of the Coup Group did little to mitigate the unfavorable response of Americans both in the United States and in Thailand to the forcible overthrow of the liberal regime. Most Americans suspected that Phibun was the instigator of the military seizure of power which intensified their rancor at this sudden turn of events. The Department of State announced that he was "the man who declared war on the Allies," and any government headed by him would be "extremely unpopular" with the Western democracies.[26] However, the announcement continued, if the former dictator remained in the background and "moderate" leaders assumed control of the government, the United States would regard the situation "differently."[27] "The political clock has been turned back . . .," a *New York Times* editorial exclaimed. "It is hoped the present setback will be only transitory and that, with the aid of the United States, the peace-loving Siamese people will soon again turn to the task of making their country a going democracy and a prosperous country."[28]

The United States Ambassador in Bangkok, Mr. Edwin Stanton, discussed the coup with Sir Geoffrey Thompson, the British Ambassador. Mr. Stanton stated: "Neither Thompson nor I liked this overthrow of the Thamrong government by force; the flouting of the constitutional processes simply set back the hands of the clock . . . We deplored the rule of force, the possibility of civil war as well as numerous diplomatic complications which might arise."[29] Alexander MacDonald, the American editor of the *Bangkok Post,* likewise commented: "To my mind, this military overthrow of even so unsatisfactory a government as Thamrong's threw Siam into a class with Latin America's banana republics. From now on, the man with the key to the arsenal would be the man in charge, regardless of politics, parliaments or constitutions."[30]

Outspoken criticism from the Americans, supplemented by similar opposition from the British, caused Phibun to resign as the Commander-in-Chief of the Thai Military Forces and to accept the more modest position of Commander-in-Chief of the Thai Army. In all probability he again counseled the leaders of the Coup Group to exercise restraint to avoid foreign intervention in internal affairs. The Allied restrictions on foreign trade had expired only two months before and a drastic change in the personnel and policies of the government might encourage a renewal of foreign controls. Also, by the end of 1947 Thailand had come to rely on the United States for economic and financial assistance, and the rapidly expanding trade with Great Britain had again become an important factor in the economy. The need to maintain good relations with the two Western powers was thus imperative.

The pressure exerted on the Thai government by the United States and Great Britain caused the coup leaders to remain in the background and enabled the "moderates" in the Democrat Party to assume a temporary role. The royalist-conservatives began by extending their control to the upper house of the legislature. Although the military leaders attempted to place their own followers in the Senate, the Regent, Prince Rangsit, ignored their request and appointed one-hundred Senators from among the nation's most venerable and highly-educated elite. Only eight Senators were selected from the 1932 revolutionary group, and no Senators were appointed from among the leadership of the recent coup.

The Coup Group was also by-passed in the selection of the potentially powerful Supreme State Council. The formation of this advisory body to the king resulted in the appointment of five members who were decidedly pro-monarchist and conservative. This move enabled the royalist-conservatives to expand their control from the legislature to the executive. When the widely-respected Prince Dhani accepted a position on the Supreme State Council he did so only on the condition that Khuang Aphaiwongse, the leader of the Democrat Party, would be appointed as Premier. The two leaders of the Coup Group, General Phin and Colonel Kach, again attempted to appoint their own followers to the new government, but the royalist-conservatives countered their demands by stressing the need to maintain good relations with the United States and Great Britain. The military leaders acquiesced and allowed Khuang to form a new regime. The conservative leader was hesitant at first to become Premier since he had no desire to serve as a puppet for the military. He now realized, however, that military power had again become the dominant force in Thai politics, and the only alternative to a government led by his party would be a resumption of military rule. He was also aware that his regime would rely largely on the diplomatic support of the United States and Great Britain. Should the policies of the Western democracies change, his government would be without a source of power.

Khuang finally agreed to form a new Cabinet with the understanding by the military that they would not interfere in politics. He probably knew he was taking a chance in trusting the coup leaders, but he decided to try and provide the best government possible. He promptly appointed many highly qualified and experienced men to his Cabinet, and the recent coup ironically brought to power one of the most honest and competent governments in Thai history. The new regime drafted plans to combat inflation and corruption, and launched another investigation to resolve the mystery surrounding the death of the late king. According to the provisional constitution this Cabinet could serve as a caretaker government only until new elections were held within ninety days.

While Khuang and his ministers made plans to stabilize the country, the army and the police suppressed many followers of the former liberal regime. The coup leaders published a series of stories purporting to prove that Pridi and the liberals were planning to set up a Communist government and murder the king. Army and police authorities arrested many persons who had participated in the Free Thai underground movement and the post-war liberal governments, some of whom were alumni of colleges and universities in the United States.[31] This suppression was generally restrained, however, as the military knew that Pridi and his followers were still popular with the Americans and the British. Also, the recognition of the new government by the Western powers was still pending.

In this atmosphere the general elections for the one-hundred seats in the new House of Representatives were held on January 29, 1948. They were reported as the most honest elections ever held in Thailand.[32] The Democrat Party had campaigned actively throughout the country and relied primarily on Khuang's growing popularity with the public. Phibun's Tharmathipat Party was actively supported by the army and heavily financed by wealthy followers who expected the military to make a political comeback. The other contenders in the election were the Prachachon Party which had formerly been a faction within the Democrat Party, and the Independents which included some of Pridi's more innocuous followers who had not been arrested or forced into hiding. Although the elections aroused less public enthusiasm than in 1946 and only 22 per cent of the electorate went to the polls, the returns gave Khuang's Democrat Party a slim majority. The results were as follows: [33] Democrat Party—53 seats, Independents—30 seats, Prachachon Party–12 seats, Tharmathipat Party–5 seats.

In Bangkok, a major contest in any national election, Khuang's party won all four seats while Phibun's party received none. Shortly after the election ten Independent representatives asked to join the Democrat Party which gave Khuang a majority of sixty-three seats in the lower house. The remaining members of the Tharmathipat Party, the Prachachon Party, and the Independents closed ranks and formed an opposition.

Khuang's Cabinet received an overwhelming vote of confidence in both houses of Parliament, and within 36 hours it obtained the long-sought recognition by the United States and Great Britain. During the next two months it removed many restrictions on foreign trade and succeeded in achieving a modest increase in rice exports. It drafted a new development program which included irrigation projects, rural electrification, and transportation. This ambitious plan, however, required considerable capital investment which the government did not have. Also, there was no change in the high cost of living. Khuang and his ministers realized that many of the economic problems which had confronted the previous liberal government offered no quick or easy solution, and they would need time and patience to put the national economy on a permanently stable basis.

In an attempt to strengthen their political position, the leaders of the Democrat Party played a dominant role in drafting a permanent constitution. Shortly after taking office the new government established a Constituent Assembly of forty members to draft a constitution and submit it to Parliament for approval within 180 days. Twenty of the delegates appointed to this body were members of the Democrat Party, while the remaining twenty delegates were selected from various professions outside of political circles. No delegates were selected from the leadership of the Coup Group. This action was strongly opposed by the military leaders who had already drafted a permanent constitution which would revert to the authoritarian political framework embodied in the 1932 constitution. The military members in Parliament promptly attacked the Khuang government as incompetent and ineffective. They also condemned the Senate as a reactionary and undemocratic body. The temporary rapprochement between the military and the royalist-conservatives had come to an end.

By March 1948 the Coup Group was becoming increasingly restive and did not appear willing to remain in the political background much longer. The poor showing of Phibun's Tharmathipat Party in the January 1948 elections had been a major insult to the military leaders and invalidated their claim that they had acted on behalf of the people in staging the November 1947 coup. Also, they were becoming more frustrated as the Democrat Party took over the Senate, the Supreme State Council, the Cabinet, the House of Representatives, and finally the Constituent Assembly. If they were to abide by the provisional constitution and the results of the latest elections, they saw themselves out of power for at least another four years. If a permanent constitution were drafted by the Democrat Party, they would continue to play a minor role in the government.

The military leaders finally decided to increase their political power regardless of possible criticism from American and British public opinion. They brashly began by seizing the executive. On April 6, 1948 they informed Khuang that he would have to resign within twenty-four hours because the progress made by his government had been unsatisfactory. The conservative leader promptly sought the support of the navy and the air force in an attempt to quell the army's bid for power, but he was informed that their manpower and weapons were insufficient.[34] His Cabinet reluctantly decided to resign. The following morning the Coup Group appointed Phibun as the new Premier.

As the first pro-Axis dictator to regain power after the war, Phibun promptly insisted that he had reluctantly taken this position only to prevent a violent clash between the young ambitious army officers in the Coup Group and the liberal regime ousted in November 1947. In an interview with Alexander MacDonald, he stated: "Public opinion wanted the change, and as it could not be done by constitutional means, the former government having a majority in Parliament, the Army decided unanimously to get rid of it."[35] In an attempt to gain popular support for the new military regime, the former army chief promised to bring an end to the instability of the country. He claimed that his government would solve the three perennial problems: inflation, corruption, and the mystery of the late king's death. He professed that he had become a "constitutional monarchist" and "the Siamese people can remove him from office whenever they want to do so."[36] Just how the people could do this he did not say. Phibun combined his quest for popular support with an appeal for closer cooperation between Thailand and the Western democracies. He stated that his government would continue to support the United Nations and pursue a firm anti-Communist policy. He stressed the emerging threat from mainland China and concluded that the United States was the only foreign power which could offer effective protection to the country. He was also eager to show his repentance for his pro-Axis leanings during World War II and anxious to prove to the Western democracies that he was really on their side.

In spite of these professions of democratic sympathy, the appointment of Phibun as Premier marked the return to military rule. By this time the militarists had developed a clever and subtle method to ease themselves into power. This process had three basic steps. The first was the forcible seizure of power in the name of the people who were allegedly demanding a change of government. This was done in abolishing the absolute monarchy in 1932 and in ousting the liberal regime in 1947. The second move was to appoint a highly-respected civilian to head an interim government in an attempt to pacify local and foreign opinion. This was accomplished in appointing Phya Manopakorn as Premier in 1932 and Khuang Aphaiwongse to head the provisional government in 1947. The third step was the direct assumption of power by the military leaders once conditions had settled and it was clear that the interim government had no internal source of support. This maneuver had been taken by Colonel Bahol in 1933 and was imitated by the Coup Group in 1948. By this time it was vividly clear that political power in Thailand depended on the control of the armed forces. Any element of constitutionalism was merely a facade to legalize the role of the military in the government.

In spite of their authoritarian methods, however, the militarists were aware of the need to base their government on a written constitution. By 1947 the symbol of a constitution as the source of political authority had become sufficiently widespread so that even they could not neglect it. Yet the essential purpose was not to establish a legal framework which would limit the exercise of political power and protect the rights of the people. Instead it was to preserve a recent change in the struggle for power and provide a legal basis for the victorious party. The military leaders were merely imitating the custom already established by the People's Party in 1932 and the liberals in 1946. By 1948 a unique combination of traditional authoritarianism and modern constitutionalism, with the major emphasis on the former, had become an important feature of the political system.

When the coup leaders ousted Khuang in April 1948 and Phibun resumed office as Premier, the government again faced the problem of gaining foreign recognition. The appearance of a serious Communist threat and the need to retain American economic aid made a prompt recognition by the United States highly desirable. Phibun originally attempted to win favor with the Western powers by seeking the reappointment of the ministers in Khuang's Cabinet. However, the refusal of these men to serve in his new government forced him to appoint many ministers who had poor reputations with the Americans and the British. Yet after little comment the United States exchanged diplomatic relations with the Phibun regime on May 3, 1948 less than a month after it had come to power. Other nations quickly followed suit.

Within a short time the reasons for the long delay by the Western powers in recognizing Khuang's government and the brief interval in extending diplomatic relations to Phibun's government became increasingly clear. The overthrow of the liberal regime in November 1947 occurred just as the United States was beginning to oppose Communist aggression in Southern Europe by providing military and economic assistance to Greece and Turkey. These moves were made before the Communist coup in Czechoslovakia and any apparent

Communist threat to Southeast Asia. With the overthrow of a weak liberal regime in Thailand, the United States could afford to wait and hope that some semblance of constitutional democracy would be preserved. By April 1948, however, the world situation had drastically changed. The United States was rushing large-scale military and economic aid to Western Europe to prevent further Communist aggression. Much of China had fallen under Communist control and Communist revolts began spreading to the newly-independent nations in Southeast Asia. Within this increasingly turbulent region Thailand was the only nation that did not have a Communist insurrection within its borders and it was the only country that remained relatively stable and calm. As the United States considered measures to deter Communist aggression in Southeast Asia, a conservative and anti-Communist regime in Thailand became increasingly attractive regardless of its internal policies or methods of achieving power. The Americans consequently became less interested in assisting the evolution of constitutional democracy and more concerned with opposing the spread of Communism. The British were also attracted to Phibun in spite of his opportunistic past, and they immediately sought his cooperation in fighting the Communist guerrillas along the Thai-Malayan border. Many segments of the British press were soon hailing the new Premier as "the strong man of Siam" whereas only a short time before he had been labeled as a "Japanese-sponsored quisling." [37] The move to recognize his government by the United States and Great Britain was also hastened by the opening of a Soviet Legation in Bangkok in the spring of 1948. This was the first Soviet diplomatic mission to be stationed in Southeast Asia.

In spite of Phibun's former collaboration with the Japanese, the Western democracies were consequently drawn closer to Thailand which had never fallen to a colonial status and had traditionally looked to the West for diplomatic support and material aid. Unlike the newly-independent nations in South and Southeast Asia such as India, Burma, and Indonesia which opposed Western military alliances and espoused a distasteful brand of neutralism, the Thai government was eager to cooperate with the United States and Great Britain in protecting the security of the region. The common objective of the Western powers and Thailand to prevent Communist aggression in Southeast Asia dictated the need for an accommodating rapprochement.

Thus, almost by coincidence the two years of liberal government in Thailand had coincided with the two-year transition in the foreign policy of the United States from the hope of peace and freedom in the early post-war period to a policy emphasizing peace and security in the new era of Communist aggression. During this time both the United States and Great Britain exerted a modest influence on the Thai government which coincided with their contrasting experiences in the country during the previous century. By 1948 the pre-eminent position of the United States in the Cold War caused the influence of the Americans to overshadow that of the British. The new era in international relations had opened the way for the United States to become more deeply involved in Thai political affairs.

CHAPTER III

THE RETURN TO MILITARY RULE

The apparent Communist threat to Thailand in 1948 caused the United States to pursue a more pragmatic policy than it had followed in the early post-war era. The Americans were no longer talking seriously of democratic ideals but were now concerned primarily with the practical matter of national security. Although some Americans retained a lingering suspicion of Phibun, many made this transition with little difficulty. The traditional admiration for Thailand's independence was again reiterated, and the unity and freedom of the Thai people was stressed. The rights of the nation were consistently voiced by the Americans in an attempt to bolster the country against Communist aggression much as these rights had been stressed before to prevent interference in Thai affairs by the European colonial powers.

These sentiments quickly took form in concrete action. In May 1949 Thailand was admitted as the forty-eighth member of the World Bank and the International Monetary Fund. Shortly thereafter a Thai military mission was invited to make a tour of army and air force installations in the United States. The Department of State complied with a request of the Thai government for a scientific mission to conduct a survey of the nation's resources.[1] The SCAP authorities in Japan also released $43,700,000 in gold as payment for goods and services which Thailand had rendered to the Japanese during World War II.[2] By the end of 1949 the United States was making plans to provide additional economic and technical aid under the Point Four program.

The strategic importance of Thailand in the new American policy in Southeast Asia was dramatically symbolized in February 1950 when Ambassador-at-Large Phillip C. Jessup arrived in Bangkok for a three-day conference with all the United States ambassadors in the Far East. The diplomats attending this meeting voiced their concern with the serious Communist threat and considered various proposals to strengthen the defenses within the region. They were not optimistic. The Communists were credited with having a "dynamic timetable" to bring Southeast Asia under their control.[3] The small countries in the were compared to a line of dominoes which would topple any one of them fall to the impending "coordinated attack."[4] Jessup talked with Phibun during his brief stay and sought his support.

From this time on the Americans sought increasingly to win Thai cooperation by stressing the "freedom" both countries enjoyed due to their common opposition to Communist aggression. On his departure Ambassador Jessup stated: "It is our conviction that we maintain our free institutions and our free traditions, our way of life and our own prosperity by steadfast unwillingness to yield to the blandishments of any foreign authority".[5] Shortly thereafter the United States provided further tangible support to this policy when President Truman approved a grant of $10,000,000 for military aid to Thailand, and the Department of State announced that swift economic assistance would be extended through the Economic Cooperation Administration.

During his first year in office Phibun seized the unique opportunity of forging closer relations with the Western democracies to bolster his own position in the internal political elite. At first his control over the government was considerably less than it had been before the war. He was now confronted with a royalist-conservative opposition in Parliament, and his power relied on the young army and police officers who had appointed him Premier. In an attempt to strengthen his tenuous position he promptly voiced the same opinion held by the Americans that the Communists posed a serious threat to Thai national security. In August 1949 he stated that foreign pressure had become "alarming" and internal Communist activity had "vigorously increased."[6]

The military and economic assistance provided by the United States also enhanced Phibun's position within the internal power structure and with the public. The offer of military aid and the diplomatic conference attended by Ambassador Jessup had a dramatic effect in illustrating to the government and people that the Americans were eager to assist them in another era of international conflict. The provision of large-scale economic aid by the United States combined with improved foreign trade enabled Thailand to enjoy its first prosperity since before the war. In 1949 Bangkok was selected as the Far Eastern headquarters for many agencies of the United Nations, a move which gave additional respectability to the Phibun regime. The former dictator received much credit for better economic conditions and he won added prestige for the assistance provided by the United States. The traditional goodwill between the Americans and the Thai likewise did much to enhance his stature.

The Move to Consolidate Military Power. As the United States strengthened Phibun's political position by providing Thailand with greater diplomatic support and foreign aid, his regime sought to consolidate and extend its power. It justified this move as a necessary measure to improve the security of the country in the face of possible Communist aggression. It began with the popular action of increasing restrictions on the local Chinese who controlled the economy and comprised the backbone of the small Communist movement. Anti-Chinese legislation was passed by Parliament, and all Chinese associations, Nationalist and Communist, were outlawed.[7] The government assumed wider powers by declaring a state of emergency and reimposing a partial censorship of the press. These restrictions were not confined to the Chinese alone as many liberals who had served in the Free Thai movement were also subject to intimidation and arrest.[8] Liberal opposition was further reduced by pushing the prosecution of former friends of Pridi who were allegedly implicated in the death of the late king. This wave of suppression was made amid official announcements that there were numerous conspiracies to overthrow the Phibun regime.

The government's fear of a coup was justified in October 1948 when a small group of army officers led by Major General Net Kemayothi attempted to overthrow the Coup Group. This scheme was uncovered before its leaders had an opportunity to act. It involved some sixty officers, many serving on the Army General Staff, who wanted to remove the armed forces from interference in politics. These professional army officers received only light sentences or suffered a forced retirement from active military service. The leaders of the Coup Group, however, used this incident as an opportunity to purge the army of disloyal followers and to assure its undivided support of the Phibun government.

This event revealed once again the major weakness of American interference in the post-war British policy in Thailand. The attempted coup indicated that the armed forces did have a large number of high-ranking officers who supported a constitutional government and wanted the military services to restrict their activities to the legitimate role of defending the nation. Had this group of officers earlier been placed at the top of the armed forces the liberal government might have survived the early post-war difficulties, and the liberal leaders, not the military, would have been the recipient of large-scale aid from the United States. Had this occurred the political system might have continued its slow evolution toward constitutional democracy instead of reverting to the authoritarian tradition.

A more serious threat to Phibun's regime occurred on February 26, 1949 when Pridi stole back into the country, and with the support of the navy and some of his Free Thai followers attempted to overthrow the government. A bitter struggle raged throughout Bangkok for three days. The fighting came to an end when Pridi's followers failed to get control of the army's tank arsenal and Phibun promised the navy a larger role in his government. Pridi managed to escape capture but coups in Thailand had ceased to be bloodless affairs. Several hundred military personnel and civilians were killed or wounded and much property was damaged. This unsuccessful attempt to overthrow the government aroused much hostility among the public and thereafter the liberals declined further as a political force. "Pridi himself," Alexander MacDonald commented, "lost incalculably by the plot's failure. His attempt to come back by force led many who had admired his vision and his statemanship to class him as a political adventurer; and the death, imprisonment, and torture of so many of his followers badly damaged his political machine." [9]

The two abortive coups in 1948 and 1949 gave the Phibun regime an additional excuse to consolidate its power more extensively than before. The failure of the professional army officers to oust the Coup Group enabled it to purge the army and assure its complete loyalty to the government. Thereafter no further opposition to military interference in politics emerged from within the armed forces. The coup attempt led by Pridi indicated that by 1949 many liberals saw the futility of trying to seek power through constitutional means and they also were willing to use force.

Previously the liberals had relied on the military leaders to provide the armed power for overthrowing the absolute monarchy and protecting the constitutional system; this time the liberals were willing to resort to arms themselves in an attempt to seize power. Pridi's abortive coup caused the Phibun government to resort to harsh measures in suppressing opponents of military rule. No longer did American or British opinion exercise any significant restraint in protecting the liberals. Within a few days two former Free Thai leaders were shot to death in their homes and many persons suspected of sympathizing with Pridi were interrogated or arrested.[10] Four ministers who had served in the liberal regime were seized and tortured by the police. Several days later they were placed in a station wagon and brutally shot.[11] The police brazenly explained that these suspects had unsuccessfully tried to escape, and they invited members of the local press to witness this sordid scene. By coincidence these four ex-ministers had been witnesses for the defense of persons accused of implication in the death of the late king. The navy was also removed as a potential source of opposition. Disloyal naval officers were imprisoned and the appropriations for the navy were drastically curtailed.

The abortive 1949 coup caused Phibun to expand the power of the Police Department. This move served two political purposes. It encouraged his regime to take more stringent measures to suppress its opponents and assure its continuation in power. It also enabled him to strengthen his own position in the internal ruling elite by balancing the influence of the army officers who had appointed him as Premier with the rapidly expanding power of the police. He selected Phao Sriyanon, now a Major-General, as the Chief of the powerful Suppression Division of the Police Department, and the clever police chief was soon a rising political leader.

Simultaneous with his endeavor to eliminate any effective opposition, Phibun sought to restore a strong spirit of nationalism as a cover for greater political authority. In May 1949 he again changed the name of the country to Thailand and his government revived many popular national customs and ceremonies. He likewise stressed the traditional respect for the monarchy in an attempt to gain broader powers for his regime. This move to increase royalist sentiment reached a climax early in 1950 when King Phumiphon returned from Switzerland amid much jubilation and pageantry. During a short stay in the country the king presided at the cremation rites of his late brother and married the daughter of the Thai Ambassador to Great Britain whom he had met while studying abroad. Phumiphon was crowned in an elaborate ceremony and shortly thereafter he returned to Europe to resume his studies. During his brief visit in Bangkok the king also opened a special session of Parliament, and Phibun prevailed on the young monarch to sign a Royal Decree authorizing his government to use the armed forces anywhere in the country to suppress "Communist-inspired" incidents. This measure gave additional legality to the military regime as it sought to remove its opponents and consolidate its expanding power.

With the removal of political opposition from within the armed forces and the elimination of the liberals, the power of the Coup Group after 1949 was limited only by the royalist-conservative Democrats in Parliament and the increasing Western influence in internal affairs. The prestige of the national legislature had suffered considerably during the unstable period after the war, but the brief experiment in constitutionalism still caused many people to view it as both a symbol of democratic rule and a channel for criticism of the government. The influence of the United States and Great Britain in the establishment of Parliament and the desire to gain additional Western assistance forced the Phibun regime to preserve the legislature and continue the appearance of governing through a constitutional framework. As the coup leaders turned to the task of eliminating their opponents in Parliament, they were consequently required to exercise more patience and tact than in their brutal removal of the liberals.

Legislative opposition to the government was at first a formidable vocal force. The Democrat Party held sixty-three of the hundred seats in the House of Representatives and it controlled a large majority in the Senate. When Phibun first presented his Cabinet for a vote of confidence in the two-hundred member joint session of Parliament, he received only seventy assenting votes. Twenty-six members opposed and 104 members were absent or abstained.[12] After this unimpressive beginning the Democrats launched bitter attacks at his regime for its favoritism to the armed forces and its interference in politics, commerce, education, and other non-military affairs of the country.[13] This opposition was supplemented by scattered criticism from the press and public opinion. Within a short time many people were again describing Thailand as a police state.[14]

Widespread discontent was further aroused by the corruption and nepotism of the military regime which soon surpassed that of the previous liberal governments. The leaders of the Coup Group took over the directorships of banks, private companies, and government corporations, and they diverted large amounts of public funds to themselves. Top-level positions in these organizations were given to members of their families and loyal followers who were lacking in experience or ability. A scandal erupted in January 1950 in which Colonel Kach, one of the leaders of the 1947 coup, was reported to have amassed a fortune of $1,000,000.[15] Subsequently public resentment forced the government to deport the colonel to Hong Kong, but other sizeable fortunes continued to be made. "The people soon saw," Alexander MacDonald observed, "that the simple raids by Thamrong's rapacious crew on the public treasury were as nothing beside the efficient system of the ring of army officers. The military had moved in precision formation into government agencies, taking over the juiciest billets for graft. They even invaded private business, young colonels becoming directors of banks and managers of semi-government industries."[16]

The royalist-conservatives in the Democrat Party made a bold but fruitless attempt to check the expanding power of the militarists by drafting a permanent constitution which was promulgated in March 1949. The new constitution expanded the power of the king and created a Privy Council of nine members to serve as the major royal advisers. It contained detailed provisions protecting civil rights and included a section entitled "State Policies" which defined military, diplomatic, economic, and social goals of the government. The new constitution placed imposing restrictions on the members of the Cabinet from interfering in economic and commercial affairs. It made the Senate completely appointive by the king and authorized the Senate to delay ordinary legislation one year.

In spite of the excellent workmanship that went into the 1949 constitution it failed to take into account the rise of the military leaders as the dominant political group in the country. It also neglected the recent changes in the distribution of power. The provisions upholding greater protection of civil rights disregarded the practice of the militarists to liquidate their opponents with little concern for legality or constitutional safeguards. The restrictions on Cabinet members engaging in commercial enterprises overlooked the practice of the coup leaders of installing themselves in directorships of public and private corporations. The provision placing the armed forces under the "supreme command" of the king was a belated and futile attempt to restore the military prerogatives of the absolute monarchy and was completely unrealistic in contemporary Thailand.

Yet the Democrats adhered to the practice already established by the liberals and the militarists, namely, the framing of the constitution again sought to protect the political position of the party drafting the constitution. This time the royalist-conservatives were attempting to restrict the military-dominated government by extending the authority of the king who was sympathetic to them and by enlarging the powers of the Senate which they controlled. In effect they tried to preserve some semblance of constitutionalism, not so much to provide a legal and political framework which could ultimately be controlled by the people, but to prevent the military leaders from interfering in commercial and financial activities—a practice which many of their own ancestors had followed with few restrictions several decades before. The men in the Coup Group were well aware that the days of the absolute monarchy were over and that constitutional government was still weak. The obstacles placed in their path by the 1949 constitution merely intensified their desire to remove the opposition posed by the royalist-conservatives and return to the authoritarian system embodied in the 1932 constitution. Only the political inexperience of the military leaders, their desire to assume power gradually, and the need to maintain good relations with the United States and Great Britain restrained them and enabled the new constitution to be promulgated.

This controversy between the militarists and the Democrats reflected a major weakness in Thai society. To a large extent this conflict represented a struggle for wealth as much as a struggle for power. The Democrats who proposed this detailed and elaborate constitution were largely members of the royal family or conservative landowners who wanted to preserve their role in the government and their personal wealth. The Coup Group on the other hand was composed almost entirely of commoners, many of whom had come from the peasantry or low-ranking military and civil service families. In a country where the economy was largely in the hands of the Chinese and the large landholdings were controlled by the royalist-conservatives, the only opportunity for a person of humble means to achieve wealth or prestige was through advancement in the military or civil service. It was essentially for this reason that the leaders of the armed forces were continually interfering in the political and commercial life of the country and endeavoring to restore the traditional authoritarian rule so their enjoyment of power and wealth would be secure.

The only notable American influence on the 1949 constitution was the detailed and lengthy section which elaborated the civil liberties of the people. Certain portions of this section were similar to the first ten amendments of the United States Constitution. An attempt to move closer toward American constitutional practice was also made in the provisions stating that the civil liberties of the people could be restricted only by a special law in time of war or national emergency, although this constitutional procedure was more like the custom used in many Latin American countries than in the United States. This change placed these basic civil liberties more in the category of constitutional rights than legal rights, but unstable conditions, both real and imaginary, made it possible for the government to restrict these liberties at almost any time by merely declaring a national emergency. Perhaps the major changes in the 1949 constitution were most influenced by nineteenth century political traditions in Britain. Many of the royalist-conservatives had received their education at British universities and they were openly sympathetic to the British political system. This influence was seen in the extensive prerogatives given to the king, the institution of a Privy Council, and the completely appointed Senate which like the House of Lords could delay ordinary legislation for one year.

Public interest in the June 1949 by-elections for additional elected seats in the House of Representatives brought democratic hopes in post-war Thailand to an all-time low. *The Bangkok Post* described the elections as "one of the dullest campaigns in the city's political history."[17] This decline in public enthusiasm was undoubtedly due to the return of the military leaders to politics and the conviction of most politically conscious Thai that their right to vote had become meaningless. The people became further disillusioned as the coup leaders resorted to corrupt practices at many of the polls. The Phibun regime rigged many of the elections and in certain areas army troops were used to vote for pro-government candidates. As expected the pro-government parties won virtually all of the new seats in the lower house, and the opposition Democrat Party failed to elect a single candidate. As a sop to local and Western opinion Phibun's ministers resigned after the election in accordance with the constitution, but it was a foregone conclusion that with few exceptions the Premier would reappoint the same cabinet. His new government was described by one observer as "a government of the military, aided by nonentities."[18]

The June by-elections caused the Democrats to lose their majority in the House of Representatives and a pro-government member was elected as Speaker of the House. Thereafter the debate in the lower house was controlled to favor government legislation and criticism of the military leaders was frequently overruled. In spite of these reverses the Democrats continued to oppose the spreading authoritarianism of the Phibun regime. They forced a general debate in both houses of Parliament where they accused the army of interfering in the June by-elections and violating constitutional procedure. They charged the government with nepotism and corruption which they claimed had weakened the morale of the military services and civil administration. They attacked the police for their harsh suppression and treatment of innocent people. Phibun and his ministers responded to these charges with weak and evasive replies. They spoke only of their intention to increase the army and the police to prevent further corruption and subversion.

Early in 1950 Phibun made a concerted effort to persuade more opposition members in the House of Representatives to join the pro-government parties. Through the use of bribery and special favors he increased the number of his followers in the lower house, and within a few months he could count on seventy-five of the 121 votes. Thereafter his regime encountered little opposition in this legislative body. By this subtle and devious method he did much to weaken the legislature and restore the traditional authoritarian system. Only the Senate remained a stronghold of opposition to his government. The wealthy and experienced men who were appointed by the king to the upper house could not be bought nor were they susceptible to his favors and persuasion.

The Impact of the Korean War. The Communist invasion of South Korea in June 1950 hastened the efforts of the United States to bolster its anti-Communist defenses throughout Asia. The unexpected outbreak of overt aggression intensified the sense of urgency among Americans which had been confined primarily to Western Europe up to this time. Thailand promptly became an important asset in this endeavor because of the conciliatory attitude of the military regime and the relative stability of the country. Under Phibun's direction the Thai government completely abandoned its traditional neutral foreign policy and aligned itself with the West. The former dictator further ingratiated himself with the Western powers by recognizing the Bao Dai regime in Vietnam and the French-sponsored governments in Laos and Cambodia. He also closed the Viet Minh headquarters in Bangkok. These moves were encouraging to the United States and France who were just beginning to intensify the struggle against the Communist guerrillas in Indochina.

The most dramatic and significant move by the Phibun regime was its offer in July 1950 to send 4000 ground troops to the beleaguered United Nations forces in South Korea.[10] The Thai government also contributed 40,000 metric tons of rice valued at $4,368,000 for Korean relief. In the United Nations Thailand joined the United States in opposing an attempt by Prime Minister Nehru to gain a seat for Communist China on the Security Council with the hope that this move would bring an end to hostilities. Thailand's proposal to send ground forces to South Korea was the first offer from an Asian nation, and the Americans promptly seized its propaganda value to counter the Communist charges that the Korean conflict was merely another example of "Western imperialism." These cooperative moves erased virtually all doubts in the minds of the Americans regarding the pro-Western sympathies of Phibun, and thereafter the former dictator was treated with great respect by the United States in the heightened tension of the Cold War.

This action also caused the United States to take additional measures to increase its material and moral support to Thailand. The first move in this direction was made in July 1950 when an educational exchange agreement under the Fulbright Act was signed by both governments.[20] Under this agreement a Fulbright Educational Foundation was established in Bangkok consisting of four Americans and four Thai with the United States Ambassador acting as honorary chairman. The Foundation was authorized to select candidates for scholarships to American universities which were to be awarded by a Board of Foreign Scholarships appointed by the President of the United States. A provision was also made for American professors and scholars to teach and study in Thailand. This action was praised by the Thai as the "greatest fellowship program in the world's history."[21] It did much to increase respect for the United States and help meet the growing demand for higher education. It also aroused a wider interest in Thailand from American scholars. By the end of the first year forty-eight students were attending graduate or professional schools in the United States under the Fulbright program, while nine Americans were teaching and studying in the country.

A second measure to bolster the internal stability of Thailand was the negotiation of an Economic and Technical Cooperation Agreement between the two governments on September 19, 1950.[22] Under this agreement the United States assented to provide economic and technical assistance, and Thailand was obligated to promote its economic development and foreign trade. The Thai government also agreed to receive a special technical and economic mission from the United States and to support its operations with counterpart funds in local currency. In making this agreement the Americans again reiterated their earlier sentiment that the United States was eager to help the Thai people because they were also a freedom-loving nation. When signing the agreement Ambassador Stanton stated: "The American people fully support this program of aid to Thailand because of their deep interest in the Thai people whose devotion to the ideals of freedom and liberty and wholehearted support of the U.N. have won the admiration of the American people."[23]

The expanded economic and technical assistance program was initially financed with $8,000,000 provided by the Economic Cooperation Administration. Within a year a Special Technical and Economic Mission (STEM) was established in Bangkok which consisted of some fifty technical experts who assisted in improving the nation's agriculture, irrigation, transportation, communications, harbor facilities, commerce, education, and public health. This mission also established an American supervised language center which provided modern facilities for teaching the English language. At the end of 1951 the Mutual Security Agency (MSA) replaced the ECA and it launched a vast global program of military, economic, and technical assistance to deter Communist aggression. Thailand was allotted $7,000,000 for economic and technical aid under this new enlarged program. In addition to direct bilateral economic aid from the United States, Thailand was given a loan of $25,400,000 from the World Bank on October 31, 1950 to assist in the construction of irrigation projects, the rehabilitation of railroads, and the development of the harbor at Bangkok.[24] This was the first loan made by the World Bank to any nation in Southeast Asia.

Perhaps the most dramatic step taken by the United States and Thailand was the signing of an Agreement Respecting Military Assistance on October 17, 1950.[25] Each government agreed to provide the other with military equipment and services. However, the agreement was made with the understanding that military aid would be supplied to Thailand under the provisions of Public Law 329 passed by the 81st Congress. The United States also agreed to provide training for the Thai armed forces in the use of American arms. The Thai were obligated to make "effective use" of this military assistance. An attempt was made by the Americans to retain some control over the use of the proffered arms with the provision that the Thai government would not "without prior consent of the Government of the United States of America, devote assistance so furnished to purposes other than those for which it is furnished." Yet the Thai inserted a provision which gave them effective control over this military equipment. Article I stated: "The Government of Thailand undertakes to retain title to and possession and control of any equipment, material, or services, received . . . unless the Government of the United States shall otherwise consent." No arrangements were made in the agreement for returning these arms to the United States should it "otherwise consent."

Most Americans assumed that the military equipment and training given to the armed forces would promote peace and unity in the country. When signing the agreement in Bangkok, Ambassador Stanton declared: "It is my sincere hope that the assistance being extended by the Government of the United States will give the armed forces and people of Thailand a feeling of greater security and will engender unity of purpose between the army, the navy, and the air force for the greater good of Thailand. By preserving peace, Thailand's armed forces will not only insure progress and prosperity for the people of Thailand but will also be making a definite contribution to world peace."[26] When the first shipment of arms arrived in January 1951 the Americans again voiced their praise of freedom in Thailand. At an impressive ceremony where much of the military equipment was displayed, Mr. Stanton formally handed the documents for the possession of these arms to Phibun. In his address the Ambassador stated: "Thailand's destiny is freedom."[27] And in a warning to the Thai people of the severe consequences of Communist aggression he added: "Your good and noble King and your democratic Constitution would be overthrown."[28] During the following year a total of twenty-eight shipments of military aid arrived from the United States with sufficient arms to equip ten army battalions. Fighter planes were provided to the air force and modern vessels were supplied to the navy. In addition to these vast quantities of arms, the United States established a Military Advisory Assistance Group (MAAG) to train the armed forces.

Many Americans believed that the educational, economic, and military programs would blend together harmoniously and benefit all the people. The programs in education and economic aid were expected to raise living standards and the military program was to protect the security of the nation. However, in a country with an authoritarian political tradition, the provision of arms to a military regime would enhance its ability to suppress internal opposition as well as to safeguard the nation from Communist aggression. Also, as more persons achieved higher educational and economic standards they would inevitably express more individualism and organize themselves into economic and social groups. In time they would almost certainly demand some voice in their government. Yet any attempt by these maturing social forces to seek a greater political role would inevitably bring them into conflict with the military regime which was primarily concerned with keeping itself in power and had been enormously strengthened by American arms. In the long run it was thus possible that the military and the non-military programs would exacerbate the internal conflicts in Thai society instead of alleviating them.

Phibun's government also received considerable assistance from the expanding post-war trade with the United States which had a significant effect in improving the national economy. By 1949 the annual trade between the two countries had climbed from its pre-war level of $3,000,000 to $60,000,000.[29] American corporations purchased large quantities of rubber and tin, and for the first time in almost a century shipments of raw materials were going directly to the United States instead of through the British entrepot ports at Hong Kong and Singapore. Fifty U.S. firms were operating in Thailand in contrast to two companies before the war. Some Americans were elated as their commercial enterprises again rivaled those of the British. One observer declared: "Whether or not it is a neighborly thing to do at a time when the British are so hard pressed for cash, the fact remains that American businessmen, ignoring recent political upheavals which have converted Siam from a shaky democracy to what seems to be a strong military dictatorship cloaked in democratic forms, are invading Siam with the headlong fervor of forty-niners rushing West to hunt gold. Every trans-ocean plane brings another load of pioneers." [30] In spite of this rapid expansion of American trade, British Commonwealth countries and other nations in Asia continued to be important customers of Thai exports.

By 1952 the American community in Thailand had expanded considerably and included a growing Embassy staff, a MAAG mission, a STEM mission, a USIS staff, a few Fulbright scholars, several hundred Protestant missionaries, and several score businessmen.[31] For the first time in history government officials outnumbered the missionaries. The increasing contacts between these Americans and the Thai people intensified earlier Western influences. The MAAG mission assisted the training of the armed forces in modern military equipment and further strengthened their determination to preserve national independence. The specialists engaged in education and technical assistance programs did much to elevate living standards and they contributed considerably to the prosperity of the country. Also, a growing number of Americans made short visits to Thailand as it became a major ally of the United States in the effort to deter Communist aggression in Southeast Asia. Between 1950 and 1952 Thailand played host to such dignitaries as Harold Stassen, Henry Luce, General Joseph L. Collins, Mrs. Eleanor Roosevelt, Justice William O. Douglas, Admiral Arthur Radford, Senator John Sparkman, Senator Bourke Hickenlooper, Senator Ernest McFarland, Senator Theodore Green, Senator Homer Ferguson, Ambassador Chester Bowles, and Assistant Secretary of State John M. Allison.[32]

The major impact on the government and people from these increasing contacts with resident and visiting Americans emphasized the precarious position of the country in the Cold War. The Thai were reminded of the horrors of life under Communist rule and encouraged to take stringent measures to protect their nation from aggression. Ambassador Stanton frequently encouraged Phibun to be alert to the allegedly increasing signs of Communist subversion among intellectuals, students, priests, and writers. Regarding this situation the Ambassador stated: "In my concern, I urged on the Prime Minister, as I had on many previous occasions, the need of trying to ferret out their plans."[33] During a brief visit in Bangkok, Henry Luce warned the Thai to beware of the "total nature" of Communism and to protect their country from its "total world-wide threat."[34] Because the Phibun government was cooperating with the United States in opposing Communist aggression some Americans went further and praised it for its devotion to democracy. In a Fourth of July edition of *The Bangkok Post* the Bank of America placed a full-page ad containing these words:[35] "COMMEMORATING THE BIRTH OF INDEPENDENCE IN THE UNITED STATES, THE BANK OF AMERICA SALUTES THE KINGDOM OF THAILAND WHERE INDEPENDENCE HAS FOR CENTURIES BEEN, THE WATCHWORD OF THE NATION. IN BOTH THAILAND AND AMERICA DEMOCRACY HAS GONE HAND IN HAND WITH NATIONAL SOVEREIGNTY. TODAY BOTH NATIONS STAND IN THE FOREFRONT OF WORLD EFFORTS TO PROMOTE AND DEFEND THE DEMOCRATIC WAY OF LIFE."

There were few Americans such as Ambassador Chester Bowles who openly declared that Communism in Southeast Asia could not be stopped by military means alone, and who stated that Thailand faced no serious internal subversive threat since the country produced a surplus of rice and most of the peasants owned their own land.

Actually the Communist threat to Thailand in 1950 was not as serious or ominous as the Americans or Thai militarists proclaimed. The officials of both governments made the mistake of assessing only the intentions of the Communists without giving sufficient consideration to their capabilities. Propaganda blasts at American "imperialism" in Southeast Asia emanating from Moscow and Peking and the confident assertion that Communism was destined to rule the world aroused an intense fear which engendered a sense of urgency and a demand for immediate concrete action. In the haste and confusion at the time the political implications of the measures taken by the United States received little consideration. Contrary to American intentions some of these actions actually increased the vulnerabilities of Thailand to Communist subversion.

While a large country such as China dominated by a Communist regime obviously posed a potential threat to Southeast Asia, an overt invasion from the Chinese mainland was the least likely contingency with which the United States and Thailand would have to contend. Yet many Americans and Thai believed that the Peking government was capable of invading the region at any moment. Actually the Chinese Communists had just finished a three-year civil war, and although they had emerged victorious in this struggle and possessed significant military power, they were in no position to launch an invasion of Southeast Asia. The victory of the Peking regime had depended to a large degree on the political support it received from the disgruntled Chinese peasants, and this cooperation would not have been forthcoming if an invasion were made into non-Chinese areas. Instead the Chinese Communists would have been confronted with bitter resistance and opposition. Mao Tse-Tung and his aides were also deterred from aggression in Southeast Asia by the threat of retaliatory action from American air power based in Japan, Okinawa, and the Philippines, and the possibility that a large-scale war would encourage the United States to support the Chinese Nationalists in an invasion of the mainland.

As the Chinese Communists became involved in the Korean conflict their prospects of invading Southeast Asia became even more unlikely, especially as the United Nations forces took an enormous toll of Chinese lives and placed a heavy burden on their limited industrial capacity. The leaders of the Peking regime were able to maintain a respectable military capability in the Korean war because of the relatively favorable transportation and communication facilities between northern China and Korea and the proximity to their major industrial centers in Manchuria. Their logistical problems were serious but they were reasonably solved. However, the Chinese Communists were not able to place this same military force in Southeast Asia because of the primitive transportation and communication facilities in southern China and the long distance from their industrial base in the north. Even if the Peking government had made the very irrational move of attempting an invasion of the region it almost certainly would have attacked Burma rather than Thailand because of its easier access and greater natural resources.

The Communist-led Viet Minh were another possible external threat to Thailand. Yet these guerrilla forces were concerned primarily with fighting the French who still hoped to retain a dominant position in their valuable Indochina colony. The Viet Minh, like the Chinese Communists, were able to wage a successful war because they received widespread support from the terrorized and disgruntled Vietnamese peasants. This assistance would not have been forthcoming if the Viet Minh had attempted to extend their military operations outside of Indochina. Also, the Vietnamese Communists did not have the industrial and logistical capacity necessary to launch a major invasion of large adjoining countries. They were a potential nuisance but certainly not a serious threat. The Communist insurgents in Malaya and Burma were likewise an important menace inside these countries but did not jeopardize the security of Thailand.

Nor was the internal Communist threat as serious as the Americans and the Thai military leaders claimed. Although Thailand had served intermittently as an important base for Communist agents operating in Southeast Asia, these activities never seriously threatened the internal stability and security of the country. The Chinese and Vietnamese Communists inside Thailand numbered only a few thousand and they were concerned primarily with the political situation in their own homelands. Very little of this activity affected Thai politics. In spite of Communist advances in the surrounding countries, the bulk of the people remained unimpressed with the appeals of Communism and the Thai Communist Party remained infinitesimal. Virginia Thompson has claimed that this condition was due to the widespread ownership of land, the lack of intense economic misery, the popular devotion to the monarchy, the pacifistic influence of Buddhism, and the absence of a colonial background.[36] This author has concluded: "Probably at no time has the number of militant communists in Thailand exceeded a few hundred."[37] Throughout the 1950's it was estimated that the Chinese Communists in the country numbered about 4000; the Thai Communists numbered approximately 200. Only one Communist has ever held a seat in the national legislature. This representative was Nai Prasert Subsunthorn who was elected as an Independent in the 1946 election, and he formed "Siam's one-man Communist party" when the political parties supporting Pridi and Khuang failed to cooperate.[38]

Yet the Communist threat was exaggerated due to the extreme sensitivity of the Thai military leaders to any possible challenge to their national independence and security. This trend was encouraged by the alarmist statements of the Americans and the belief that Communist aggression was imminent almost anywhere in Asia. This distorted assessment caused both governments to concentrate most of their effort on the least likely contingency and to overlook the major Communist threat, namely the backward political, economic, and social conditions inside the country which could be exploited by the Communists and used to spread anti-government hostility. In spite of the widespread ownership of land and the general well-being of many people, the Phibun regime failed to make sufficient progress in reducing such vulnerabilities as the depressed economic and social conditions among the Laotian-speaking Thai in the northeastern provinces who harbored latent separatist tendencies. The government likewise maintained discriminatory practices against the local Chinese who controlled the bulk of the national economy and were susceptible to influences and pressures from the mainland. Little action was taken to improve economic opportunities for the 500,000 Thai Moslems living in the four southern provinces bordering on Malaya. The peasants continued to receive only one-third of the price obtained for their surplus rice. The people continued to earn an average per capita income of about $90 a year. They were likewise deprived of any voice in their government by the authoritarian practices of the military leaders. Other serious internal problems received insufficient attention or were completely ignored.

Thus Thailand in 1950 did not have any large number of Communists inside the country who posed a serious threat to the nation's security, but it did have certain internal vulnerabilities which provided an opportunity for the spread of Communism. Consequently the major effort in protecting the country should have been directed toward the removal of these weaknesses by political, economic, and social reforms and not toward the massive build-up of the military and police forces which would be concentrating on the least likely threat. The suppressive measures taken by the military regime after 1950 and the increasing funds devoted to the armed forces indicated that these serious weaknesses in the society would receive less instead of more attention. This policy was almost certain to increase popular discontent. If this trend continued it could result in a vicious cycle of devoting more effort to the least serious threat which in turn would intensify the conditions which contributed to the most likely threat.

Yet the Americans were taking no chances in Thailand. They were determined to stress a general and total Communist threat when this threat was limited and specific. The bitter experience in defeating the Axis powers in World War II convinced the government of the United States that it was better to exaggerate a threat to world peace and security than to minimize one. By 1951 this attitude had developed into an obsession with Communism and Americans thereafter assessed almost every action in both foreign and domestic affairs in terms of its possible effect on the global struggle with the Communist bloc. This feeling was intensified by the growing disillusionment in the post-war era, the reaction to the Alger Hiss trial, the heavy loss of American lives in Korea, the recklessness of the McCarthy era, and the general elusiveness of world peace. Within a short time many Americans became victims of their own propaganda and were willing to undertake almost any concrete action that appeared to deter the supposedly rising tide of Communism. The offer of military and economic aid to a small country such as Thailand located near the periphery of the Communist bloc gave tangible expression to this sense of urgency and enabled Americans to feel that "something" was being done.

In effect the impact of the Korean conflict caused the United States to intensify the fear of Communism in a country which had few Communists and was fairly well protected from aggression by external political and geographical factors. At the same time Americans flattered the leaders of the government for their devotion to freedom and democracy when in fact the country was just emerging from centuries of absolute rule and still had made no significant progress in establishing democratic institutions. The military leaders were actively converting the political system into a more powerful and ruthless form of authoritarianism due partially to the availability of large quantities of American arms. The influence of the United States gave additional material and moral support to the Phibun regime and discouraged its political opposition. It strengthened the executive and administrative structures and further weakened the legislature and the courts. It likewise encouraged the military leaders to take even stronger measures in suppressing local opposition using the excuse that all anti-government activity was Communist-inspired. Within a short time the stress on nationalism, the fear of Communism, and the presence of American arms discouraged all but a few people from opposing the policies of the military-dominated government.

Phibun again seized the unique opportunity provided by extensive American aid to enhance his own political position. The former dictator, like most Americans, was a stanch pragmatist, and he readily justified the increased authority assumed by his government on the basis of the alleged Communist threat. He rightly and shrewdly judged the reaction of the United States to his offer to send troops to Korea, and he used his growing stature among the Americans to strengthen his role within the internal ruling elite. By 1951 the expanding channels of military and economic aid were partially accredited to his intimate collaboration with the United States which made him almost indispensable to the Coup Group supporting his regime. The enhanced position of the military leaders resulting from the increased American aid after the Korean war enabled them to complete the task of eliminating all effective political opposition.

A first step in this direction occurred when Phibun increased the nation's military and security forces. His government instructed the Board of Defense and Peace Maintenance Corps, both led by General Phin and General Phao, to draft plans for the defense of the country and to devise more effective methods of suppressing internal subversion.[39] In April 1951 national conscription was started and the government established a Home Guard to be trained and stationed in strategic provinces. By 1952 full mobilization was under consideration.

The expansion of the armed forces placed an enormous financial burden on the national treasury in spite of the very extensive military assistance received from the United States. The 1950 budget of 1,949,350,-355 baht ($97,500,000) was increased to 3,685,725,783 baht ($184,300,-000) by 1952 with Phibun explaining that the deficit would be made up by foreign and internal loans.[40] The appropriations to the Ministry of Defense and the Ministry of Interior were the largest in the budget each year. The government was helped to some extent during the Korean war with additional revenues from the high prices for rice, rubber, and tin. By 1951 Thailand had become the world's largest rice exporter which brought the income from foreign trade to an all-time high.[41] With this expanding prosperity, however, the country experienced more inflation which posed new problems for the government and placed additional hardships on the people.

The new era of economic prosperity aroused widespread discontent when the leaders of the Coup Group expanded their personal enterprises which caused a corresponding increase in nepotism and corruption throughout the country. By this time these profiteering operations had become an indispensable source of income to the military leaders in maintaining the loyalty of their growing body of followers. This trend exacerbated the personal rivalries among the various factions within the armed forces and caused numerous rumors of plots against the government. In November 1950 the police arrested seventy-six young army officers who were charged with forming a conspiracy against the Phibun regime.[42] Bitter clashes also erupted between the military and civilian factions within the pro-government parties with each group demanding that their opponents be ousted from the Cabinet. Phibun was able to mediate these disputes but much antagonism remained.

The rivalries within the armed forces flared into open violence on June 29, 1951 when Phibun was kidnapped by the navy while officiating at a ceremony aboard the dredger "Manhattan" as it was being turned over by American officials to the Thai government.[43] A broadcast from the naval headquarters promptly announced the formation of a new government and demanded the removal of the leaders of the Coup Group from the Cabinet. The navy rebels politely apologized to the Americans for interfering with the ceremony on the "Manhattan".

They declared: "We did not intend to insult much appreciated good-will to Siam, but we were compelled by patriotic motives."[44] An attempt was made for several hours to negotiate the differences between the navy rebels and the government, but this effort failed with each side accusing the other as being "Communist." The following day bitter fighting broke out in Bangkok with the army, police, and air force pitted against the navy and the marines. The army and police shelled naval installations while the air force bombed naval strongholds, including the flagship "Sri Ayudhya" on which Phibun was held captive. The Premier escaped from the ship as it was sinking and swam ashore. He eventually made his way to territory controlled by the government and broadcast an appeal to the navy rebels to stop fighting. Shortly thereafter the navy surrendered. The abortive coup lasted three days and caused a reported 603 civilian and 3,000 military casualities in addition to extensive destruction to public and private property.[45] Many of the 1200 persons killed in the fighting were civilians.

A few days after the coup the Phibun regime began an extensive investigation which enabled it to suppress its opposition and consolidate its power even further. General Phao was promoted to the powerful post of Director-General of the Police Department, and the police arrested over one thousand naval officers and enlisted men in addition to fifty students from the University of Moral and Political Science. The navy was completely reorganized and its personnel was reduced by 75 per cent. Phibun claimed that the Communists were the cause of the attempted coup and he linked the navy rebels to Pridi and his Free Thai followers.

In spite of the claims by both sides that Communists were involved in this abortive coup, most observers agreed that it had been caused by the increasing rivalry among the military services. The navy had been deprived of what it thought was its fair share of the spoils in the government, and it consequently sought to rectify the situation by the only effective means available—the use of force. Regardless of the hope of the United States that American arms would unite the armed forces and encourage them to work for the welfare of the nation, this coup attempt showed the vulnerability of the military leaders to petty factionalism and their willingness to resort to violence in pursuing their personal ambitions regardless of the consequences to the country. Regarding this situation John Coast commented: "Whereas, before, Siam had been famous for the non-violence of her political changes, now several hundred innocent civilians were apt to suffer death or wounds everytime her responsible leaders sought to change the Government. The political development of Siam since this most recent attempted coup suggests that the situation has deteriorated." [46]

The abortive navy coup revealed several important deficiencies in American policy. Most obviously it showed that in spite of the military agreement with the United States the military leaders were willing to use American arms in their personal rivalries. The provision in the agreement that the United States could regain control over these arms should they be used for any purpose other than opposing the Communists was meaningless. The attempted coup also showed that the desire of the Thai leaders to maintain the goodwill of the United States was overweighed by their endeavor to eliminate their rivals in the internal struggle for power. Also, the reduction of the navy to one-fourth of its former strength indicated that the size of the armed forces in the future would be determined by their successes or failures in internal politics, not by the need to protect the country from Communist aggression.

Phibun attempted to smooth over the implications of the coup with a prompt announcement to the United States that there would be no change in Thailand's pro-Western foreign policy and that no American arms had been used by either side in the recent fighting. Actually this latter statement was contrary to the facts. The Premier had been kidnapped by the navy in an American-made landing craft and American arms had been extensively used by the army, the police, and the air force in suppressing the revolt. In effect the military equipment given to the government to protect the country from Communist aggression was being used to make the internal clashes among the contending military and political forces more violent than before. In the aftermath of the coup many persons criticized the United States for giving large quantities of arms to a regime dominated by military officers. The charge "American guns killed our people" was voiced in Bangkok for many days.[47]

After the abortive navy coup some Americans developed a unique attitude toward their relations with the Thai government. Thereafter it became almost fashionable within the American community to talk jokingly about the rivalry among the military leaders and the violent action they had taken against each other. This was true even of the Americans who had quickly scurried to their homes after Phibun's kidnapping and who feared for their own safety and that of their children during the three days that Bangkok became the scene of bitter fighting. Some Americans became more fascinated with the local power struggle than in the much more important matter of the Cold War. Ironically no Americans voiced the opinion that the provision of large quantities of arms by their government to the militarists had anything to do with the recent attempted coup. No one declared that the United States was responsible in some degree for the increasing destruction caused by the rivalries among the military leaders. The only apparent concern was the announcement of the Phibun government that there would be no change in Thailand's pro-Western foreign policy. The shipments of arms from the United States continued. The armed forces received more excellent training from the MAAG mission. The Phibun regime was again praised for its devotion to human freedom and the cause of democracy.

Complete Military Rule. The abortive coup served to weaken Phibun's position in the ruling elite and thereafter he became even more dependent on the leaders of the Coup Group. The suppression of the navy rebels vividly illustrated that the real power behind his regime was wielded by General Phin, General Phao, and General Sarit. For the first time the air force entered the internal political struggle and Air Marshal Fuen Ronapakat became a junior partner in the military leadership of the government. In the past the air force had been a relatively small and insignificant military group and it had maintained a policy of strict neutrality in the previous feuds between the army and navy. However, by 1951 the air force possessed a considerable number of American-made combat planes that were manned by competent American-trained pilots, and this augmented military power enabled it to play a major role in bringing victory to the government side. The leaders of the Coup Group decided to retain Phibun as Premier primarily because he had become extremely popular with the United States which enabled Thailand to receive the much-desired military and economic aid. The coup leaders, however, were highly displeased with their minor role in his government and the obstructive bicameral legislature. With their enhanced power and prestige after the attempted navy coup they became even more determined than before to expand their authority. By this time they had also gained considerable political experience which gave them a sense of confidence that they had lacked before.

The Coup Group took it first step toward greater political power in November, 1951, as the Thai people were eagerly awaiting the return of King Phumiphon from Switzerland. The royal family was returning by sea and they intended to remain in the country. This would be the first time the Thai monarch had taken permanent residence since King Prajadhipok left for Europe in 1934. At Singapore King Phumiphon transferred from his chartered ocean vessel to a Thai naval ship and he was expected to arrive in Bangkok in a few days. While the king was enroute between Singapore and Bangkok the leaders of the Coup Group seized the government and established themselves as a "Provisional Executive Committee." [48] They abolished the 1949 constitution and replaced it with an amended version of the 1932 constitution. They dissolved the bicameral Parliament and appointed a new Assembly of 123 representatives which was to act as the national legislature until elections were held for an equal number of elected members within ninety days. They also banned all political parties and placed the press under government censorship. Phibun was again retained as Premier, but almost all important ministerial posts were given to leading members within the Coup Group. The military leaders took thirteen positions in the new government whereas they had only four before. They also appointed ninety-six army and police officers to the newly-created legislature.[49]

When seizing control of the government, the Provisional Executive Committee revealed the extent to which it had been motivated by the American obsession with Communism, and it justified the seizure of power as a move to protect the country from Communist aggression. It issued the following announcement: "Because of the present world situation and because of Communist aggression and widespread corruption, members of the armed forces, the police and leaders of the 1932 and 1947 coups d'etat had decided to put the 1932 Constitution in force in the kingdom." [50]

The Committee also claimed that the 1949 constitution did not give the government effective power in suppressing Communism and the members of Parliament did not have the sense of responsibility to carry out their duties properly. The Senate was cited as a serious obstacle to effective action. Two days after the coup the Provisional Executive Committee formally transferred its powers to the newly-constituted Cabinet and the newly-appointed Assembly.

While converting the political system to a completely authoritarian basis the militarists also voiced the statements they had heard from the Americans that their government was democratic and devoted to human freedom. The new regime issued a communique denying the charge that the country was moving toward a dictatorship and it claimed that the 1932 constitution would provide full freedom to the people. It announced a new ten-point program which stated in part: [51]

"Point 1. The government will be democratic and abide by the constitution.

"Point 5. Freedom and equality of the individual will be upheld and respect paid to the United Nations Declaration of Human Rights.

"Point 10. Freedom of the courts and the individual."

Thus while the government was becoming completely authoritarian the military leaders were claiming that their regime was actually democratic. To the bulk of the less educated and inexperienced Thai people a modicum of reality was given to this questionable claim by the increasing cooperation between Thailand and the United States, the leading Western democracy.

The timing of the November coup was well planned. The militarists knew that the monarchy wielded little political power but that it was still a widely respected social and religious institution. In the era of heightened international tension the king could serve as an important stabilizing force. As in pre-war Japan the monarchy could also uphold a dignified facade for authoritarian rule, provided the king himself exercised no political power. Yet under the 1949 constitution a liberal and pro-democratic king who had spent most of his life in Western Europe might have asserted his extensive prerogatives and become a serious obstacle to the rapidly growing power of the Coup Group. The Senate, dominated by the royalist-conservatives, would undoubtedly have cooperated closely with the young monarch and it might have imposed even greater limitations on the government. The leaders of the Coup Group decided to take no chances and consequently altered the political system in their favor while they had the opportunity. They wanted the king back in the country to serve as a stabilizing force so they waited until just three days before his return to make this change in the government. Had the coup leaders seized power sooner the royal family might have returned to Switzerland or refused to return to Thailand thereby jeopardizing their newly acquired power. The young, inexperienced king was thus confronted with a fait accompli on his arrival in Bangkok, and on December 6, 1951 he issued a Royal Proclamation restoring the 1932 constitution.[52]

The November 1951 coup also brought an end to the royalist-conservatives as a significant political force. They were the last obstacle to complete authoritarian rule which the military leaders had patiently sought since they first ousted the liberals in November 1947. The royalist-conservatives had played a skillful delaying action for four years, but by 1951 the coup leaders had become so powerful that they would tolerate no effective opposition to their expanding authority.

A few members of this group, such as Prince Wan Waithayakon, were retained in diplomatic and advisory positions where they continued to serve their country with honor and distinction. Most of them, however, turned to professional and cultural activities and no longer sought an active role in politics.

This group was actually paying this high price for its failure to cooperate with the liberals earlier in the post-war era. At that time the constitutional framework established by the liberals gave the royalist-conservatives the opportunity to exercise some influence on the government even though they did not control it. They were able to serve in many executive and administrative positions and maintain themselves as an organized political force. Yet they short-sightedly allowed their personal animosity toward Pridi and his liberal followers to overshadow the urgent need to establish a stable political framework which would enable them to continue their needed services to the country. They opportunistically joined with Phibun and his military followers to bring about Pridi's downfall which gradually ended the second attempt to establish a constitutional system. Thereafter the growing interference of the military in politics made the return to authoritarian rule merely a matter of time. The royalist-conservatives were able to play a restraining role for about four years due to the expanding influence of the United States in internal affairs and the need to please Western opinion by keeping some "moderates" on the national scene. Yet by the end of 1951 the military leaders could readily see that the United States was much more concerned with protecting the country from the Communist threat than in keeping "moderates" in the government. With this change in American policy the royalist-conservatives lost this external support and the militarists promptly removed them from participation in politics.

Thus by the end of 1951 the Coup Group was exercising virtually unlimited political power. Since their overthrow of the liberal regime the military leaders had used a revival of nationalism, an exaggerated fear of Communism, and reliance on American arms to remove the major opponents in their quest for complete authoritarian rule. The leaders of the Coup Group, like the absolute monarchy before them, readily accepted the innovations of Western technology and new administrative techniques which enhanced their military and political power. But they strongly rejected Western political values in spite of their lip service to the contrary. The frequent attempted coups by the professional army officers, the liberals, and finally the navy leaders illustrated that virtually all politically conscious groups had likewise discarded the Western system of constitutional democracy, and military power had become accepted as the primary basis for political authority. The remnants of constitutionalism which remained after 1952 were used largely as a facade to retain respectability in the eyes of local and foreign opinion.

However, by 1952 a new generation of enthusiastic liberal-minded Thai was emerging which wanted to restore the democratic goals of the 1932 revolution and again move the political system closer toward some form of representative government. Many of these young liberals had been educated in the United States and Western Europe. Yet this emerging progressive group became increasingly disillusioned with the United States as it extended moral and material support to the Phibun regime and many Americans voiced their approval of its internal suppressive measures.[53] These persons continued to show a sincere respect for genuine constitutional government as practiced in the West, and they appreciated American economic and social aid. However, they strongly opposed the policy of the United States in providing large quantities of arms to the military and police forces which were used more to increase the political power of the coup leaders and to suppress their opponents than to protect the country from Communism. Some Americans, recalling Phibun's opportunistic past and the suppression of political freedom by the former military leaders, also opposed large-scale military aid. One American stated: "American aid to Thailand means aid to Phibun's government and the bolstering of his regime . . . American aid will help our erstwhile enemy entrench himself more deeply and will embitter the liberals, our former friends."[54]

Not all American aid provided direct support to the military regime, however, and the non-military programs helped to elevate economic and social standards. By 1952 the total cost of economic and technical assistance was $16,100,000 in addition to aid provided through the United Nations and the World Bank.[55] This assistance increased the size and skill of a slowly expanding middle class that was playing a larger role in the national economy. For the first time in history sizeable numbers of Thai (not Chinese) were becoming involved in commercial enterprises. American aid programs promoting agriculture, industry, commerce, public health, public works, and education encouraged the growth of organized groups in each of these fields. This trend appeared to promote a more sophisticated political and social consciousness which in time could provide a foundation for the development of constitutional government.

The education program was especially significant in arousing a more mature political attitude. Many of the Thai students returning from the United States and Western Europe became competent specialists in the civil administration. As of 1952, however, none of these Western educated returnees took an active role in politics; many of them became increasingly frustrated as military officers with little education or experience ran the government in an arbitrary and inefficient manner. Many Western-influenced Thai joined the rising criticism of the military regime, and some of these persons looked forward to the time when the country might resume its endeavor to achieve some form of democratic government.

By 1952 the only significant internal limitation on the Coup Group was that imposed by the inherent personal weaknesses within the military regime itself. With the removal of all effective opposition the coup leaders themselves split into two factions, one based primarily on the police headed by General Phao and another within the army led by General Sarit. To mediate this growing schism within his government, Phibun sought increasing support from the United States. This development began a trend toward a tenuous triumvirate rule and in some degree it restricted the freedom of action of the three military leaders.

The increasing influence of American and European opinion also restrained the Thai government to some extent, and at times it mitigated the harshness of authoritarian rule. It was due largely to Western influence that the Assembly was allowed to continue the motions of parliamentary procedure, and the protection offered by the courts, though weakened, remained reasonably intact. Increasing cooperation with American economic and technical aid programs also altered many policies of the Phibun regime by causing it to devote more attention to education, public health, and social welfare. Modest and scattered criticism of the government was tolerated and for many people the return to complete authoritarian rule was not unduly severe.

Chapter IV

THE IMPACT OF THE EISENHOWER ADMINISTRATION

The 1952 presidential campaign in the United States had important implications regarding the future of American policy in Thailand. The Republican Party which gloried in the widespread prestige of its popular candidate, General Eisenhower, accused the Truman administration of being "soft" on Communism, especially in Asia. The Democrats were excoriated for the victory of the Communists in China and the bitter experiences of the American military forces in Korea. Much more should be done, the Republicans claimed, to prevent further Communist aggression in other parts of Asia and throughout the world.

After the election President Eisenhower promised that his administration would follow "a new, positive foreign policy" to block any further advances by the Communists and to bolster the nation's anti-Communist allies.[1] A "new look" would be given to the American military posture, and a new stress would be placed on deterrent military power and collective regional security. In his inaugural address the new president stated:

"We hold it to be the first task of statesmanship to develop the strength that will deter the forces of aggression and promote the conditions of peace.

"Appreciating that economic need, military security, and political wisdom combine to suggest regional groups of free peoples, we hope, within the framework of the United Nations, to help strengthen such special bonds the world over."[2]

While stressing a more dynamic and aggressive foreign policy, President Eisenhower also upheld the need to economize on the expenditures of the United States government. He condemned the large deficits of the Truman administration as inflationary, and he declared in his State of the Union message that "the first order of business is the elimination of the annual deficit."[3] The leaders of his administration called for a reduction in the number of American troops stationed overseas and a corresponding increase in the armed forces maintained by the non-Communist countries on the Sino-Soviet periphery. The economy-minded Republicans cited elaborate statistics illustrating how Asian military forces could be maintained at a much smaller cost than American military forces. They emphasized the dollars that could be saved by increasing foreign ground forces and supporting them with American air and naval power. This aspect of United States foreign policy was soon labeled by some critics as "more bang for a buck". No serious thought was given by the new administration to the political implications of this proposed policy change on the countries in Asia. It was generally assumed that the non-Communist governments in the region would benefit greatly from an increased emphasis on military power, and that the Asian countries would willingly cooperate in advancing these objectives of American foreign policy.

The implementation of these policy changes was placed in the hands of the new Secretary of State, John Foster Dulles. In his first major speech Mr. Dulles stated that the primary concern of the United States was the "deadly serious" threat of "encirclement" by the Soviet Union and its Communist-dominated allies.[4] He declared that there would be no major changes in the foreign policy of the former Truman administration, but he claimed some attempts would be made to enlarge and sharpen it. He added that more attention would be given to Asia in the future and he voiced his concern for the security of Indochina whose fall to the Communists would jeopardize the security of other countries in Southeast Asia. Shortly after taking over as the head of the Department of State, Mr. Dulles made a personal tour of the non-Communist countries in the region to determine the willingness of their leaders to join a military alliance with the West. The refusal of the neutralist leaders in India, Burma, and Indonesia to support this venture caused the United States to turn increasingly to the pro-Western governments in the Philippines, Indochina, and Thailand to augment the local ground forces.

On January 12, 1954 Mr. Dulles delivered the most important address of his career to the Council on Foreign Relations in New York.[5] It was his famous "massive retaliation" speech which defined the foreign policy goals of the Eisenhower administration and with few exceptions guided its actions throughout its eight years in office. The Secretary of State reiterated the urgent need for the United States to increase its deterrent power against Communist aggression at a reduced cost. To achieve this objective he claimed the United States must place greater stress on "community deterrent power" and less stress on "local defensive power." Local defensive forces in the non-Communist region would be increased but their real effectiveness would be to detain any armed in-

vasion long enough for the United States Air Force to strik
vital industrial and communication centers of any Communist aggressor with "massive retaliatory power." Mr. Dulles added: "The way to deter aggression is for the free community to be willing and able to respond vigorously at places and with means of its own choosing."[6] The result would be "more security at less cost." He specifically warned Communist China that aggression in Indochina "would have grave consequences which might not be confined to Indo-China." He also proposed that this "basic decision" by the Eisenhower administration to cut the costs of government would be supplemented by a reduction in economic and technical aid to the underdeveloped countries. Economic assistance in the form of grants, the Secretary of State claimed, was not effective nor in accordance with the free enterprise system. Thereafter the United States would rely largely on private trade and investments as the best means to promote the economic and social well-being of these people.[7] Ironically, President Eisenhower at the same time requested Congress for an additional $1,000,000,000 for military and economic aid for Asia.

These policy changes by the Eisenhower administration indicated that it entertained a greater fear of the Communist threat than its predecessor. The increasing emphasis on Asia and the desire to enlarge the ground forces in the region meant that pro-Western countries such as Thailand were precisely the areas where the new administration wanted to expand its influence and support. The added stress on military power and regional collective security likewise revealed that the United States would augment its assistance to the Phibun regime and attempt to align it even more closely with the Western bloc. This policy change caused Americans to become even more reluctant than before to voice their opinion of the authoritarian practices of the coup leaders. The militant anti-Communism of both governments gave Phibun and his aides more influence in the implementation of American policy. The Republican leaders had few twinges of conscience in praising the former pro-Axis dictator as did some of the officials in the Truman administration. Their only concern was that Thailand remain firmly committed to the West. The only important criteria in assessing American policy were quick results and the appearance of success.

The Eisenhower administration did not have long to wait to give concrete expression to its new policy in Thailand. The end of the Korean war enabled the Chinese Communists to transfer sizeable quantities of military equipment to the Viet Minh forces in northern

Vietnam where they had been waging a bitter anti-colonial struggle against the French for over seven years. In April 1953 the Viet Minh suddenly launched an invasion of Laos which brought their forces to within a few miles of the Thai border. Many observers felt that Thailand would be the next target of Communist aggression in spite of a sudden and voluntary retreat by the Viet Minh invaders.[8] This feeling was intensified when Communist troops in December 1953 again invaded Laos and captured the town of Thakheg on the Mekong River directly opposite from Thailand. Western concern for the security of Southeast Asia reached a new high in May 1954 when the fall of Dienbienphu to the Viet Minh caused the collapse of French resistance in Indochina. With the partition of Vietnam at the Geneva conference in July 1954, the United States looked increasingly to Thailand as one of the most secure bases for the military defense of the region.

The apparent threat to Thailand from the Viet Minh forces was supplemented by the possibility of subversion instigated from Communist China. On January 31, 1953 Peking announced the formation of a "Thai Autonomous People's Government" at Sibsongpanna in southern Yunnan province which had been the original homeland of the Thai people and was still inhabited by some 200,000 Thai tribesmen.[9] This move was interpreted by many Western observers as an attempt by the Peking regime to establish a base in southern China for subversive operations and possible guerrilla warfare against the Thai government and other Thai minorities in Burma and Laos. This fear was exacerbated in July 1954 when Pridi suddenly emerged in Communist China after his mysterious disappearance from Singapore almost five years before. The Peking radio quoted an article that the former Thai leader had published in the official newspaper of the Chinese Communist party, the *People's Daily,* in which he urged the Thai people "to wage a struggle against their rulers—American imperialism and its puppets, the government of Thailand." [10] Shortly thereafter the Peking radio referred to him as the "Public Leader of Thailand." [11] This dramatic move caused many Western and Thai officials to believe that Pridi would be used by the Chinese Communists to head the Thai Autonomous People's Government in Yunnan province against the Phibun regime.

The threat of military invasion from Indochina and subversion from Communist China made the security position of Thailand look even more precarious than before. While the propaganda charges emanating from the Communist capitals intensified this feeling, an objective analysis of these allegedly threatening forces would again have made this assessment appear somewhat exaggerated. As mentioned previously, the Viet Minh was a formidable guerrilla force in Vietnam in its struggle with the French due to the widespread support it received from the Vietnamese people who considered it a genuine nationalist movement. An invasion of Thailand by the Viet Minh forces would have required strong logistical support which they lacked and the invaders would obviously have received no political support from the Thai people. The Viet Minh incursions into Laos were almost certainly made to enhance their bargaining position in the negotiations with the French and they did not actually pose as a serious threat to Thailand. Mr. Dulles himself admitted as much in December 1953 when he minimized the danger of the Viet Minh troops on the Thai border and declared that they "are not now, according to our information, in such numbers as to carry any present threat to Thailand." [12] Shortly thereafter the Viet Minh forces withdrew to North Vietnam.

The alleged menace of Communist subversion from the Thai Autoonomous People's Government in Yunnan province was even less of a threat than the Viet Minh in Indochina. The inhabitants in this area are backward tribesmen who number only 200,000 and have been isolated for many centuries from the more advanced people in Thailand.[13] The terrain between Yunnan province and the Thai border is extremely rugged and the launching of subversive operations from this area by Thai tribesmen who have little prestige or support in Thailand would have been extremely difficult. The possibility of Pridi leading these primitive people in a struggle against the Phibun regime was very remote. In all probability the establishment of a Thai Autonomous State in southern China and the emergence of Pridi in Peking were part of a propaganda campaign launched by the Chinese Communists to discourage the Phibun government from cooperating too closely with the Western powers.

In spite of these conditions in the area surrounding Thailand, the intense fear of Communist aggression by the Eisenhower administration and the extreme sensitivity of the Thai government to Communist propaganda made these threats appear ominous. Consequently the United States again increased its material and moral support to cope with the least likely threat to Thai national security. Thereafter the Americans turned primarily to a military defense of the country and almost all non-military assistance was subordinated to military objectives.

The Expansion of Military Aid. The move by the Eisenhower administration to strengthen the military forces in Thailand came at the conclusion of the Geneva conference which partitioned Vietnam and removed the French as a significant power in Southeast Asia. Shortly after this military and diplomatic debacle the United States announced its intention to build Thailand into a powerful "bastion" for the defense of the region. The MAAG mission was enlarged from 300 to 400 men and more Thai military officers were trained in the United States. Military assistance was increased by $28,200,000 and reports were made that the United States was considering an expenditure of $50,000,000 to double the size of the Thai army.[14] The training of junior officers, non-commissioned officers, and technical personnel in Thailand was expanded, and the United States supplied more tanks, artillery, small arms, and jet fighter planes to the armed forces. Construction began on a 297-mile highway from central to northeastern Thailand. An extension was added to the northeastern railroad line from Udorn to Nongkhai and modern airfields were built to handle jet aircraft.[15] As before, the Americans justified this sudden expansion in military assistance in light of the alleged threat from Communist China and the strong pro-Western policy of the Thai government. "Government in Thailand," a *New York Times* editorial exclaimed, "has been and is strongly anti-Communist. But militarily Thailand is not yet strong enough to be a bridge-head that can be held against a southward and westward Communist advance. The need for help, therefore is plain. Fortunately, we are dealing with a people and a Government to which it can be given with confidence." [16]

In addition to the rapid expansion of military aid, the Eisenhower administration converted much of the economic aid program to the support of larger military forces. Economic assistance thereafter was divided into "technical cooperation" and "defense support." Technical cooperation consisted of the same developmental projects which had been initiated since 1951 and had done much to advance the economy. In 1954 this program was reduced to approximately one-half of its former size. Defense support consisted of money and supplies which were given to the Thai government so it could maintain a larger number of troops than the national economy could otherwise sustain. The funds devoted to this activity by the Eisenhower administration were increased to more than six times the money spent on technical cooperation. More dollars were expended on defense support in 1955 alone than all the funds provided to technical assistance during the preceding four years. The following table shows the amounts of money spent for each program by the United States.[17]

AMERICAN EXPENDITURES IN THAILAND: 1952-1955

U.S. Fiscal Year	*Technical Cooperation*	*Economic Aid (Defense Support)*
1952	$7,200,000	....
1953	6,500,000	....
1954	8,800,000	....
1955	4,600,000	$29,700,000

These figures actually reveal only a fraction of the funds devoted to military aid. The dollars spent in direct support of the armed forces was a classified secret, but it was undoubtedly several times the amount given to defense support.

A major factor in stressing the need for more military aid was the influence exerted by Major General William J. Donovan who replaced Mr. Stanton as the United States Ambassador in 1953. General Donovan was already well known in Thailand as the former head of the O.S.S. which had achieved one of its most notable successes during World War II by collaborating with the Free Thai underground movement. Ironically, he was now assisting the Thai government headed by Phibun who had been an ally of the Japanese, while Pridi, who had courageously assisted the O.S.S., was in Peking cooperating with the Chinese Communists. The O.S.S. chief had been personally selected for this diplomatic assignment by his close friend, President Eisenhower. According to one source Donovan had been picked for this post "to prepare the country for an eventual Communist assault." [18]

During the one year that General Donovan served as Ambassador he made frequent trips to Washington and held numerous talks with President Eisenhower and Secretary Dulles. In these consultations he continually stressed the need for more military support to Thailand. In the summer of 1954 while the French were withdrawing from Indochina, he brought General Sarit to Washington where they appealed to the leaders of the Eisenhower administration for larger military forces. Donovan was instrumental in adding $28,200,000 in military aid and one hundred instructors to the MAAG mission. He was also responsible for the reports proposing that the size of the armed forces be doubled.[19] In both countries the Ambassador stressed the serious external and internal threat to Thai national security. On one occasion he stated that "our enemy might make another effort in Indochina not only to destroy Indochina but to do its best to direct its attempt upon Thailand itself." [20] At a press conference in Bangkok he declared that the United States could help protect Thailand from external aggression but the Thai government itself must take more stringent measures to suppress internal subversion. He added: "This country must prevent itself from becoming Communist from within."[21] Donovan frequently traveled to the border provinces with the Thai leaders and emphasized the need to maintain strong military and security forces. Even after he retired as Ambassador and returned to the United States, he continued to stress the serious Communist threat. In an article entitled "Our Stake in Thailand" published in the July 1955 issue of *Fortune* magazine the general appealed for more military aid and hailed the country as "the free world's strongest bastion in Southeast Asia."[22]

In December 1954 Mr. John E. Peurifoy was appointed as United States Ambassador to Thailand. He had formerly served as an ambassador in Greece and Guatemala, and he had recently won wide acclaim in Central America for assisting in the ouster of the pro-Communist Arbenz regime. His primary objective in Thailand was to assist its development into a major defense base for the security of Southeast Asia and to keep the leaders of the government alert to the Communist threat. The new ambassador also continued the policy of his predecessors in praising the military leaders for their devotion to the cause of liberty and the free world. Within the triumvirate regime Peurifoy tended to favor Phibun and sought to enhance his position within the ruling elite. He generally distrusted General Phao and indicated a desire to curb the police chief's rapidly expanding power.

The role of General Donovan and Mr. Peurifoy in gaining additional military aid was assisted by the influence of Mr. Stanton who had retired from the Foreign Service. The former ambassador told an audience in the United States that Communist activity in Thailand had greatly increased and the internal threat was a "covert underground thing which is being stepped up all the time."[23] In an article entitled "Spotlight on Thailand" published in the October 1954 issue of *Foreign Affairs* he cited the alleged attempts of the Communists to subvert the Thai government. He praised the stringent measures taken by the military leaders in suppressing these apparent signs of Communist activity and appealed for the United States to increase its assistance to the armed forces. He labeled the Thai as "our best friends in South Asia today."[24] Mr. Stanton supported the move by the Eisenhower administration to create a military pact in the region and claimed that Thailand would willingly serve as the major center of such an alliance. He concluded: "If Thailand's freedom and independence can be preserved, the heart and much of the body of Southeast Asia will have been saved."[25]

The three men who served as United States Ambassador to Thailand from 1946 to 1955 had nothing but good intentions in attempting to help the government and people, and in stressing what they felt was a serious threat to the nation's security. They were men of extensive experience in public affairs and were deeply devoted to the anti-Communist policies of their government. They spoke with great authority on Thailand and their diplomatic tours were hailed as eminently successful. Unfortunately Mr. Peurifoy's tour ended in one of the major tragedies in American-Thai relations when he was killed in an automobile accident in August 1955.

While these ambassadors deserve much credit for their devotion to duty, their influence on the political progress of Thailand had serious deficiencies. With the partial exception of Mr. Stanton, none of these diplomatic officials had a significant knowledge of the internal workings of the government or a genuine understanding of the deep-seated characteristics of the people. During their tours they confined most of their contacts to top-level officials in the government. This was especially true of General Donovan who spent most of his one year as ambassador traveling to the United States or in consultation with the military leaders. Their diplomatic role consisted primarily of maintaining friendly relations with the Thai government by promising larger grants of foreign aid and in serving as a messenger between the military establishments of the two countries. They looked at the Communist threat largely through the eyes of their superiors in Washington instead of making an objective and realistic assessment of the situation from within Southeast Asia. They were primarily concerned with quick results and the appearance of success. They generally accepted the validity of the reports of the military leaders regarding the internal threat and assumed that any opposition to the government was Communist-inspired. This was especially true of Mr. Stanton who relied almost entirely on the Thai leaders for his information on internal Communist activities and frequently urged them to suppress these apparent signs of subversion.

These three ambassadors felt that the rapid expansion of the armed forces served as a major bulwark against the spread of Communism. They likewise believed that the modest economic and social progress promoted by the non-military aid programs would satisfy the demand of the people for higher living standards. Yet each of these diplomatic officials failed to recognize the antithetical nature of the military and non-military aid programs sponsored by their government. They did not see that large-scale military aid to the Phibun regime was pushing the political system backward toward a more ruthless form of authoritarianism. They did not emphasize sufficiently the vulnerabilities in the economic and social system which continued to provide the Communists with an excellent opportunity to exploit anti-government sentiment. They did not encourage the military leaders to provide a channel for the people to exercise some influence on the policies of their government. Perhaps most serious was their failure to inform their superiors in Washington that the move toward greater reliance on military power and less emphasis on economic and social development was a move precisely in the wrong direction. In effect these ambassadors facilitated a change in emphasis in American policy which further diverted attention from the most serious threat to Thai national security to a threat which was the least likely to materialize.

What was true about the three ambassadors was also generally true about many other Americans who exerted some influence during this same period. Many officials talked with great authority on Thailand while very few had made a serious study of Thai society. By 1955 the number of resident Americans was higher than at any time in the intercourse between the two countries. The MAAG mission of more than 400 men comprised the vast majority of officials, while the missionaries and businessmen were the largest groups among non-officials.[26] In addition to the increasing influence exerted by Americans living in the country, Thailand continued to be visited by numerous high-ranking officials from the United States who received widespread attention. Between 1952 and 1955 these dignitaries included Vice-President Nixon, Secretary of State Dulles, Adlai Stevenson, Harold Stassen, several Senators, numerous Congressmen, and many generals and admirals.[27] Even a few movie stars such as Danny Kaye, Ava Gardner, and William Holden made their way to Bangkok for brief visits.

A notable trend throughout this period was the growing intimacy between the Thai military leaders and the top-level military officials from the United States. In the amicable consultations between these two groups only military considerations were seriously assessed. To gain even closer cooperation both groups frequently bestowed important national decorations on each other. While visiting in the United States in July 1954 General Sarit and Lt. General Jira Wichitsongkhram, the Thai Chief of Defense General Staff, were each awarded the Legion of Merit by General Ridgway, the Chief of Staff of the United States Army. Shortly thereafter General Phao was given the Legion of Merit by Secretary of the Army, Robert B. Stevens, for "exceptionally meritorious service" in fostering American-Thai relations. The Thai government was even more generous in bestowing national decorations and within three years it conferred more national honors on American officers than in the entire previous century. These honors ranged from the Most Exalted Order of the White Elephant to Commander of the Order (Third Class). These decorations were awarded to virtually every high-ranking official in the United States military establishment including Secretary of the Navy, Robert B. Anderson, Admiral Arthur W. Radford, General Mathew B. Ridgway, Lt. General Lyman L. Lemnitzer, General John E. Hull, General Nathan Twining, Admiral Felix B. Stump, and numerous other lesser-known American military officers. Only a few honors, usually of less distinction, were awarded to American officials engaged in non-military programs. This activity revealed how deeply impressed the Phibun regime had become with the role of the American military leaders in obtaining large-scale foreign aid which in turn bolstered their political power.

The United States continued to impress upon the Thai government the precarious position of the country in the Cold War and the need to maintain a strong defense. In April 1953 Adlai Stevenson visited Thailand as a state guest at the time the Viet Minh launched their first invasion of Laos. He warned the Thai leaders that their country was the real target of the Communists and added: "I hope that Thailand, its government and people fully appreciate the threat." [28] In June 1955 Senator Everett Dirksen inspected the American aid programs and claimed that they were "being wisely and profitably utilized for the mutual benefit of Thailand and the United States." [29] He added: "The young Thais I have seen in uniform impressed me immensely by their capacity for discipline and their capabilities as soldiers." The Senator from Illinois said nothing about their capacity to think for themselves or to understand the real nature of freedom for which their country and the United States was fighting. Some Americans, especially military officers, intensified the previous efforts to make Thailand appear as a democratic nation which shared the same political and social values as the United States. When leaving the country after heading the MAAG mission for over three years, Colonel Charles A. Sheldon stated in his farewell message: "Thailand's borders are threatened by armed aggression by people who do not believe in democracy, who do not believe in freedom or the dignity of the individual man as do the people of Thailand and my country." [30] And when arriving in Bangkok in December 1954 for consultation with the military leaders, Admiral Radford declared that "closer arrangements between democracies will be much better." [31]

The Impact of the SEATO Alliance. The culmination of the attempt by the United States to bolster the security of Thailand and the surrounding countries was reached in the formation of the Southeast Asia Collective Defense Treaty, more popularly known as SEATO. The Eisenhower administration was prompted to this action by the partition of Vietnam at the Geneva conference in July 1954 and the general feeling that the non-Communist countries in Indochina would be quickly absorbed into the Communist bloc. A Soviet veto in the United Nations Security Council in June 1954 of a Thai request to dispatch an investigation commission to Indochina combined with an urgent appeal from Thailand for more military aid also hastened the move by the United States government to erect a collective security alliance in the region. After much hesitation the Americans were finally willing to expand their security commitments from the island defenses in the Pacific to the mainland of Asia.

The major driving force behind this endeavor was that exerted by Mr. Dulles who advocated a policy of "united action" even before the Geneva conference began.[32] The British and the French balked at this move until the final compromise to partition Vietnam. The British at first sought an alliance which would stress economic and social development rather than military power with the hope that India, Pakistan, Burma, Ceylon and Indonesia would join and contribute to the stability and progress of the region. Mr. Dulles promptly quashed this idea by insisting on a purely military alliance which would "build a dike" between the Communists and the non-Communists in Southeast Asia.[33] The heavy emphasis on military power caused all the Colombo nations except Pakistan to refuse to join this pact. Throughout these preliminary negotiations the Thai government consistently supported the position of the Secretary of State by stressing the serious Communist threat and offering military bases to the proposed alliance.

The SEATO treaty was formed at Manila on September 6-8, 1954 among eight nations: Australia, New Zealand, the United States, Great Britain, France, Thailand, Pakistan, and the Philippines. This conference provided an additional channel for the Americans to stress the Communist danger to the security of the region. Upon his arrival in Manila Mr. Dulles declared: "We are united by a common danger, the danger that stems from international communism and its insatiable ambition . . . We feel a sense of common destiny with those who have in this area their life and being." [34]

The diverse interests among the member nations caused them to negotiate a flexible alliance such as the ANZUS pact instead of a tightly coordinated organization such as NATO. Both the Americans and the

British opposed a joint military command or combined military forces. In spite of the looser organization Mr. Dulles assured the delegates at the conference that in the event of Communist aggression the United States would quickly support them with its mobile air and naval power. During the negotiations he advocated that the alliance be directed only against Communist incursions whereas the other nations wanted a broader interpretation of aggression. The Secretary of State also wanted the three non-Communist countries in Indochina covered by the treaty, a proposal to which only Thailand at first agreed.

In the final draft of the SEATO treaty Mr. Dulles was forced to make several modest concessions, but he got most of what he originally sought in the alliance. The treaty stated that the member nations agreed to uphold the "purposes and principles" of the Charter of the United Nations, and each party vowed "to strengthen the fabric of peace and freedom and to uphold the principles of democracy, individual liberty and the rule of law, and to promote the economic well-being and development of all peoples in the treaty area." In Article II each member agreed to "maintain and develop their individual and collective capacity to resist armed attack and to prevent and counter subversive activities directed from without against their territorial integrity and political stability." Article III upheld the aim of each member "to strengthen their free institutions" and to promote "economic progress and social well-being." Article IV contained the essence of the treaty with the provision that in the event of acts of aggression each member would "meet the common danger in accordance with its constitutional processes." This was the first regional alliance signed by the United States which formally authorized collective action in dealing with internal subversion in any member nation.

A Council was established to implement the treaty and to hold consultations periodically on "military and any other planning". The United States succeeded in defining the treaty area as "the entire territory of the Asian Parties" and "the general area of Southeast Asia (and) the Southwest Pacific." Since the area north of 21 degrees 30 minutes latitude was excluded, Hong Kong and Formosa were not covered by the treaty. The three states of Indochina, however, were included. The United States did not succeed in confining the alliance only to Communist aggression. Secretary Dulles consequently included a special "Understanding of the United States of America" stating that his government adhered to the treaty with the stipulation that it would "apply only to communist aggression." In the event of other aggression the United States agreed to "consult" with the member nations.

At the instigation of the Filipino delegation a Pacific Charter was also signed by all members of the alliance except France. This proclamation was designed to "uphold the principle of equal rights and self-determination" for the people of Southeast Asia as the famous Atlantic Charter had done for the nations Western Europe.

From February 23-25, 1955 the SEATO Council held its first meeting in Bangkok to implement the treaty. Phibun used this occasion to impress on the visiting delegates what he believed to be the grave Communist danger to the nations of Southeast Asia. Just before the conference opened he declared that 20,000 "Free Thai" troops were being massed by the Chinese Communists near the northern Thai border. These forces, he claimed, were sufficient to invade Thailand and conquer the region. The Premier did not provide any evidence to support this startling announcement. Yet he included a similar threat in his welcoming address. "So far as international peace and security are concerned," he stated, "the situation in our treaty area, as at no other times in its history, requires greater watchfulness and preparedness, for while the danger of armed aggression clearly exists, there also is manifest an acute threat of infiltration and subversion which forms a more insidious mode of aggression."[35]

In his opening speech Mr. Dulles supported Phibun's position and explained the basic purposes of American foreign policy:

"United States foreign policy, in its basic aspects, has always rested on two propositions. The first is that we want our own people to enjoy, in peace, the blessings of liberty. The second is that we cannot assure liberty for ourselves unless others also have it. Freedom cannot thrive in an environment that is hostile to freedom.

"It is appropriate that we should be meeting here in Thailand, a country whose very name means "land of the free." May our action here be such that this happy land wherein we meet and all of the lands with which our treaty deals shall be forever 'lands of the free.'"[36]

During the conference the delegates representing Thailand, Pakistan, and the Philippines sought to insert more "teeth" in the alliance and urged the establishment of a unified military command, a joint mobile striking force, and token American troops stationed at strategic posts within the treaty area. In accordance with his doctrine of massive retaliation Mr. Dulles again voiced his preference for larger ground forces in the local countries supported by mobile American air and naval power. He explained that SEATO was only one force in the containment of Communism in Asia. Formosa, Japan, and South Korea, he added, were other closely related fronts which had to be bolstered by massive retaliatory power. The United States consequently could not overextend its limited military resources to any single region.

The SEATO Council decided to meet annually in the treaty area. Bangkok was selected as the headquarters for a permanent secretariat of the alliance, and the ambassadors of each member nation in the Thai capital were designated as Council Representatives who would meet more frequently to discuss current problems. Four committees were established to deal with military affairs, subversion, economic affairs, and information, cultural, educational and labor activities respectively.

In the formation of this alliance an additional channel was provided between the United States and Thailand to emphasize such Western values as democracy, individual liberty, and the rule of law. The Pacific Charter also stressed the ideas of equality and national self-determination. Since its inception, however, the major impact of SEATO in Thailand has emphasized the need for more military power and police action to protect the security of the country. The alliance has provided the military leaders with another justification to suppress internal opposition and at the same time to claim that the intimate relations between Thailand and the SEATO members make these actions "democratic."

Thereafter the Phibun regime frequently timed the suppression of internal political opponents so it would coincide with an important meeting of the SEATO alliance, thereby minimizing local and foreign criticism. This practice was used for the first time just before the Council conference in February 1955 when the police executed three men who had been accused of implication in the unsolved death of King Ananda. Two of these men had been released in 1951 for lack of evidence. The other defendant had been sentenced to death even though the Criminal Court admitted that the "assassin" was still at large. In 1954 when Pridi emerged in Peking and the fear of Communism in Thailand reached a new high, the military leaders again arrested these men and sought capital punishment. The Criminal Court complied with the government's request and the king refused to commute these heavy sentences. The executions took place just six days before the first SEATO Council meeting—a conference held to uphold respect for law and the dignity of the individual. The reasons for this harsh action have never been adequately explained nor has sufficient evidence been uncovered to implicate these three men in the death of the late king. It is not unlikely that the Thai militarists had these men executed to prove to the Americans that they too could be "tough" on the "Communists."

The SEATO treaty had other serious deficiencies in promoting the long-range objectives of the United States in Southeast Asia. Perhaps most obvious was the narrow military approach to the defense of the region which was promoted by the Americans and forced the British to drop their proposals for a broader and more progressive alliance. The primary stress on military power again concentrated the major anti-Communist effort on the least likely threat and further diverted attention from the real danger in the depressed economic and social conditions in the three Asian members. The economic provisions included in the treaty received no serious consideration from the United States until 1957. The pact further encouraged an increase in the conventional military forces in each Asian member which placed an additional financial burden on the United States and the local economies.

A more effective move would have been the conversion of the local armies into small mobile striking forces capable of countering guerrilla warfare—the most likely form of military action in the area. Also, since all the nations in the alliance except Thailand were already members of a Western military pact, a wiser policy would have been the negotiation of a bilateral defense treaty between the United States and Thailand instead of the establishment of a cumbersome piece of international machinery such as the SEATO organization. Such a treaty could have assured the Thai leaders of American determination to defend their country, and it might have reduced their exaggerated fears concerning the nation's security. Thereafter both governments could have acted with greater freedom of action in the event a genuine Communist threat did materialize.

The membership of the alliance also indicated that it would have enormous difficulties in opposing any serious Communist threats in the region. The inclusion of Great Britain and France made it almost certain that no nation which had formerly been a European colony would join. Also, the British were much more concerned with their mounting problems in the Middle East and Africa, and the French were beginning a bitter struggle against the nationalist rebels in Algeria. The inclusion of these two European powers almost guaranteed that they would pursue a conservative and cautious policy and avoid any additional commitments in Southeast Asia. The Thai and the Filipinos on the other hand were vitally concerned with any Communist threat and could be expected to demand immediate action in the event of a danger to their national security. The absence of India as one of the most influential Asian nations was a serious deficiency. The participation of Pakistan was an enormous liability as its leaders openly admitted that their primary purpose in joining Western military alliances was to strengthen their position in their struggle with India and Afghanistan. Pakistan's concern with Communist aggression was a secondary matter.

Finally, the SEATO treaty tended to split South and Southeast Asia into two blocs, one neutralist and one pro-Western, and it made the highly desirable goal of promoting unity and cooperation within the region more difficult. Shortly after the formation of the alliance, the neutralist bloc reacted by organizing the Afro-Asian conference at Bandung which won widespread support among many influential uncommitted nations.

The attempt to counter subversion was one of the better aspects of the new alliance. However, these provisions had dangerous implications if they were merely to strengthen the local police forces and exchange information on Communist agents operating in the region. While some activity along these lines could be useful, a more effective method of countering this threat would be the launching of urgently needed political, economic, and social reforms to meet the expanding needs of the people and contribute to the popular support of the governments in the treaty area. The comments made by Mr. Dulles at the first SEATO conference indicated that no serious attempt would be made to launch these reforms. His position that Southeast Asia was only one front in the containment of Communism meant that the United States was looking only at the military defense of the region and giving little consideration to the economic and social problems in each country. This policy also assumed that each of these Asian nations opposed Communism in the same way and to the same degree as the United States. Needless to say, this defensive and conservative policy neglected many forces operating in the region and the demand of the people for political, economic, and social change.

Authoritarian Triumvirate Rule. Throughout the period from 1952 to 1955 the Thai government was dominated by the triumvirate rule of Field Marshal Phibun Songkhram, General Phao, and General Sarit each of whom received extensive material and moral support from the United States. Phibun's position within this power elite was enhanced to some extent by the increasing rivalry between Phao and Sarit. The two junior contenders also accepted the Premier's meditating role in their occasional disputes. To strengthen his position further Phibun usually held several portfolios in the Cabinet including the post of Minister of Defense, Minister of Economic Affairs, and Minister of Culture. He likewise attempted to instill a spirit of cooperation in his regime by stressing the national welfare, loyalty to the king, and the threat of Communism. In effect, he was playing much the same role after 1952 that Colonel Bahol had played from 1933 to 1938 when he and Pridi were the contending aspirants for power. Phibun's position in the 1950's, however, was much more precarious than Bahol's as he had no significant power from within the armed forces and he was relying largely on the diplomatic support provided by the United States. Also, both of his subordinates wielded enormous influence whereas only the military faction within the former People's Party had commanded any significant power. If the Americans withdrew their support or if the internal rivalry between Phao and Sarit erupted into violence the Premier's position within the triumvirate regime would be seriously jeopardized.

Phibun's major competitor for political power throughout this period was the young forty-two year old police chief, Phao Sriyanon, who had been promoted to the rank of General in July 1952 and was hailed by many observers as the "strong man" of Thailand. General Phao's training and experience had been entirely within the army until he was transferred to the police force when it expanded after the war. His rise to power had been facilitated by the assistance of his father-in-law, General Phin, who had planned the 1947 coup. One of his major assets was the extensive assistance he received from the American-owned Sea Supply Corporation which enabled him to build the police force into a powerful military organization which was better led, better paid, and more efficient than the army. The United States provided the police with their own tanks, artillery, armored cars, air force, naval patrol vessels, and the only training school for paratroopers in the country. By 1954 American assistance enabled Phao to increase the police force to 42,835 men or one policeman for every 407 people. This was one of the highest ratios between policemen and citizens of any country in the world. Although the police at the time were a slightly smaller force than the army, the police officials were able to play a more active political role due to their direct contact with the public and their ability to intimidate and suppress anti-government opponents with the claim that they were protecting the internal security of the country.

Phao's political position was also enhanced by his dynamic and aggressive personality. He was highly ambitious, an excellent administrator, and he loved politics. His charm and affability made him a good mixer among foreigners. His very un-Thai characteristics made the colorful police chief strongly admired by the Americans and passionately feared by the Thai people. In spite of these assets, however, he was poorly informed and his approach to internal and international affairs was extremely narrow and crude. As late as June 1953 he exclaimed that the Soviet Union did not possess an atomic bomb and only the United States had succeeded in mastering atomic energy.[37] The only possible method of opposing Communism, he claimed, was the use of military power. He believed that permanent peace was impossible to achieve and mankind should be prepared for the inevitability of another war. His idea of democracy was a regime established by a majority of the Assembly (under the authoritarian 1952 constitution) administering the country according to the laws made by the government-controlled legislature. His suspicion of persons he thought were sympathetic to Communism knew no bounds. In 1952 he claimed that the Communists had been the cause of every attempted coup in Thailand since the end of World War II. He even blamed the Communists for the occasional brawls between army personnel and the police.

Phao relied largely on his monopoly of the opium trade and his extensive commercial enterprises for the income he needed to support his personal political machine. He was ably assisted in this endeavor by several "knights" who held high positions in the police force and whose loyalty he retained by lavish gifts and an undisclosed private income. As Phibun and the Americans urged more stringent internal security measures, the police chief was able to expand his power into virtually every aspect of government policy. By 1953 he held the post of Director-General of the Police Department, Deputy Minister of Interior, and Deputy Minister of Finance. He was also appointed to head a special security committee of the Cabinet called the Political Affairs Bureau which was given the same status as a ministry and was assisted by a Central Intelligence Agency assigned to the task of reporting on political agitators. He headed a Foreign News Collecting and Correcting Committee established by the government to correct "incorrect" information which had been published about Thailand abroad.[38] He was selected as Director-General of a special committee created by the Cabinet entitled the Civil Service Code Department which was authorized to rewrite the regulations of the civil service to prevent Communist infiltration. Phao also served as the leading spokesman for the government in the Assembly and led the attack against anti-government representatives. The Communist threat, he emphatically insisted, justified increasingly more stringent laws and harsher suppression by the police. He continually countered the charges that the government was becoming a dictatorship by explaining that Thailand was closely allied to the most democratic nation in the world, the United States. His insatiable lust for power was perhaps most clearly revealed in his appointment in June 1953 to another special committee established by the Cabinet to investigate all laws which had not been fully enforced. This trend reached ludicrous proportions in May 1955 when Phao was appointed to head an Anti-Corruption Committee which cautioned all government officials to cease from corrupt practices and luxurious living. Instead, the committee proclaimed, these leaders should set an example to the people.

With his expanding authority Phao led one of the most ruthless and thorough suppressions of internal opposition in recent history. In 1952 he ordered the police to take into custody any person suspected of aiding the Communists, a move which aroused widespread fear and suspicion of any one who voiced opposition to the government. The notorious Criminal Investigation Division and the Crime Suppression Squad secretly arrested scores of people and obtained quick confessions of Communist conspiracy. Yet whenever these victims were released for lack of evidence they invariably claimed that they had no sympathy with Communism or any connection with a Communist organization. The police intensified their suppression by establishing an informer system in which the public was instructed to send any information on Communist suspects to "Box 777" so these persons could be investigated.[39] The police also announced that they were seeking young people from twelve to twenty years of age to serve in a "youth detective organization" where they would be trained to inform on anyone disturbing internal peace and order. Within the brief span of two years General Phao almost single-handedly converted Thailand into a police state.

The third member of the triumvirate regime was Sarit Thanarat who also had been promoted to the rank of General at the early age of forty-two and whose training and experience had been entirely in the army. He had gradually risen as a major political figure since his supporting role in the 1947 coup. After the November 1951 coup he took the position of Deputy Minister of Defense in Phibun's government, and in 1954 he replaced General Phin as Commander-in-Chief of the army just before his visit to the United States. His stature was greatly enhanced by his trip to Washington and the warm and sympathetic reception from the leaders of the Eisenhower administration. Sarit received much of the credit for the rapid expansion of American military aid. In March 1955 he was given the rank of Admiral of the Navy and Air Marshal of the Air Force. The following year he was promoted to the rank of Field Marshal.

Sarit, like Phao, relied heavily on his private income to finance his own political organization. While the police chief derived most of his funds from the opium trade, the army chief received an enormous income from the national lottery. Until 1955, however, Sarit did not appear as extensively involved in politics as Phao. This was due partly to the fact that the army did not have direct daily contact with the public as did the police, hence it was not actively suppressing the opponents of the triumvirate regime. This condition was also due to Sarit's retiring and sullen personality which gave the impression that he wanted to remain aloof from politics. The army chief was not as good an administrator as Phao nor was he an especially competent military commander. At times he did not appear as concerned about the Communist threat as the police chief or the Americans, and he favored the visit of Thai assemblymen to Communist China. Unlike Phao he did not speak good English and he often felt uncomfortable in the presence of foreigners. He usually confined his contacts to his army cronies with whom he frequently engaged in heavy drinking, causing him to suffer from an acute case of cirrhosis of the liver. To the Americans he appeared as a rugged and dour army officer to whom they paid considerable respect but with whom they did not enjoy the same intimate relationship as they did with the more cooperative and affable police chief, General Phao.

In spite of the personal rivalry within the triumvirate regime, the three military leaders were united in their desire to maintain themselves in power and to suppress any opposition to their expanding authority. To retain their dominant political position they promptly sought to legalize their authoritarian rule. This was partially accomplished by extending military control to the legislature, promulgating the 1952 constitution, enacting more restrictive laws, and taking prompt suppressive action against actual or potential opposition. In the elections held in February 1952 for the 123 elected seats in the Assembly, they began to move for complete legal authority. With political parties abolished the candidates were forced to run on an independent basis and they were permitted to campaign only with the tacit understanding that they would not excessively criticize the government. One candidate in Saraburi province who engaged in a bitter denunciation of the military regime was called in by the police for questioning.[40] Khuang Aphaiwongse and the Democrat Party boycotted the elections claiming that they were not "ethical." [41]

As election day approached the public appeared so apathetic that Phibun personally appealed to the people to exercise their right to vote. In spite of this plea his government took no chances in allowing the people to elect many anti-government representatives. Some of the elections were rigged and in crucial areas army troops were again used to vote for pro-government candidates. The results were as follows: [42] pro-government members—85 seats, independent members—9 seats, opposition members—29 seats. Shortly after the election some of the independents and opposition members realized that their position in the Assembly was hopeless and they requested to join the dominant pro-government bloc. Only a few determined opposition members, most of whom represented the poverty-stricken northeastern provinces, continued to criticize the policies of the government.

The promulgation of the 1952 constitution also enhanced the legal facade erected by the triumvirate regime. The new constiution had been drafted by a committee headed by Phin, Phao, and Sarit and it bore the deep imprint of their influence. The king succeeded in inserting a provision stating that the return to an authoritarian-type constitution had been caused by international tension. This action implied that the latest change in the political system would be only temporary and a democratic constitution would be restored when the world situation became less tense. This platitude did not deter the militarists from asserting their dominant political power. The major features of the new constitution were the numerous additional powers granted to the government and the reduced authority of the legislature and the king. The provisions enumerating civil rights upheld the freedom of religion, speech, publication, and assembly, but as before, these rights were "subject to the provisions of the law." Political parties could be established only according to law.

The military leaders introduced an entirely new concept in Thai constitutional practice in the provisions which upheld the same rights and liberties to members of the military and police forces and government officials as to other nationals "unless they are subject to restrictions imposed by law, by-laws or regulations issued by virtue of law in so far as it concerns political activity, efficiency or discipline." Since military and police leaders now controlled the government and the legislature it was almost certain that no laws restricting military, police, or government officials in political activities would be passed.

The constitution reverted to a unicameral Assembly of People's Representatives composed of equal numbers of elected and appointed members for a term of five years. The parliamentary immunities of the representatives were weakened to the point where the government could readily intimidate them or restrict their activities. The new constitution concluded with the usual "Transitory Provisions" which stated that after five years the appointed representatives would be replaced by elected members when more than one-half of the people in any province had received a primary school education. After ten years the appointed representatives would not be retained and the national legislature would be completely elective.

As before, the new constitution provided its creators with a legal framework designed to preserve a recent change in political power and to protect their dominant position. It enabled the military leaders to control both the government and the legislature for the first time since World War II, and it provided them with the legal basis for exercising virtually unlimited power. The king was able to insert several minor modifications which retained some of the democratic features of the 1949 constitution, but in practice these restrictions on executive power could be readily circumvented. The military leaders understandably deleted the restrictions prohibiting government officials or members of the Assembly from holding directorships in private or public corporations. In effect the new constitution formally concentrated almost all military, political, and economic power in the hands of a few men which had been the major objective of the military leaders since they overthrew the liberal government in November 1947. Upon returning from a short leave in the United States, Ambassador Stanton described the situation as follows: "I learned of disheartening developments which had taken place and had set back the slow progress being made toward a more democratic form of government . . . Friends of Thailand as well as serious-minded Thai were exceedingly unhappy over these events. However, the Prime Minister and his supporters took the position that the country was not yet ready for full democratic government and that some of the elected members of the Lower House had been obstructive. They professed to be supporters of democracy but asserted that the dangers surrounding the country called for strong leadership . . . The shell of constitutional government remained but the people had little voice in the Assembly."[43]

Some Americans agreed with this discouraging trend and reiterated similar sorrowful comments. However, none openly declared that the enormous quantities of military aid provided by their government had greatly strengthened the hands of the militarists and encouraged them to push the political system back to where it had been in 1932. The military leaders actually had no more right than any other Thai citizens to claim that the country was not yet ready for democracy or that some of the elected members in the former legislature had been "obstructive." Yet the arms given to them by the United States enabled them to assert such a right. No other group was able to stop them.

In accordance with the new constitution Phibun's government resigned and the role of the military in the new Cabinet was further increased. The Premier himself had disapproved of the Coup Group's seizure of complete power in November 1951 and he hinted that he might retire from politics or take some minor position in the legislature. By this time, however, the military leaders were well aware that they needed a person of Phibun's stature to retain the support of the United States and he was persuaded to head a new government. In March 1952 his Cabinet was unanimously approved by the Assembly.[44] A major consideration in forming the new regime was to maintain the favor of the United States which was suspected of disapproving of the recent seizure of power by the Coup Group. Consequently the important post of Minister of Foreign Affairs was given to Prince Wan Waithayakon who had served as the Thai Ambassador to the United States since 1947 and was highly respected by the Americans for his ability and cooperation at the United Nations.[45] Phibun retained his former portfolios as Minister of Defense and Minister of Culture while General Phao became the Deputy Minister of Interior and General Sarit took over as Deputy Minister of Defense. The new government was comprised of nineteen military and police officers and seven civilians.

Before enacting more suppressive laws the triumvirate regime converted the Assembly into a rubber-stamp body where government policies were announced and quickly approved. Like the Cabinet, the legislature consisted almost entirely of military and police officers who merely parroted the position of the government and voted as they were told. In the 1952 legislative session the pro-government bloc reduced the meeting time to four hours a week with the excuse that the Cabinet ministers were too busy to come to the Assembly any more frequently. All bills presented by the government were approved with overwhelming majorities, and only a few elected representatives dared to voice their opposition. The perversion of the national legislature by the triumvirate regime is illustrated in the following table showing the voting on several typical bills under the 1949 constitution as compared with the 1952 constitution: [46]

COMPARISON OF ASSEMBLY VOTING UNDER THE 1949 AND 1952 CONSTITUTIONS

1949 *Constitution*	*Vote*
Supplementary Budget Bill Increasing the Salaries of Civil Servants (Approved).	41-32
Military Agreement with the United States (Approved)	42-29
Rent Control Bill (Defeated)	32-15
1952 *Constitution*	
Government Electoral Bill (Approved)	80-1
Government Bill Creating Rank of Brigadier-General in the Police Department (Approved)	100-3
Opposition Bill to Repeal Press Act (Defeated)	86-10
Opposition Bill to Repeal Press Censorship in Press Act (Defeated)	116-9

At a meeting of the Assembly in January 1953 the government was able to obtain seven bills at one sitting. On another occasion during the following year the legislature approved eight bills in four hours with four of these bills passing through all three readings. By this time constitutional government in Thailand had become a complete farce.

The first major act to expand the legal authority of the triumvirate regime was an emergency law approved in February 1952. This law was justified as a necessary measure to cope with the serious Communist threat. It gave the government wide powers to place foreigners in restricted areas, deport undesirable aliens, impose curfews, search suspicious residences, ban public meetings, and establish a censorship of the press.[47] The emergency law was loosely worded and authorized the government to resort to almost any measure to maintain peace and order. In October 1952 after Phibun had publicly announced that conditions in the country were returning to "normalcy," General Phao ordered a strict suppression of alleged Communist agitators claiming that subversive activities were becoming more widespread. It was at this time that the police chief ordered his officers to investigate and arrest any person suspected of Communist sympathies. The following month the police made one of the most sweeping mass-arrests since World War II claiming that they had uncovered a plot to establish a Communist dictatorship in Thailand. The police announced that "those arrested are members of a clique seeking to overthrow the government by force and change it into an undemocratic regime with the collaboration of a foreign power." [48] A total of 104 persons were arrested, including politicians, writers, students, government officials, military personnel, and relatives of former liberal leaders. Forty-nine of these persons were subsequently sentenced to twenty years in prison. One of the persons who received this heavy penalty was Pridi's son. The police again claimed that the Communists had been behind every attempted coup since World War II. As before no evidence was given to support these charges.

The authority of the triumvirate regime was further increased when a stringent anti-Communist law was passed by the Assembly in November 1952.[49] This measure had been prepared by General Phao who personally presented it to the legislature in his capacity as Deputy Minister of Interior. He urged prompt passage of the bill claiming that it had been patterned after anti-Communist statutes in Turkey, Singapore, and the United States. To support the government's position he called attention to the recent Communist "plot" uncovered by his police officers which he claimed was directed at the establishment of a Communist dictatorship. The debate on this law lasted only one hour and it was passed by a vote of 131 to 2. It provided for prison terms ranging from ten years to life for membership in the Communist Party, and heavy penalties were imposed for persons attending Communist discussion groups who did not report them to the police.

Additional suspects were arrested under the new anti-Communist law within forty-eight hours after it came into effect. Three newspapers were closed. Several persons were questioned for spreading rumors that the police were using "third degree" methods in obtaining confessions and claiming that the recent Communist plot was only a "farce."[50] The following month the Premier ordered Phao to place "strong men" at strategic positions in the provincial police administration where they could give special attention to those areas where opposition to the government or "democracy" was suspected.[51] The increasingly arbitrary authority of the police was vividly illustrated during a debate in the Assembly when General Phao was asked why his subordinates had arrested the editor of a local newspaper. The police chief replied that the editor had denied news reports issued by the Public Relations Department of the government. The government department, he added, could not be wrong.[52]

The triumvirate regime further extended its authority through administrative action which it again justified as necessary to protect the country from Communist aggression and infiltration. An attempt was made to purge the ranks of the civil service of any person suspected of harboring Communist sympathies. Phibun instructed the members of his Cabinet that they were personally responsible for any disloyal activities by the personnel in their ministries, and each minister established his own investigating committee to examine suspected employees. The government also established a new security plan in which a directory was compiled of all persons engaging in political activities.[53] Each individual was listed according to his political beliefs and those persons whose loyalty was in doubt were placed under police surveillance.

Having consolidated its authority at the national level the triumvirate regime in 1953 turned to local government where some vestiges of democracy still remained. It abolished all elected provincial assemblies and announced that new elections would be held for one-half of the members of these local legislative bodies. As in the National Assembly, the government was authorized to appoint the other representatives in the provincial legislatures. The municipalities also became the victims of the same centralizing process. The Ministry of Interior arbitrarily dismissed the elected mayor of Bangkok, Khun Lert, and under a new Municipal Reform Act it was authorized to appoint the mayors of all municipalities and one-half of the members of the municipal assemblies.[54] The government could dismiss any mayor or dissolve a municipal assembly at any time. Provincial police officials were given the same authority over the local village chiefs and their advisory councils.

Minor Limitations on the Triumvirate Regime. In spite of the vast centralized power exercised by the triumvirate regime, it did permit a modest opposition to its rule, and in practice several internal forces were able to exercise minor restraints on its extensive authority. One of the most important checks was that exerted by the pro-government members in the Assembly. After the February 1952 elections these representatives held private weekly meetings at the Manangasila Villa in Bangkok to discuss legislation which the government proposed to submit to the national legislature. Since political parties were not permitted, this body called itself the "Legislative Study Commission" and its approval of government-sponsored legislation was tantamount to its acceptance by the Assembly. In effect the Legislative Study Commission operated as a pro-government political party as it was headed by Phibun and his ministers and its organization and management was carefully controlled by General Phao.[55] Under the police chief's leadership the body adopted regulations which required that all pro-government members must obtain the approval of the Commission before submitting any question to the government, introducing any bill, or supporting any motion in the Assembly. All pro-government representatives were required to attend the legislative sessions whenever a government proposal was up for discussion, and they were required to vote in favor of all government bills. All meetings of the Commission were held in secret. The triumvirate regime retained the loyalty and services of the pro-government members by providing them with 2000 baht in "pocket money" each month in addition to their regular salary as members of the legislature. Their allegiance was further strengthened by numerous favors including special housing facilities, medical care, junkets to Europe, and educational opportunities for their families.

In spite of these controls, the Legislative Study Commission did not completely succumb to the role of a rubber-stamp body. The elected members in the Commission occasionally voiced their opposition to government proposals and at times they succeeded in modifying executive action. The Commission, for example, forced the triumvirate regime to delete a provision from a bill exempting Chulalongkorn University from the restrictions included in the Rent Control Act. On another occasion the government was forced to modify a law banning small rice mills in the provinces. Opposition to a new "basic" method of teaching the Thai language in the public schools became so intense that the entire program was dropped. The Commission, like the Coup Group, was also limited by rivaling factions within its membership which served at times to moderate the policies of the government.

The small group of opposition members in the Assembly were able to exercise only minimal restraint on the triumvirate regime. They organized themselves informally into a group called "His Majesty's Opposition" and they continually charged the government with corruption, nepotism, and incompetency.[56] They advocated a socialist doctrine and attacked the military leaders for neglecting public health, education, and rural economic development. Most of the opposition representatives criticized the pro-Western foreign policy of the Phibun regime and advocated a policy of neutralism. They denounced the large quantities of military aid provided to the armed forces by the United States. They likewise opposed Thailand's adherence to the SEATO alliance. When the pro-government representatives organized the Legislative Study Commission, the opposition members established themselves into a group called the "Opposition Legislative Study Commission" which they later changed to the "People's Legislative Study Commission." An element of validity was given to this latter title as this group was composed entirely of elected representatives and it opened its meetings to the public and the press. It was able occasionally to exercise a modest influence, and the government at times did modify its action after hearing criticism from the opposition. The government permitted opposition members to travel inside and outside the country. However, their activities were restricted by intermittent harassment from the police.

The two most prominent leaders of this small group were Thep Jotinuchit and Klaew Norapati, both elected representatives from northeastern provinces. Their debates with the military leaders on the floor of the Assembly for almost three years provided the only significant public criticism of the triumvirate regime and the only meaningful discussion in what otherwise would have been a colorless and apathetic legislature. Their attacks on the government were well publicized and won scattered support as popular discontent with the Phibun government slowly increased.

Thep Jotinuchit had formerly served as Deputy Minister of Commerce and his primary interest was in the economic development of the underprivileged areas of the country, especially the poverty-stricken provinces in the northeast.[57] He drafted much of the legislation presented by the opposition group which was quickly voted down by overwhelming pro-government majorities. In July 1953 he proposed a bill to legalize political parties in accordance with a provision in the 1952 constitution. This bill was promptly defeated by the pro-government bloc on the grounds that it would open the way for the Communists to organize a political front in Thailand. Shortly thereafter he presented another bill which provided that village chiefs be popularly elected instead of appointed by provincial officials. This proposal was likewise rejected by the pro-government representatives who claimed that it would enable "influential men" to use the elections to put unqualified persons in power. In spite of these obstacles Thep continued to lead some of the most vicious attacks against the government and his polemic duels in the legislature frequently brought him face to face with General Phao. On one occasion the pro-government Speaker of the Assembly placed a bill on the agenda without the required three-hour notice because the police chief had labeled the matter as "urgent."[58] Thep thereby led a dramatic walk-out by the members of the opposition during which he declared: "We call ourselves a democratic country. We must listen to views and not force people to be silent." Phao promptly admonished him to refrain from inciting the people against the government. The police chief claimed that his subordinates had information linking Thep with the Viet Minh and replied: "Let me warn him to be careful."[59] Phao added: "I am democratic and anti-Red."

Klaew Norapati likewise voiced bitter criticism of the triumvirate regime and he refused to be silenced by the intimidation of the police.[60] He served as the major opponent of the government as it increased its authority to suppress internal "subversion." He likewise opposed the move to augment the size of the armed forces. He criticized American military aid and the SEATO alliance. He urged the government to reduce its expenditures to the military and police forces so it could expand the economic development of the country. He favored trade with Communist China. He also denounced the government for censoring the local press. He attacked the triumvirate regime for permitting luxuries such as a television station in Bangkok while people in the provinces were living in abject poverty. Klaew directed his charges at all three military leaders. On one occasion he criticized Phibun for allowing members of his Cabinet to hold more positions than they could effectively administer. He denounced Phao for using plain-clothes policeman as spies in the halls and lounges of the Assembly building. And he opposed a bill presented by Sarit to draft all university graduates into the armed forces for two years. Klaew's outspoken opposition frequently caused him to be interrogated by the police. At one time he explained that his political activities were motivated by his attempt to reduce military expenditures so that more money could be used to help the people in the northeastern provinces. The police announced that these actions were part of a Communist plot.

The efforts of Thep, Klaew, and their small opposition group involved the United States in another paradox in its extensive support to the anti-Communist but authoritarian triumvirate regime. This small socialist group was either publicly ignored or privately denounced by many Americans in Bangkok and considerable attempts were made to have it stigmatized as "Communist." Yet these few determined men were the very persons who were striving against overwhelming odds to preserve some form of constitutional government. Admittedly, some of their ideas on internal and international affairs were extreme and naive, especially their illusion that Thailand could profit enormously from a closer relationship with Communist China. But by almost any standard they were fearless and courageous men in the midst of a hopeless situation. They expressed qualities that Americans had traditionally admired. To the best of their ability they were attempting to preserve a political system such as they had seen or studied about in the West. Had they been serving in the United States Congress they would in all probability have found themselves among the liberal Democrats. Under the authoritarian triumvirate regime in Thailand they could be considered nothing but left-wing extremists. The overriding policy of the Eisenhower administration that the Thai government must be kept closely aligned with the Western bloc regardless of its internal policies ironically caused the Americans to ignore or debase a small group attempting to retain some of the liberal elements of the Western political tradition. If a few Thai socialists had to be sacrificed for this supreme objective it was only one of many inevitable misfortunes in the Cold War. The Americans somehow felt that the end would justify the means.

The courts to some extent placed modest limitations on the triumvirate regime although the intense fear of Communism promoted by the military leaders and the Americans served to weaken the judicial process. However, in many cases the courts did continue to offer some protection to individual liberty. According to law the police were required to present imprisoned suspects to the Criminal Court every twelve days and justify the retention of these persons for a longer period. On most occasions the police merely informed the Court that the suspects had contributed to a serious Communist threat and with few exceptions the police were authorized to hold them for an additional twelve days. Requests by these persons for release on bail were usually denied. By law, however, no one could be held for more than eighty-four days unless sufficient evidence had been presented. In most cases the police were unable to obtain adequate evidence and the suspects were released.[61] Occasionally the courts went so far as to check arbitrary administrative actions of the military leaders themselves. In July 1952 the Civil Court ruled that General Phao acting in his role as "Press Officer" had gone beyond the limits of the law in imposing censorship on the Thai-language newspaper *Naew Na*.[62] Yet this act was the exception rather than the rule. The triumvirate regime frequently corrupted the channels of justice to enhance its power as vividly illustrated in its ability to obtain capital punishment for the three men allegedly implicated in the death of King Ananda.

In all probability King Phumiphon placed minor restraints on the triumvirate regime, although he kept aloof from politics in his ceremonial role under the constitutional monarchy. As mentioned previously he persuaded the military leaders to retain some of the democratic features incorporated in the 1949 constitution. These included several provisions protecting civil rights and the directive principles of state policy.[63] After the triumvirate regime was formally established in

March 1952 the king requested briefings from the Cabinet members on the administration of their ministries to become better informed on the actual operation of the government. It is possible that he used these briefings to impress on the ministers the need to govern in the interests of the nation and the people. In his public appearances the young monarch also stressed the need for responsible government, and he urged the Cabinet, the Assembly, and the people to work together for the welfare of the nation. These consultations and public proclamations may have served to check in some degree the rapacity of the triumvirate regime.

Public opinion played no significant role throughout this period, although modest criticism of the government was permitted. This vocal opposition served to remind the military leaders that at least some segments of the public continued to watch the conduct of the government and take an active interest in political affairs. A few prominent individuals stood out in this activity. Khuang Aphaiwongse, the leader of the defunct Democrat Party, remained out of politics after the promulgation of the 1952 constitution, but he continued to voice his opinion of the government with restrained and subtle frankness. At times he supported certain policies of the triumvirate regime but he often voiced criticism of the military leaders, especially their ineptitude in administering the national economy. Seni Pramoj returned to his law practice and remained quietly critical of the Phibun government. In spite of his previous intimate connections with the United States during World War II, Seni opposed Thailand's pro-Western foreign policy on the grounds that the country was too small and underdeveloped to participate actively in the military alliances sponsored by the Western powers. Kukrit Pramoj also retired from politics and led an active role as one of the most influential journalists in the country. Through his popular newspaper, the *Siam Rath,* he continued his own clever criticism of the military leaders by the use of wit, satire, and subtle innuendoes.

By 1955 discontent with the triumvirate regime was intensified by the increasing number of Western-educated Thai who were returning from American and European universities and assuming responsible positions in the civil administration. This group comprised the most alert and competent officials in the country and provided the government with its technical and administrative experts. On their return from abroad many of these persons became frustrated as they saw the military leaders misuse American aid, siphon off some 12 per cent of the national income for their personal fortunes, and give the peasants only one-third of the income received from the sale of their rice. Many were eager to initiate reforms and assist their people with the knowledge they had acquired in the West. Yet they were confined to purely administrative tasks as the enormous power wielded by the military leaders prevented them from exercising any significant political influence. A returned Fulbright student voiced his feelings as follows: "I came back from America full of ideas and enthusiasm to help my country. But every day I see that nothing is done here except by personal influence and favoritism. Every bit of policy is controlled by people put into their jobs by political friends, regardless of their ability. They are always making promises but they never fulfill them."[64]

The educated Thai were quick to see through the perversion of the national legislature and the deception of the triumvirate regime in using the Communist threat as justification to attack and arrest its political opponents. A junior civil servant expressed this attitude in these terms: "Only half of our members of parliament are elected. The others are appointed. And the elections—such strange things happen that nobody believes in them any more. I love Thailand. Yet if I say freely what I say to you, they will say I am Communist."[65]

These comments perhaps more than anything else proved that the American military and non-military programs were releasing antithetical forces which as early as 1955 were coming into sharper conflict. Young Western-educated Thai who were vastly superior in intelligence and integrity to the military leaders were forced to stand aside while their government continued to be operated in an authoritarian and incompetent manner. The situation was similar in many respects to the frustration experienced by the young Western-influenced idealists who formed the People's Party in 1932 and overthrew the absolute monarchy. Like the reactionary princes around Prajadhipok, the leaders of the triumvirate regime were concerned mainly with enhancing their personal wealth and keeping themselves in power. While the former princes had received much of their wealth and power from their intimate connections with Europeans, the military leaders were receiving much of their wealth and power from the large-scale aid provided by the United States.

As these two diverse forces came into increasing conflict the general tendency of most Americans was to declare that the ruthless suppression of political opposition by the military leaders was a purely internal affair. Only a few Americans, mainly scholars and journalists, openly stated that the United States had some moral responsibility for the security and welfare of the growing number of liberal-minded Thai who were being suppressed by the triumvirate regime. One American scholar stated: "The unpleasant fact must be faced that American aid to Thailand, our only active partisan in Southeast Asia has largely made possible the arming and training of a para-military police force that eclipses the country's army and is dedicated to suppressing any opposition to the Phibun regime." [66]

Perhaps the most significant and dangerous aspect of this growing conflict was the possibility that Western-influenced liberals who realized that they could do nothing by themselves to improve their government might turn to the Communists for assistance. The extensive material and moral support provided by the United States to the Phibun regime only intensified this disillusionment with the Western democracies and strengthened the feeling among some liberals that their only hope was to gain the cooperation of the Communist bloc. Pridi had already taken this drastic step and others might follow. One American observer described this situation as follows: "An ever-increasing number of Siamese liberals and socialist patriots, believers in democracy, are giving up all hope that anything can be done to help their country under the present regime. If their voice is not heard by America and Britain they will surely turn to Red China. Continued reliance on the military strengthening of Thailand, to the exclusion of political, social, and economic reforms long overdue, will not resolve the tragedy of Thailand. It can only weaken the will of the people to resist the clever promises of the Communists and make the true defense of the country vastly more difficult." [67]

The real tragedy of this situation was that these young Thai liberals actually detested the ideology and practice of Communism as readily as they opposed the triumvirate regime. However some were tempted to take the chance that they could use the Communists to assist them in ousting the military leaders and then later free themselves from Communist control. They failed to realize that in all probability the Communists would gain control over them and establish a totalitarian regime in Thailand. By 1955 an element of reality was given to this ominous possibility by the rising anti-government sentiment which was also becoming increasingly anti-American. Contrary to the intentions of the leaders of the Eisenhower administration and many conscientious Americans who sought to bolster the security of the country, the rapid increase in military aid and the exaggeration of the Communist threat was increasing, not decreasing, the vulnerability of many Thai people to Communism.

Chapter V

THE DECLINE OF TRIUMVIRATE RULE

The changes which took place on the international scene during the spring and summer of 1955 had a significant effect on the relations between the United States and Thailand. The Soviet Union appeared to be somewhat less intransigent since the death of Stalin and a policy of "peaceful coexistence" became the dominant party doctrine with the rise of Khrushchev as the new Communist leader. This apparent change in Soviet foreign policy was due primarily to the atomic stalemate with the Western bloc. It was also caused by the rising influence of the uncommitted nations who were demanding greater efforts by the major powers for a permanent peace. The Soviet Union accordingly altered its policy from a stress on military threats to non-military courses of action, and it proclaimed that peaceful relations with the non-Communist world had been the only objective of the Communist camp since the Bolshevik revolution in October 1917.

To give concrete expression to this new policy the Soviet rulers agreed to meet with the leaders of the Western alliance at the "summit" conference in Geneva in July 1955 where both parties vowed their unbending devotion to world peace. This conciliatory gesture was followed by the Austrian peace treaty and the evacuation of the Porkkala naval base in Finland. The Soviet Union paid a tacit compliment to the United States as it endeavored to expand its influence in the underdeveloped countries by imitating the American policy of providing the uncommitted nations with sizeable grants of economic and military aid. These modest concessions did not indicate a fundamental change in the long-range goal to spread Communism throughout the world. They were primarily a change in tactics to expand Soviet influence and power through non-violent means. The Russian leaders gave no serious indication that they wished to halt the Cold War. They merely revealed that they wanted a slight relaxation in world tensions.

The response of the United States to the new trend in international relations was one of guarded skepticism. When convinced that some relaxation of tension might result from a meeting with the Soviet leaders, President Eisenhower agreed to attend the Geneva conference

...he returned stating that there was "evidence of a new friendliness in the world." [1] Yet like the Soviet Union, the United States wanted to maintain adequate influence in the uncommitted nations. In light of the nuclear stalemate with the Communist bloc, some Americans began advocating that more economic and technical assistance be given to these underdeveloped countries to assist them in meeting the rising demand of their people for better living conditions and that the previous stress on military power be reduced. However, the Eisenhower administration did not make any significant changes in its large military aid programs in the non-Communist countries in Asia. Secretary of State Dulles insisted that the modest economic and technical assistance these nations were already receiving through bilateral programs, the United Nations, and the Colombo Plan, was sufficient. Perhaps the only notable concession made by the United States to the new era of "peaceful coexistence" was the agreement to negotiate informally with the Chinese Communists on their disputes in Asia and the release of American prisoners. Actually American military aid to the pro-Western nations in Asia was increased. In April 1955 President Eisenhower requested Congress to grant $3,500,000,000 for foreign aid, the bulk of it designated for military assistance to the "Arc of Free Asia." [2]

American policy in Thailand reflected this conservative attitude, and the previous attempt to prevent the spread of Communism primarily through the use of military and police power remained essentially the same. In 1956 the United States provided the modest sum of $4,800,000 for technical aid and in 1957 this amount was further reduced to $4,500,000. Defense support in 1956 cost $29,500,000 and in 1957 these funds were increased to $30,000,000. By the end of 1957 the United States had spent a total of $138,000,000 for foreign aid in Thailand with most of this money devoted to the armed forces. A much larger undisclosed amount had been used for direct military assistance since the aid programs had been launched in 1950. According to the new United States Ambassador, Max Bishop, the amount spent on direct military aid was "in the hundreds of millions of dollars." [3]

In addition to bilateral aid the United States continued to provide extensive economic and technical assistance through the World Bank. In August 1955 the World Bank loaned Thailand $12,000,000 for the improvement of its railroads; in September 1956 it provided a loan of $3,400,000 for the development of Bangkok harbor; in May 1957 it began considering a loan of $100,000,000 for the Yanhee hydro-electric power project in northern Thailand.[4] The Bank also assisted the government in developing a long-range economic program. Additional loans and assistance from the Bank of America and other private American corporations further aided the Phibun regime in promoting the economic progress of the country.

In spite of this extensive assistance, the rapid expansion of the armed forces encouraged by the Eisenhower administration continued to place a heavy burden on the national economy. Between 1950 and 1957 the Thai government was forced to increase its annual defense budget from approximately $33,000,000 to $93,000,000. After 1955 the leaders of the triumvirate regime themselves began to request that more American aid be transferred from military assistance to the economic and technical aid programs. Secretary Dulles strongly opposed these appeals. On a brief visit to Bangkok in March 1956 he declared that "the United States military and economic aid programs for Thailand are well-balanced and there is no reason for any change."[5] This opinion was supported by Admiral Radford who visited the Thai capital shortly thereafter and stated that the large military program would be maintained just as before.[6]

The SEATO alliance continued to provide the United States with another channel to stress the Communist threat and the importance of military power. On his return to Washington after the SEATO conference in Bangkok in February 1955 Mr. Dulles informed the American people in a radio broadcast that he had just "visited the forward positions against which the waves of communism are beating and where the issues of war and peace, of freedom and captivity, hang in precarious balance."[7] The Secretary of State described the non-Communist countries of Southeast Asia as "a gallant band of independent and freedom-loving nations" who were opposing 600 million Chinese Communists. He specifically referred to Thailand as the "land of the Free."[8]

As the new era of "peaceful coexistence" caused Thailand to soften its attitude towards the Communist bloc and veer closer toward neutralism, the United States used the SEATO organization to instill an even stronger fear of Communism in the minds of the Thai leaders and people. From 1955 to 1957 the meetings of the Military Advisors and the Committee of Security Experts were the only activities of the alliance which received any serious consideration by the United States. The threat of Communist subversion was most frequently stressed. A SEATO sub-committee meeting at Manila in September 1955 reported that "subversion is on the upswing" in Southeast Asia and the internal threat to the member nations was much more serious than during the previous year.[9] As before no evidence was provided to support this claim. The Committee of Economic Experts supposedly considering methods of improving the economic development of the three Asian members received little attention from the Americans. Yet as economic difficulties in Thailand increased after 1955, the Thai government used this committee as an additional channel to appeal for more economic aid. This practice became increasingly embarrassing to the United States as these requests were supported by similar appeals from the Filipinos and the Pakistanis. The Committee on Information, Cultural, Education and Labor Activities did little more than issue platitudinous resolutions from time to time and offer a few research scholarships to promote an understanding of the treaty organization.

While the SEATO alliance undoubtedly gave some people in Thailand a greater sense of security, the government continued to use it as a cover for its suppression of internal opposition. The concurrence of Thailand's participation in important events sponsored by the treaty organization and more suppressive action against opponents of the triumvirate regime soon became too common to be merely coincidental. Two weeks after the first SEATO conference in Bangkok forty-nine persons arrested in the November 1952 "plot" to establish a Communist regime were sentenced to twenty years in prison.[10] Perhaps the most obvious example of this policy was the dramatic arrest of Thep Jotinuchit, Klaew Norapati, and their small party in February 1956 when they returned from Communist China just a few days after an impressive SEATO military maneuver near Bangkok. Thep and his party had received the approval of many top-level government officials including Marshal Sarit before they made their journey to Communist China. On their return in the midst of the pro-Western enthusiasm aroused by the SEATO military display they were charged with violating the Anti-Communist Act. The attitude of the military leaders on this occasion was clearly revealed in the words of the Chief of the Criminal Investigation Division: "The Thai government does not want the Communist ideology because it stands firm with the free democracies. It does not want anybody to propagate Communism in this country . . . There is considerable Communist movement in Thailand at present, with Communists inside the country contacting Communists abroad, like trips to Communist China."[11]

While the visit to Communist China by Thep and his party was a questionable political move, the government had no evidence that they were propagating Communism in Thailand. Yet the intimate relationship between the triumvirate regime and the SEATO nations encouraged the former to take this "anti-Communist" action. Additional examples of this same suppressive policy will be cited later.

Throughout the period from 1955 to 1957 most Americans living in Thailand continued to stress the Communist threat and bolster the military regime. Until his untimely death in August 1955 Mr. Peurifoy supported Phibun as the ideal anti-Communist leader in Southeast Asia and praised him for his devotion to the "free world." [12] The Ambassador emphasized the Communist threat with little knowledge of the country or an objective assessment of the political and economic conditions in the surrounding region. Yet his words and actions strengthened the exaggerated fear of Communism entertained by the Thai leaders. After only a few weeks in Thailand, Ambassador Peurifoy made a brief tour of the northeastern provinces and declared that the Vietnamese refugees living in the area were ninety per cent "pro-Communist." [13] He gave no information on how he arrived at this high figure.

A police official stationed in this area later admitted that the bulk of the Vietnamese refugees were strong nationalists who had fled their homeland when the French returned to Indochina after World War II.[14] With few exceptions these people had lived peacefully in Thailand for almost ten years where most of them had become excellent farmers. Many of these refugees voiced their admiration for Ho Chi Minh because he was fighting the French, but they knew nothing about Communism nor did they support any Communist organization. This police official claimed that at the most only a few hundred of the Vietnamese refugees were pro-Communist. Mr. Peurifoy predicted that approximately 35,000 of these refugees were pro-Communist. Yet the exaggerated fear of Communism among the Thai and the Americans enabled the popular ambassador to make this questionable assessment with an air of conviction and credulity.

In January 1956 Mr. Max W. Bishop was appointed as United States Ambassador to Thailand. Mr. Bishop was a career Foreign Service Officer and had served at various diplomatic posts in the Far East for fifteen years. He was recognized in the Department of State as an expert on Asia. When he took his oath of office, Assistant Secretary Robertson declared: "No one is more aware of Communist intentions and tactics than he." [15] This was Mr. Bishop's first assignment as an ambassador and he appeared extremely anxious to impress his superiors by maintaining the same close relations with the Thai militarists as his predecessors. Yet he arrived in the country just as a nationalist reaction toward United States policy was emerging. In spite of the good intentions of the Americans, their excessively intimate contacts with the military leaders had caused the rising tide of anti-government sentiment to engender a growing manifestation of anti-Americanism. Opponents of the government increasingly criticized American military aid and the SEATO alliance. The United States was blamed for almost all of Thailand's economic ills: the low prices of rubber and tin, competition in the rice trade, and insufficient economic progress.[16] Some of these critics went so far as to charge the United States with controlling the Thai government. High-ranking American officials and the Thai military leaders did much to encourage this censure by their frequent public appearances together and their lavish praise of each other.

Mr. Bishop tried diligently to stem the rising tide of opposition toward the triumvirate regime and his own government. As the criticism mounted he became even more outspoken than his predecessors in lauding the military leaders and defending the large military program. At one of his early press conferences he vigorously upheld the need for more weapons in preference to greater economic assistance: "A country must first have strength—a shield to protect it from those who aim to destroy it."[17] After sufficient armed strength has been achieved, he added: "I would agree economic development is more important." The new ambassador unfortunately did not indicate just when sufficient military power in Thailand would ever be achieved. Ambassador Bishop also justified the large quantities of American military aid by stressing the Communist menace. He declared that in spite of reduced world tension the Communist threat had not diminished but had "assumed a different and possibly more dangerous form—that of pretending friendship while working and plotting through secret conspiracy the death of free governments and the enslavement of free people."[18] He answered critics of Thailand's close relationship with Western powers by stating that he could not imagine any role for the country with its "glorious history of freedom and independence, but that of sovereign independence and full partnership with its allies."[19]

Mr. Bishop likewise reiterated the praise heaped on Thailand by Mr. Dulles and numerous other Americans. "Thailand," he declared at a SEATO committee meeting, "is a most auspicious place of the meeting of your committee. With its long history of freedom, its illustrious traditions of valor, and its profound and devout religious life, it is indeed an inspiration."[20] And the ambassador frequently stressed the traditional American admiration of Thai national independence to the ludicrous point of disparaging his own country and Western civilization. "Asia," he stated on another occasion, "was a civilized and cultured world long before many of our ancestors gave up their bear skins and clubs . . . For my part, I wish not only to learn the facts about Thailand but also to come to understand the problems and aspirations of the Thai people." [21]

In effect Mr. Bishop quickly became an ardent and unyielding apologist for the military leaders and their policy of close collaboration with the Western bloc. This practice intensified the feeling among many Thai people that the United States had a vested interest in the Phibun government and would support it regardless of public opinion. This impression combined with the harsh suppression of internal opposition by the police whose aggressiveness and efficiency were widely attributed to the Americans did much to increase hostility toward the triumvirate regime and the United States. In all probability less frequent public appearences by important American officials and the military leaders and less eloquent praise of the latter's "achievements" would have made relations between the two countries appear more normal and might have discouraged some of the rising hostility.

Resident and visiting Americans continued to emphasize the Communist threat to the country. During the period from 1955 to 1957 Thailand was again visited by many prominent Americans including Vice President Nixon, Secretary of State Dulles, Under-Secretary of State Christian Herter, Director of ICA John B. Hollister, many Senators and Congressmen, and numerous Generals and Admirals (who continued to be showered with military decorations from the grateful Thai government.) [22] Other visitors from the United States included Mrs. Eleanor Roosevelt, Justice William O. Douglas, former Governor Thomas E. Dewey, Mrs. Pearl Mesta, William Randolph Hearst, Jr. John P. Marquand, Martha Graham, Cecil B. deMille, and Marlon Brando. A special group representing President Eisenhower known as the "Citizens Committee on Mutual Security" headed by Benjamin Fairless, President of the American Iron and Steel Institute, visited Phibun and brought him the greetings and support of the chief executive.

The major impact of this personal contact was to counter any serious attempt by the Thai government to veer toward neutralism or weaken its allegiance to the Western bloc. Most Americans sought to maintain close relations between the two countries and pledged even greater efforts to prevent the spread of Communism. When Vice President Nixon visited Bangkok briefly in July 1956 and held short consultations with the military leaders, they hinted at a policy of neutralism. They also appealed for "more and quicker economic aid." [23] Mr. Nixon succeeded in opposing the trend toward neutralism by praising the "political stability" and "economic progress" in the country and urging a continuation of intimate relations with the United States.

"On the basis of conversations and study of Thai policy," the Vice President stated, "I have no doubt about Thailand's dedication to independence and freedom and that Thailand would not adopt policies which would mean destruction of that independence by Communist colonial imperialism.

"It is particularly gratifying and a source of moral strength to the American Government and the American people to have such a staunch ally as Thailand has been these past years." [24]

Secretary of the Air Force Quarles likewise exclaimed that the only way to stop Communist aggression was to maintain the strength of the "free world." [25] He added that this "means the United States and its allies, including Thailand." During a brief visit former Governor Dewey declared: "There is a settled, orderly situation in Thailand . . . There has been a steady improvement toward stability." [26] William Randolph Hearst, Jr. met briefly with Phibun and labeled Thailand an "oasis of security." [27]

While it is impossible to assess precisely the effect of these expressions of American moral support for the triumvirate regime, they undoubtedly had some influence in encouraging the military leaders to continue their repressive internal policies. These complimentary statements were made by eminent Americans who had very little knowledge of Thailand and only a superficial impression which they had gained after a few days in the country. Yet they again indicated that the primary concern of the United States was "order," "stability," and "security." By strengthening these values through an exaggerated stress of the Communist threat, the Americans hoped to retain Thailand as a strong pro-Western ally.

The Impact of Phibun's "New Democracy". The most profound American influence on Thai politics during this period came from Phibun's world tour from April to June 1955 during which he spent three weeks in the United States. This journey was the Premier's first travel outside the country in twenty-eight years. The invitation to visit the United States was almost certainly initiated by the Americans to enhance his international stature as a leader of the "free world" in Southeast Asia. It was perhaps more urgently prompted by their desire to maintain his leading role within the triumvirate regime. It is highly possible that this invitation was the idea of Mr. Peurifoy who opposed the growing influence of General Phao and wanted to bolster Phibun's position. Unlike his two subordinates, the Premier did not have an internal military organization of his own as a source of political power. Consequently American military aid to the police and the army had been alloted to seek a balance of power between Phao and Sarit so Phibun could maintain his influence and control. However, the continual aggressiveness of the police chief created the impression that he might use his extensive power to crush the army and take over the government. While the Americans admired Phao's efficiency and enthusiasm, they did not want him to head the government. He was charming and anti-Communist, but even their obsession with Communism did not prevent them from seeing that he was too ambitious and too crude. In all probability he would have carried the suppression of internal opposition to the point where it would arouse more anti-government hostility and contribute to the instability of the country. Sarit was largely an unknown figure at the time. He appeared to be the quiet army chief who was indifferent to politics. The Americans thus felt that they had no choice but to strengthen the Premier's position within the ruling elite, and they sought to do this by illustrating even more vividly than before the strong moral support he enjoyed from the United States. However, noting the lesson taught by history that triumvirate regimes are short-lived, they maintained good relations with his two subordinates in the event that the delicate balance of power was upset and one of them emerged as the victor.

Throughout his tour in the United States Phibun repeatedly spoke of the serious Communist threat to Southeast Asia and the effort of his government to defend Thailand's independence. During his visit he was at his charming best and he convinced many Americans that his country was a part of the "democratic" world. In San Francisco he declared that the Communists would "inevitably" try to invade Thailand and "drive for world domination." [28] In Los Angeles he stated that the Communist menace will never be stopped by negotiations and "to halt communism it will have to be by force." [29] In a speech before the National Press Club in Washington, he told his audience that he hoped for reduced tensions in Asia without causing the people there "to lose faith in the strength of the free world." [30] He declared that the American officials believed Thailand would be the next target after Vietnam. In a forty-minute conference with Secretary Dulles he appealed for additional military and economic assistance and cited the Communist threat to his country emanating from southern China, Laos,

Burma, and Malaya. Afterward he declared that the "people of Asia desire their political freedom and self-government." [31] In a brief speech before the United States Congress, Phibun expressed the gratitude of his government for American aid and reminded the Congressmen that Thailand had sent troops to Korea. He said that his people admired Americans because "they love freedom" and he declared "my country will always be on your side." [32] In the House of Representatives he stated: "We are trying to achieve fully representative government which is directly responsible to the people." [33] The Premier was invited to a special interview with news correspondents in the U.S. News and World Report conference room in Washington where he further stressed the Communist threat and discussed the measures he had taken to increase the military and police forces. He summarized the attitude of his government by stating: "Within my country they [the Communists] are not successful, because we watch them very, very carefully and arrest them." [34]

At a press conference in New York City, Phibun praised the United Nations and the SEATO alliance. He aroused a brief furor when he predicted that World War III was "inevitable." [35] An indication as to how deeply the Premier had thought about this problem was revealed a day or two later when he publicly announced that the criticism aroused by his gloomy prediction had caused him to change his mind and state that another world war was not inevitable. At the same time when he addressed the Far East-American Council of Commerce and Industry, he declared: "We are clear in our minds as to what kind of life we want, just as you are clear in your minds that the American way of life is what you cherish. Let there by no mistake about our intention to belong to the free democratic nations." [36]

In addition to these public addresses, his tour was highlighted by playing golf with President Eisenhower, talking with United Nations' Secretary-General Dag Hammarskold, laying a wreath on the grave of Franklin D. Roosevelt, visiting West Point Military Academy, observing a steel plant in Pennsylvania and an automobile factory in Michigan, and receiving an honorary Doctor of Law degree from Columbia University. [37]

Phibun's tour in the United States provided the leaders of the Eisenhower administration with another opportunity to eulogize the Premier for his strong opposition to Communism and his close collaboration with the Western bloc. At an impressive ceremony on the White House lawn he was awarded the Legion of Merit by President Eisenhower "for outstanding services to the United Nations and the cause of freedom."[38] The citation described him as "a resourceful and inspiring leader" whose "outstanding professional skill, sound judgment, and keen foresight, contributed significantly to the missions and objectives of the United Nations command."[39] At a dinner given in his honor, Secretary Dulles lauded his government because it "dares to stand fast for the cause of liberty and freedom."[40] In New York City Mayor Wagner gave the Premier the city's scroll for distinguished public service and declared that his "outspoken friendship for the United States and the United Nations had made him one of us."[41]

After leaving the United States Phibun went first to Spain where he heaped praise and bestowed a military decoration on a man he had long admired, General Franco.[42] Thereafter he toured virtually all of the Western nations during which he dined with Queen Elizabeth, conferred with Prime Minister Anthony Eden, met the heads of other Western governments, and had an audience with the Pope. After brief stops in Egypt, Pakistan, and Ceylon he returned home. He conspicuously avoided India, Burma, and Indonesia all of which had recently played a major role in sponsoring the Afro-Asian conference in Bandung and espoused a distasteful brand of neutralism. It is not unlikely that he avoided these neutralist countries to intensify the opinion of the Americans that he was firmly committed to the Western bloc. He probably felt that a brief visit with another anti-Communist military leader such as Franco would not be frowned on by the United States.

Besides the obvious attempt to cement closer relations with the Western powers, Phibun's purpose in undertaking this world tour was undoubtedly motivated by his own desire to bolster his position within the triumvirate regime. As mentioned previously this was almost certainly the major reason why the invitation was extended to him by the United States. By 1955 both Phao and Sarit were becoming extremely powerful political figures because of the rapid expansion of American aid to the military and police forces. They had also received much prestige from their missions to the United States during the previous year where they had been instrumental in obtaining additional military and economic assistance. With his two subordinates relying on their extensive power in the internal political struggle, Phibun was forced to turn more closely to his major source of political power—the diplomatic support of the United States. Consequently the world tour was used by the Premier to enhance his prestige and illustrate even more vividly than before his important role in obtaining large quantities of American foreign aid.

On his return from abroad Phibun ushered in one of the most colorful and confusing episodes in Thai political history. From his recent efforts to impose an increasingly repressive form of authoritarianism he suddenly attempted to shift the political system toward a new and unique style of popular democracy. He began by announcing that he would be a candidate for an elected seat in the Assembly in the February 1957 election.[43] Some indication that this move had been influenced by his observations in the United States was shown when he publicly mused how he could run for an elected office and at the same time hold the rank of a Field Marshal. He indicated that he might follow the example of President Eisenhower who had resigned his military rank as a five-star general to be eligible for election to the office of president.[44] Phibun later requested that the law be amended so that he could run for an elected office and retain his military rank. Yet he remained determined to seek office through a popular election.

Thereafter the Premier engaged in a series of public addresses in which he sought to explain the meaning of democracy to his people and arouse a wider interest in political affairs. In many of his speeches he subtly criticized the younger military leaders in his own regime and appealed for support of the original democratic ideals of the 1932 revolution. On one occasion he urged a larger popular turnout in future elections and stated that "democracy is government of the people by the people for the people . . . people should concern themselves with government."[45] In an address before a class of newly commissioned naval officers he declared:

"In a democracy, soldiers should not interfere in politics . . . government officials, whether soldiers, civil service or police, whether permanent or political, should not engage in business effecting the general economy of the nation and the lives of the people . . . I feel that we should promote the democracy of this country . . . in setting up a government, they [the Western democracies] do so by elections to a Parliament and without having to use military or police force . . . Military or police force is only used to save a country when it is in danger. In some countries the army set themselves up in the middle and do not take sides in politics. With regard to our Thailand, the type of administration was changed 23 years ago. As head of the government I call for a halt to use of military police force to set up a government, because such is an act against democracy."[46]

In remarks directed more pointedly at his own subordinates, he announced that coup d'etats had become "outmoded."[47] He added: "Any coup now would mean overthrowing the King as constitutional head of the nation and setting up a republic. This, we cannot allow." As he took over as Minister of Interior shortly thereafter he promised that "elections in future shall be just, true, and democratic." [48]

Phibun supplemented these appeals for democracy with a series of political reforms that rivaled those brought about after the overthrow of the absolute monarchy in 1932 and the return of the liberals at the end of World War II. He resigned his own position as Inspector-General of the armed forces and sold his stock in private companies. He claimed these actions were to set an example of the need to separate the military from political and economic affairs. He ordered the army tanks removed from in front of his office and reduced the armed guard. Thereafter the Premier appeared in the streets driving his own automobile without an escort. In addition, he abolished the trade monopolies and special privileges of his Cabinet ministers and ordered them to sever their connections with private corporations.[49] To place his government in closer contact with the people he freed the press from police censorship and held regular press conferences similar to those he had observed in the United States and Western Europe. Phibun went further than the Americans or Europeans, however, by requiring the members of his government to attend the press conferences and answer direct questions about their ministries.[50] He further encouraged the local reporters to establish a "Press Club" such as he had seen in the United States.

To increase popular participation in politics the Premier established a "Hyde Park" debating center in Bangkok and in the large provincial towns similar to the one he had observed in London. He ordered the police to permit speakers at these public discussions to criticize the government in accordance with the rights of the people in a democratic country. He gave more liberty to opposition representatives in the Assembly and restricted the police in interfering with their political activities. At a press conference he stated: "Opposition politicians have the right to meet and discuss legislative bills, questionaires and other business of people's representatives. They have as much right as pro-government politicians." [51] In September 1955 Phibun persuaded the Assembly to pass a statute legalizing political parties. Within a short time numerous parties had registered with the government and began campaigning for the February 1957 general election. In an attempt to increase the electorate the Premier urged the pro-government representatives to lower the voting age to twenty years and abolish all educational requirements. When they balked at his proposal, he stalked out of their meeting and threatened to resign from the government. His request was accepted shortly thereafter and the voting requirements were accordingly reduced. He also extended his democratic reforms to local government. He ordered the provincial governors and officials to "get close to the people" and "eat with the people" so they could discuss their problems and consider their views.[52] He urged that Bangkok and the provincial cities establish a "Town Hall" such as he had seen in the United States and Western Europe to increase the participation of the people in public affairs.

A major obstacle to Phibun's "new democracy" was the enormous power wielded by General Phao and the police. The Premier accordingly sought to reduce the authority of the police chief in his attempt to improve his own position within the triumvirate regime. He accomplished this by a very shrewd move in which he again relied on the United States. Shortly after returning from his world tour he sent Phao to Washington in his capacity as Deputy Minister of Finance to negotiate a new loan. As soon as the police chief was out of the country the Premier reshuffled his Cabinet to increase his own influence and reduce that of General Phao. Phibun took the powerful post of Minister of Interior while the police chief was removed as Deputy Minister of Finance, the very position in which he was sent to the United States to negotiate another loan. Field Marshal Phin, Phao's father-in-law, was removed as Deputy Minister of Interior.[53] Other supporters of the police chief were also dropped from the Cabinet and replaced by persons loyal to Phibun and Sarit. General Phao's authority as "Press Officer" was transferred to the Governor of Bangkok. Police officials were specifically warned by the Premier to abolish their connections with private and public commercial enterprises. As Minister of Defense and Minister of Interior Phibun announced that thereafter he had the sole power to declare a military or police alert and order troop movements except in the event of war or open revolt .Within a short time he removed many police and army troops from Bangkok declaring that "they should not remain in the midst of the civilian population."[54]

Phibun's action to reduce the extensive power of General Phao won wide popular approval as it took place during one of the most notorious scandals involving the police force in the nation's history. Assisted by the United States Embassy, the government exposed an opium deal in which Phao had authorized more than $1,000,000 in rewards to police officials in northern Thailand who had seized over twenty tons of opium but had failed to arrest a single smuggler. This exposé revealed more emphatically than ever before the vast opium racket that had been operated by the police for many years. The scandal aroused widespread criticism from the public, and in the wake of Phibun's well-publicized world tour it made a bad impression abroad. The Premier joined in denouncing the police chief and his subordinates and stated that the "nation's honor is more important than any profit from opium."[55] He promised to close the opium dens by 1957 and he used this incident to deflate even further the prestige formerly enjoyed by General Phao.

The exact reasons for Phibun's sudden democratic reforms and his efforts to reduce the power of the police chief are somewhat difficult to assess in light of the increasingly fluid international and internal political situation. To a considerable extent, however, they did indicate another unique blending of external and internal influences on the evolving political system. The Premier had undoubtedly been impressed by the democratic institutions and practices he observed during his visit in the United States and Western Europe, and on his return he probably felt that after almost five years of close contacts with Western nations it was time for Thailand to adopt some democratic practices. Also, after ruling the country for many years in an authoritarian manner, he possibly thought that he might try to establish a government based on popular rule. On his world tour he heard of the relative ease with which the democratic governments in the West changed hands, and he felt that perhaps he could establish the same procedure in Thailand. One American observer commented: "Prime Minister Pibul, recounting these incidents of democratic life abroad at a press conference like President Eisenhower's, an institution which he inaugurated upon his return, seemed genuinely impressed by the way other great men of the world entered into and departed from power."[56]

Phibun's recent talks with President Eisenhower, Prime Minister Eden, and other Western leaders probably made him feel that he too was one of the "great men of the world." This tour consequently gave the Premier a new sense of self-confidence and encouraged him to expand his limited political power.

A more important purpose behind Phibun's reforms was his intense desire to strengthen his own position within the triumvirate regime. In addition to the enhanced prestige he had received from his visit abroad, he undoubtedly felt that the best way to maintain a balance of power between Phao and Sarit and extend his personal influence was to obtain a wider base of popular support. It was probably for this reason that the Premier sought to reduce the power wielded by the police chief and increase public participation in politics which he thought he could personally manipulate and control. He somehow assumed that the growing anti-government sentiment was directed largely at his subordinates, especially General Phao, rather than towards himself. He possibly felt that the lavish praise he had recently received abroad at the same time made him a popular figure within his own country. Actually his democratic reforms smacked of demagoguery as he probably intended to use the popular discontent to discredit the younger military leaders in his regime and obtain a mass appeal for himself. It is certain that he hoped to receive an overwhelming vote in the February 1957 general election. It is highly doubtful that the Premier really intended to establish a permanent democratic system. Instead his major goal was to get a broad popular mandate so that neither Phao nor Sarit would dare to challenge his political position. In effect, he was trying to supplement his only source of political power which up to this time was the diplomatic support of the United States with a large internal political base of his own. The democratic institutions and practices he had observed in the West provided him with precisely the means he needed to achieve this important objective.

In launching these reforms and unleashing the channels of public opinion, Phibun shrewdly undercut the influence of General Phao who became even more unpopular due to his relentless and brutal suppression of internal opposition. The upsurging wave of criticism was directed largely at the police who were bitterly attacked for political assassinations, torture, intimidation, and the imprisonment of innocent people. Most Thai were elated as the zealous police chief was shorn of some of his extensive powers. The people, however, were not prepared for the sudden shift from militant authoritarianism to representative government and virtually all of Phibun's reforms led to gross perversions of what was supposed to be a democratic process.

The Premier himself contributed to this trend by subjecting the members of his government to gruelling cross-examinations at his press conferences where they were expected to answer immediately any question posed by a news reporter. Obviously even the most competent members of the Cabinet could not give well-prepared replies or defend their administrative action with sufficient factual data. Within a short time opponents of the government were paying some of the news reporters to ask embarassing questions to unpopular Cabinet ministers and then to attack them for their brief and vague replies. Some members of the local press also used the question-and-answer period to launch long and bitter attacks against the government rather than to gain information on its policies. Phibun often appeared amused as his ministers became the targets of irate and scathing criticism, an attitude which reduced the morale and unity within his own regime.

The role of the Cabinet and the Assembly was further weakened as the Premier gave more attention to the critics at his press conferences and the "Hyde Park" debating centers than he did to the members of his government or the legislature. His desire for mass popularity became increasingly evident as he encouraged even greater criticism of his regime and at the same time refused to support his ministers. Some of the denunciations of Cabinet members appeared in one of Phibun's own newspapers. On one occasion he summarized his attitude toward this new political trend by stating: "Public opinion is the most powerful influence in the nation."[57]

The "Hyde Park" debating centers became another channel through which the Premier hoped to extend his popular appeal. However, the bitter anti-government reaction which reverberated back through this medium was more than he had expected. Perhaps no other innovation in the post-war era caused more groups to enter the political arena and make demands on the government for the achievement of their economic and social objectives. Within a short time sixteen labor unions were organized, and a newly-formed Thai Labor Party requested a law protecting the rights of workers. In response to this trend an employers association was formed to deal with the new leaders of organized labor. Unfortunately these public debates quickly fell into the hands of extremists who made many demands which the government could not possibly meet even if it had been sincerely susceptible to public opinion. Yet after several years of repressed political liberty it was almost certain that many persons would take advantage of their newly-won freedom and launch bitter criticisms of the triumvirate regime. The "Hyde Park" debates became extremely popular with the large crowds who gathered for the entertainment provided at these meetings which further encouraged demagoguery and dramatic displays of opposition to the government. On one occasion, Pethai Jotinuchit, the younger brother of Thep Jotinuchit, slashed his arm with a razor "as a sacrifice to democracy."[58] The bleeding orator exclaimed that he had just returned from Great Britain where he had observed genuine democracy in action. He called for a dissolution of the Coup Group and the abolition of the appointed representatives in the Assembly. Incidents such as these soon led to violence and within a few weeks several persons watching these debates had been beaten or stabbed. It was later proved that some of this violence was instigated by the police who were angered by a public airing of their nefarious activities. On several occasions General Phao was sent by Phibun to defend the government at the public debates in Bangkok. The police chief merely succeeded in attracting larger crowds and creating additional violence. His replies were impulsive and vague. They ranged from a promise to submit proposed legislation to the crowds at the "Hyde Park" center to a flippant defense of the large incomes received by the military leaders on the grounds that many local Chinese businessmen were also very wealthy.

By February 1956 the patience of the triumvirate regime was growing thin. The increasingly bitter remarks by their critics caught Phibun and his subordinates by surprise, and they began to have second thoughts about the "new democracy." Then with little warning they suddenly banned all political gatherings and arrested a group of hunger strikers protesting the presence of appointed representatives in the Assembly. It was at this time that they imprisoned Thep Jotinuchit and his party as they returned from their visit to Communist China. Two opposition members of the Assembly who had been arrested for visiting Communist China and later released were again seized by the police. The triumvirate regime justified this suppressive action with the usual claim that it was protecting the country from Communist subversion. This time, however, the military leaders issued a new charge, namely that the opponents of the government were abusing their rights in a democracy. Phibun declared: "The Government for the sake of continued peace, has decided to arrest those persons who have been using democracy as a mask to break the country's laws and create internal disturbances." [59] Phao said these persons would be held without bail on charges of being "Communists propagating communism, supporting communism and conferring with a Communist organization." [60] In his order banning public gatherings, the police chief further declared: "The Ministry of Interior has been permitting public gatherings for the purpose of expressing opinions with [sic] the limits of the law but some groups of people have been holding meetings and expressing opinions beyond the limits of the law, in order to create public unrest, which is one of the methods of the Communists. This may cause disorder in the nation." [61]

At the same time local newspapers were warned not to violate the Press Act, and certain reporters were barred from Phibun's press conferences. The ban on public gatherings was soon lifted to permit political campaigning for the February 1957 general election, but the government watched these activities closely to prevent opinions which were "beyond the limits of the law."

The vehement criticism which erupted with virtually unrestricted political freedom illustrated that many of the articulate segments of Thai public opinion lacked a sense of restraint and moderation at a time when such an attitude was the only realistic way to influence a military government allegedly attempting to relax its authoritarian rule. Much of the animosity expressed toward the triumvirate regime was due to the long period of political suppression, and many of the charges against the government were undoubtedly justified. However, the extremists who served as the major anti-government spokesmen used their role merely to dramatize their opposition and lead their followers into sensational but ineffective action. This fruitless practice prevented the moderates or gradualists who might have proposed realistic alternative policies from emerging within these opposition groups. These moderate leaders might have captured Phibun's political reforms and turned the country toward some form of representative rule. Instead the extreme measures used by a few outspoken critics were almost certain to arouse a harsh reaction from an authoritarian regime which was unaccustomed to public criticism and was still determined to keep itself in power. A possible opportunity to broaden the popular base of the government and impose some checks on its virtually unlimited power was thereby missed.

This suppressive action also indicated that the military leaders were still adhering to the traditional idea that specific groups working for their own interests were automatically betraying the welfare of the nation. Like military officers in most countries who think primarily in terms of "national security" and "the national interest," the Thai military leaders failed to understand or probably did not want to understand that modern democratic government inevitably involves a conflict among many contending economic and social groups. The purpose of a democratic framework is to provide a peaceful channel so these groups can compromise their conflicting interests and at the same time serve the general welfare of the nation. Yet the narrow and rigid attitude of the triumvirate regime caused it to assume that anyone opposing their concept of the national welfare was contributing to public "unrest" and "disorder."

The suppressive reaction of the government likewise revealed the precarious basis of civil liberties under an authoritarian regime. The military leaders took it for granted that they had arbitrary authority to control all political activities of the people. Phao clearly revealed this attitude in his statement that the Ministry of Interior had "been permitting" public gatherings since the inauguration of the democratic reforms. He made no indication that the people might enjoy some of these liberties as part of their basic human rights. Also, the charge made by the government that opinions had to be within "the limits of the law" really meant that the military leaders could be criticized only until they were personally offended. This vague standard thus depended on the tolerance and benevolence of the government leaders themselves. Under a regime of military officers who often displayed considerable personal pride and short tempers it meant that the political freedom of the people would continue to be narrowly construed and drastically curtailed. The desire of the militarists to preserve internal "peace," "order," and "stability" at any cost likewise discouraged any strong resurgence of individualism or pluralism. In effect the reaction of the Phibun government to the opposition aroused by its own political reforms illustrated the enormous difficulty of attempting to promote democracy "from above" under a military regime.

Within the rising anti-government sentiment released by Phibun's democratic reforms was a growing criticism directed toward the United States. As this trend continued many Americans became alarmed and believed that their anti-Communist programs were in jeopardy. Through the local press and the "Hyde Park" debating centers some critics demanded a neutralist foreign policy, more trade with Communist China, and the recognition of the Peking regime. The United States was denounced for providing Thailand with military aid and insufficient economic assistance. The SEATO alliance was bitterly attacked and many opponents of the triumvirate regime repeated their charge that the Americans were actually controlling the Thai government. In May 1956 Nai Lewlalong Bunnag, the defense counsel at a trial in the Appeals Court, charged that American and British diplomatic pressure had caused General Phao to order sweeping arrests of Communist suspects. The attorney claimed that the police chief had no documentary evidence proving that his clients had been part of any Communist conspiracy and he declared that "definitely foreign pressure was brought to bear for the arrests." [62] On another occasion the popular critic, Pethai Jotinuchit, questioned the government on the possibility of trade with Communist China: "Has the American Government, which has very close relations with the Thai Government and is comparable to a big brother of the Thai Government, given views or advices to the Government on this matter?" [63]

A spokesman for the Free Democratic Party in February 1957 went so far as to praise Communist China and label the United States "a treacherous ally."[64] Ironically, two of the newspapers spreading these caustic statements were owned by Phibun and Sarit who claimed they had no control over the editorial policies of their papers. Yet as anti-American sentiment continued to spread the Premier was forced to deny that the United States was controlling his government. On one occasion he sent Marshal Sarit to the "Hyde Park" debating center in Bangkok to answer charges that Thailand was "an American colony."[65]

Anti-American hostility was further intensified as the triumvirate regime frequently justified its actions by stressing the need to please the United States and the members of SEATO in the conduct of certain internal affairs. When many critics demanded the release of political prisoners, the government replied that it would first have to consider "foreign views" since Thailand was a member of the SEATO alliance.[66] This appearance of American interference in Thai internal affairs aroused additional hostility toward the United States and increased the opposition to the Phibun regime. A few acts of misconduct by American military personnel in Bangkok further contributed to this criticism. Many Thai also became increasingly apprehensive as the United States began informal negotiations with the Chinese Communists following the Geneva summit conference in 1955. Some persons felt this move might precede American recognition of the Peking regime. A decline in Thai foreign trade likewise aroused stronger demands for more commercial relations with Communist China, a move which many people felt would solve all the nation's economic ills. Phibun encouraged greater popular hostility as he continued to oppose these demands on the grounds that Thailand must maintain close relations with the United States. When the British in Malaya began selling large quantities of rubber to Communist China the pressure to sell Thai rubber to the Chinese Communists rapidly increased. The Premier maintained his opposition to these requests and stated that Thailand could not offend the United States. He claimed that American aid and trade far outweighed the advantages of trading with the Chinese mainland. In spite of increasing criticism, in October 1956 he ordered a complete ban on goods imported from Communist China.

While Phibun's assessment of the value of trade with Communist China was much more realistic and far-sighted than that of his critics, his stress on the need to placate the United States gave rise to bitter recriminations which were aroused by the natural feeling that a foreign government was controlling the nation. His desperate attempt to maintain his own political position which depended heavily on American diplomatic support consequently clashed with the growing resentment toward the United States.

This internal opposition was supplemented after 1955 with an open and growing criticism among some Americans. For the first time since the large foreign aid programs began in 1950 prominent Americans began to question the value of extensive military assistance to the authoritarian triumvirate regime. Some Americans realized that their own government bore some of the responsibility for the suppressive measures of the Phibun government. These persons assessed more objectively the impact of the foreign aid programs on the internal politics of the country, and recognized that the military leaders were using their enhanced powers to oppress their opponents with the excuse that they were fighting Communism. After a brief visit in the country Senator Theodore Green stated: "There is a growth of democratic feeling here but it hasn't shown up yet in the Government. . . . Democracy needs a stronger, broader base." [67] At the conclusion of a tour in the region Senator Allen J. Ellender was especially critical of the oversized military program. He declared: "The U.S. military aid program there [Thailand] is far too big. It's too big for what they've faced in the past. We're giving them modern weapons they don't know how to use." [68] In the summer of 1956 the *New York Times* correspondent for Southeast Asia, Robert Alden, wrote a series of articles denouncing the corruption and authoritarianism within the Thai government. The hostile reaction to this criticism, even among many opponents of the government, caused Ambassador Bishop to apologize publicly for these articles. It encouraged General Phao to take the unusual action of restricting Alden's visits to Bangkok to two hours. Phao claimed that his articles were "not the truth." [69]

Perhaps the most objective and penetrating assessment of the impact of the foreign aid programs on internal affairs was that made by Mr. Clement D. Johnston, President of the United States Chamber of Commerce, who testified before a special committee of the United States Senate in 1957 after he had completed a tour of Southeast Asia. Mr. Johnston declared that some of the governments in the region, including Thailand, were keeping themselves in power with American arms and making "windfall profits" from American foreign aid.[70] He appealed for "substantial" reductions in military aid to these countries even though the governments concerned would "strongly protest." "More than one of these nations," he stated, "is using U.S. funds to build and equip armed forces some of whose officers and men seem to think of their mission only in terms of ancient hostilities and rivalries . . . Communism and Communist aggression do not alone provide sufficient challenge to motivate current military programs . . . As long as the Southeast Asia Treaty Organization (SEATO) with its implied promise of unlimited American support, offers security against Communist aggression, it would appear that the military forces of Cambodia, Laos, Thailand and South Vietnam are in every case larger and more heavily equipped than the needs of mere internal security would dictate . . . Control of the army and the police is a conventional effective means of protecting the political situation as well as maintaining security."[71]

In his testimony Mr. Johnston further declared that the great need of the people in Southeast Asia was to be "let alone militarily so as to devote maximum effort to correcting a deplorably low level of education, sanitation, and economic productivity." He requested that American economic and military aid in the region be reduced "by at least half during the next two years."

These statements by prominent Americans added to the growing internal opposition to the triumvirate regime. While many critics in Thailand actually agreed with much of this censure, they were offended when some persons from a nation which they thought was closely allied to the country criticized the policies of their government. National pride and the feeling that the close cooperation between the two countries placed the Thai leaders beyond reproach exacerbated this expanding sentiment of anti-Americanism. The criticism by Americans also placed Phibun in an embarrassing position as he still depended on the diplomatic support of the United States in the internal power elite. Yet he was forced to defend a country in which more spokesmen were becoming increasingly critical of his regime. Unfortunately many Thai did not understand the practice of freedom of speech and press in the United States. They failed to realize that these opinions were not those of the American government. They also fell victim to a common human failing as they eagerly defended their own right to denounce the policies of the United States, while at the same time they became greatly offended when a few Americans criticized the actions of their government.

The February 1957 General Election. The democratic reforms launched by Phibun intensified the campaigning in the general election in February 1957. As mentioned previously the government took a major step toward political freedom in September 1955 when the

Assembly passed the first political party law in the nation's history. During the following year more than twenty-five political parties were officially registered. The Premier again promised the people that they were well on their way toward democracy, and General Phao assured the voters that in the forthcoming election there would be "no political tricks." [72] When opening the Assembly in June 1956 King Phumiphon praised the Political Party Act as "a step forward in democratic government" and urged the people to work for the progress and unity of the nation.[73] At the beginning of 1957 the king reminded the people that the coming year was the celebrated 2500th year in the Buddhist Era and they should strive to conduct themselves according to the teachings of their religion. He hailed the forthcoming general election and praised the government for its effort to remove the appointed representatives from the Assembly. In spite of these promises of more political freedom, however, the police frequently harassed the candidates who criticized the triumvirate regime. A candidate of the Economist Party was arrested shortly before the election for using "vehement oratory" and labeling Thailand a "land of slaves." [74]

Under Phibun's direction the Legislative Study Commission was transformed into the major government party called the Seri Manangasila Party. The Premier requested that his Cabinet ministers run for office in the forthcoming election, and he entered the contest for one of the elected seats in Bangkok. Both Phibun and Phao campaigned actively for the government party, although the police chief decided not to run for elected office until 1962. Marshal Sarit played only a minor role in the election and usually remained in the background. The Seri Manangasila Party established branch offices in every important province throughout the country, and its chances for an impressive victory appeared good as it won a highly publicized by-election in Uttaradit province in July 1956 which was judged "clean" by foreign observers. It spent approximately 20,000,000 baht in the campaign, and in spite of its pledge to stage an honest election it used civil servants and members of the armed forces to support pro-government candidates.[75] It also bought the services of prominent opposition leaders. Through the use of persuasion and money Phao succeeded in bringing Pethai Jotinuchit, the leader of the Hyde Park Movement Party, and Liang Jaiyakal, the leader of the People's Party, to the government side. These moves aroused bitter antagonism among the opposition parties who charged the government with bribery. Regardless of these criticisms Phao predicted that the Seri Manangasila Party would win an overwhelming victory throughout the country and capture all nine seats in the crucial election in Bangkok.

The Democrat Party was revived by Khuang Aphaiwongse among the royalist-conservative groups, and it became the major contender of the government party. Although Khuang and his followers lacked the enormous financial resources of the military leaders and the assistance of the civil and military services, they consistently attracted larger crowds than the pro-government candidates. The conservative leader was an effective campaigner and won widespread support for the programs advanced by his party. When the government candidates stressed the rapid material progress which Thailand had made in the post-war era, he claimed that much of this advancement had been due to American foreign aid. He criticized the lack of democracy and attacked the continued use of appointed members in the Assembly. He likewise denounced the triumvirate regime for its misuse of American aid and extensive corruption. He upheld a pro-Western foreign policy, although he advocated that Thailand should be more independent of the United States.

Most of the other political parties formed around attractive personalities attempting to increase their political influence. The former Tharmathipat Party was revived and campaigned for Phibun, while a newly-formed National Democratic Party composed of junior military officers supported Sarit. Most of the small opposition parties advocated socialism, neutralism, and trade with Communist China. A Free Democratic Party was organized by left-wing socialists who claimed that they wanted to serve as "the conscience of the government."[77] An Economist Party was established by Thep Jotinuchit and Klaew Norapati which also upheld a socialist program and was composed primarily of political leaders from the northeastern provinces. Other small opposition parties included a Thai Labor Party, a Hyde Park Movement Party, and a Utopia Party.

This sudden upsurge of political activity again revealed some basic weaknesses in the political system. The large number of political parties indicated that these emerging forces were again focusing on a few attractive personalities rather than formulating some realistic programs to promote the progress of the people. The members of the contending parties again moved from group to group as opportunity and money dictated. There was no serious attempt by any of these parties to merge their organizations or campaigning efforts even when they indicated a similar political orientation. The election was largely considered to be a popularity contest between the major candidates rather than a process of selecting a political party capable of governing the country. Perhaps the only hopeful sign in the campaign was the emergence of Khuang Aphaiwongse and the Democrat Party as a moderate political force advocating many realistic alternatives to the policies of the triumvirate regime.

Although the Phibun government was assured of a majority in the Assembly due to the continuation of the appointed members, the public response to the February 1957 election brought more voters to the polls than at any time in the history of the country. The election also drew much attention from abroad. "The real significance of this election," a *New York Times* editorial stated, "lies in the fact that the Premier has, for the first time, called for a popular mandate. He has submitted his leadership to the electorate. If it be argued that he has nothing to lose, since appointments could control the Assembly in any case, it can also be urged that he had much to gain. The gain, moreover, is not his personally but is a gain for free and representative government. A free election is another important stride. Thailand may not yet be a "democracy" in the fullest sense of the word, but the movement is in that direction." [78]

The major local attention was on the contest between the Seri Manangasila Party and the Democrat Party in Bangkok where Phibun and Khuang were each seeking a decisive victory. In the early afternoon on election day (February 26) the returns showed that the votes for the candidates of these two parties were about equal. In some districts, however, Khuang was reported to be ahead of Phibun and only two or three government candidates appeared likely to be elected.[79] At this point no further returns were announced and the final results were not published by the government until two days later. In the meantime there were numerous reports of fraudulent voting with the use of "firecards" and "paratroops," and many eligible voters appearing at the polls were told that their names were not on the register.[80] Many polling stations were visited by hoodlums (nakheng) who intimidated voters suspected of supporting opposition candidates, and in one district a man was killed on the street after declaring publicly that he had voted for Khuang. The Governor of Bangkok who was responsible for supervising the election resigned his position before the balloting was finished for "failure to effectively control the situation." [81]

The final results of the election were announced on February 28. Phibun had received 137,735 votes while Khuang got 118,457 votes.[82] In the closely contested Bangkok election the Seri Manangasila Party had received seven seats and the Democrat Party had won two seats. The nationwide results were as follows:

Seri Manangasila Party	85 seats
Democrat Party	28 "
Independents	13 "
Free Democratic Party	11 "
Tharmathipat Party	10 "
Economist Party	8 "
National Democratic Party	3 "
Hyde Park Movement Party	2 "

The opposition parties charged the government with cheating and claimed that the elections were the "dirtiest ever."[84] Khuang said the government party had used "forged ballots," and the Democrat Party immediately announced that it would contest the elections in court. In his influential *Siam Rath Weekly Review* Kukrit Pramoj denounced the triumvirate regime with unprecedented vigor: "By robbing the people of their sovereign rights during the election, the present government has committed the most serious crime against humanity . . . In our estimation Field Marshal Pibulsonggram and General Phao Sriyanond have been raised to the criminal level of Stalin and Beria."[85] The military leaders replied that if any cheating had been done in the elections, it had been accomplished by individuals and not by the Seri Manangasila Party.

The election was a moral defeat for the government. It indicated that in spite of the traditional apathy of the people toward politics and the enormous weaknesses of the opposition political parties, the triumvirate regime actually enjoyed little public support after many years of authoritarian rule. And Phibun did not get the broad popular mandate he so highly desired. Regardless of its vast expenditures, the use of the civil service and the armed forces, and alleged interference in the elections, the Seri Manangasila Party received only a slight majority of the elected seats. Khuang and the candidates of his party made a surprisingly good showing in many provinces. In Bangkok more than half of the government candidates, including four Cabinet ministers, were defeated. Many persons felt that if the military leaders had not interfered with the elections Khuang and his Democrat Party would have won many additional seats. Further charges of fraud and rumors that the police had distributed 50,000 counterfeit ballots to hoodlums the day before the elections added greatly to anti-government hostility.

Instead of attempting to mollify this mounting opposition, the military leaders sought to suppress public criticism and within a few days they took the extreme action of declaring a state of emergency. Their excuse for this action was the usual charge that internal opposition groups were collaborating with a foreign power and seeking to overthrow the government. An official communique stated: "The Government has received evidence that a group of persons, with the assistance of foreign nations, has been conspiring to create internal disturbance and to finally take over control of Thailand."[86] Phibun accused the opposition of leading "the people and Government officials to misunderstand and disdain the Government, and organizing rallies and demonstrations with a view to overthrowing the Government by force for their own selfish ends and to further the interest of their political party."[87]

As before the government did not reveal any evidence of this alleged plot. However, the Premier disclosed the duplicity behind his democratic reforms when his failure to win a popular mandate in the general election caused him to accuse the opposition parties of pursuing "their own selfish ends." These remarks made it obvious that he had no real intention of transferring political power to opposition leaders even if they had won the election. His charge that these political parties sought to overthrow the triumvirate regime by force was ridiculous in light of the vast quantities of arms possessed by the military leaders.

Nevertheless the government launched another harsh suppression of political opposition. Marshal Sarit was made Supreme Commander of the armed forces and the police and charged with the responsibility of maintaining peace and order. All public meetings were banned. Several editors were arrested for making speeches and printing articles critical of the triumvirate regime. Army troops equipped with American tanks and machine guns seized strategic positions throughout Bangkok while the Royal Air Force using American jets flew low-level flights over the capital city. This prompt and convincing display of military power at first discouraged most people from any further overt criticism of the government. Kukrit Pramoj claimed these intimidating actions by the armed forces "put terror into the hearts of the people and destroyed their morale."[88]

The most determined opposition to the triumvirate regime in the aftermath of the general election came from an unexpected source—the students at Chulalongkorn University. In spite of the official ban on public gatherings and the impressive display of military power, more than 2000 students gathered at a mass rally on the university campus to protest the alleged corruption in the recent election. They lowered the flag to half-mast "in memory of dead democracy." [89] As they were about to march on the Ministry of Interior, Sarit arrived on the scene and consoled the students by stating that the elections were "completely dirty from all sides." [90] He told them that although public meetings had been banned they could go to the Ministry of Interior in small groups. The students staged a mass demonstration before Phibun's office and demanded that he resign. They insisted that the United States stop interfering in Thai internal affairs. They requested new elections and the formation of student committees to supervise the balloting. The Premier replied that the election could be invalidated only by the courts. The students disbursed only when requested by Sarit.

The demonstration by these university students illustrated in some degree the influence of Western political ideas on the growing middle class. It indicated that some Thai wanted greater political freedom in addition to the significant economic and social progress of the country. One slogan voiced by the disgruntled students was: "We don't want air conditioning, we want democracy." This incident also revealed the liberal ideological force behind much of the opposition toward a government dominated by a reactionary military regime. Contrary to the claim of many Thai and American officials, the student demonstration and the expanding criticism of the triumvirate regime was Western-inspired, not Communist-inspired. This action was the strongest outburst of public indignation toward the military leaders since they had seized complete power in 1951, and it has been compared by Pickerell and Moore to the 1932 coup which overthrew the absolute monarchy.[91]

The suppressive action against the opposition coincided with another meeting of the SEATO alliance, and it is almost certain that the Thai government again used its membership in this treaty organization to justify its harsh measures. The general election in Thailand occurred just a few days before the second annual SEATO conference in Canberra, Australia. At this meeting greater stress was placed on Communist subversion and each member was to be made more "Communist-proof." [92] When preparing for this conference a military spokesman of the Thai government admitted that it had received a report from the SEATO Committee of Security Experts stating that a plot had been discovered to overthrow the pro-Western triumvirate regime.[93] The Thai military leaders did not disclose any details regarding this report nor did any spokesmen of the SEATO organization elaborate on its reliability. Although the government decree declaring the state of emergency did not specifically claim that the alleged threat was Communist-inspired, this attitude certainly prevailed within the triumvirate regime. Just two days after the emergency was declared General Jira Wichitsongkhram, the Chief of the Defense General Staff, left Bangkok for the SEATO conference in Canberra. He stated: "Thailand is on the side of the free world, therefore you can guess it must be a country in the Communist bloc which engineered and supported the trouble." [94] This brief remark aptly described the general feeling of the Thai military leaders. The alleged Communist threat continued to be a convenient excuse to suppress all democratic tendencies on the grounds that any opposition to the government was Communist-inspired. Thailand's participation in the SEATO alliance reinforced this opinion. No thought was given to the possibility that internal opposition could also be anti-Communist.

Further developments at the SEATO meeting in Canberra undoubtedly encouraged the triumvirate regime to take even more stringent action against its critics. One report issued at the conference stated:

"The relative stability which prevailed in the Treaty Area should not obscure the fact that the Communist threat has assumed a more insidious, but equally dangerous form.

"We have observed that the main effort of the Communists to subvert the peoples of countries in the Treaty Area consists in the infiltration of political, youth, and cultural movements and trade unions." [95]

Again no evidence was given to support this assessment of Communist infiltration into political, economic, and social groups in the region.

In addressing the conference Secretary of State Dulles also commented on the progress of the alliance during the preceding year: "SEATO is an effective force against aggression and subversion. This fact has encouraged constructive developments in many fields. Increased stability in the treaty area is fully evident . . During this period of SEATO's existence, the free countries of the area have conducted orderly elections on a nationwide basis and have been able to implement their ideals of universal suffrage and free elections. Substantial social and economic progress has been made by all members states." [96]

While there was some truth in Mr. Dulles' claim that substantial economic and social progress had been made by the Asian members of the treaty organization, his judgment regarding political progress in Thailand was directly contrary to the facts. In effect the Thai government was being praised by American officials for reforms that did not exist. For almost ten years the political system had been moving further away from, not closer toward, free institutions and genuine representative government. Assisted by American military aid the triumvirate regime in four brief years had obliterated the modest and painful progress made toward constitutional democracy since the overthrow of the absolute monarchy in 1932. The rapid increase in military assistance sponsored by the Eisenhower administration had given the military leaders uncontested political power. And just a few days before this SEATO conference, Thailand had experienced one of the most corrupt and fraudulent elections in its entire history. It had not conducted an "orderly" and "free" election as the Secretary of State claimed. The only reason the Thai government had been able to maintain "increased stability" during this period was due to its control of the weapons provided by the United States. Yet the desire of the Americans to maintain a strong military defense against Communist aggression in Southeast Asia caused them to overlook these realities in Thai internal affairs. The position of the United States at the SEATO conference in Canberra also implied approval of the recent suppressive action taken by the Thai government, and many Americans continued to accept the claim that all opposition to the triumvirate regime was Communist-inspired. This conference again revealed the ironical state in which American arms and diplomatic support were encouraging the Thai government to suppress political groups that had been aroused by Western political ideas and Phibun's democratic reforms.

In spite of the repressive action of the military leaders and the continuing moral and material support of the United States, Phibun's political position declined rapidly after the February 1957 election. The Premier tried desperately to halt this trend by restoring Phao's former powers to balance the rapidly growing popularity of Sarit. The state of emergency was ended within twelve days and Sarit's authority as Supreme Commander of the armed forces and the police was terminated. In an attempt to enhance the power of the police chief, Phibun gave him his own Cabinet post as Minister of Interior. Yet Sarit's popularity caused the Premier to give the army chief his post as Minister of Defense. At the same time Phibun sought to undercut the growing political power of Sarit by urging the members of his government to resign their permanent official positions, a move which would have caused Sarit to give up his control over the army. The Premier likewise requested that his ministers relinquish all private commercial interests, a move which would have deprived the army chief of his extensive income. Sarit balked at these requests. At the same time he continued to increase his popular appeal by disassociating himself from the discredited Seri Manangasila Party and proclaiming his disdain for politics. On one occasion he stated: "I do not like politics and I have not concerned myself with the party or done anything for it."[97]

Sarit's political position was further enhanced by his quiet and retiring personality and the general impression that he remained largely indifferent to the internal struggle for power. His army troops were not directly involved in the suppression of political opposition as were the police. His popularity was greatly increased by his shrewd conduct during the state of emergency and his ability to place the blame for this crisis on the misconduct of Phibun and Phao. The army chief also won much support by favoring less dependence on the United States and more trade with Communist China.

In March 1957 Sarit was able to use his stronger political position to add several of his own followers to the government. Shortly thereafter some of his supporters formed the Sahabhum (Unionist) Party. This new party was at first led by Sarit's half-brother, Nai Sanguan Chandrasaka, and its avowed purpose was to bring about the overthrow of Phibun and Phao. Many observers suspected the army chief of secretly backing the Sahabhum Party although he disclaimed any official connection. He continually declared that his loyalty to the Premier was "unwavering."[98] The Sahabhum Party at first held only ten seats in the Assembly, but it was soon joined by the Democrat Party, the Free Democratic Party, and the Economist Party which formed an increasingly effective opposition. By August 1957 an increasing number of pro-government representatives began leaving the Seri Manangasila Party to join the new party supporting Sarit. The following month the government was faced with the possibility of losing its majority in the Assembly.

The triumvirate regime was further weakened by a series of setbacks which soon led to its downfall. One of these reverses was the failure of Phibun and Phao to halt the rising tide of opposition to their authoritarian rule. The police chief contributed to this trend by ordering his subordinates to maintain a strict control of all public gatherings and the local press. Bitter feelings toward the government were increased as the police arrested all persons returning from visits to Communist China. After the disappointing election results Phibun and Phao pushed the selection of thirty-seven additional appointed representatives in the Assembly to balance the 160 elected members, a move which the opposition parties declared as unconstitutional.

King Phumiphon also introduced a modest reverse to the beleaguered triumvirate regime when he delayed its attempt to select the additional appointed representatives. This action by the king encouraged the opposition to intensify its criticism of the government. The Dika Court likewise handed Phibun and Phao a severe setback by ruling that the constitution prohibited any additional appointed representatives in the Assembly. Although this judgment was issued at the same time that the high court upheld the validity of the general election, the adverse decision regarding appointed representatives was another moral defeat for the government and a boon to the opposition.

Perhaps most damaging to Phibun's political position and the delicate balance of power between Phao and Sarit was the increasing popular hostility directed toward the United States. This trend reached its climax in the summer of 1957. Many local newspapers accused the United States of war-mongering and praised the Soviet Union and Communist China for promoting world peace. The two newspapers owned by Phibun and Sarit continued to publish some of the most bitter attacks against the United States while their owners again claimed that they had no control over the editorial policies of their papers. At the May Day parade in 1957 many signs bore such slogans as: "Thailand is not an American colony," "Quit SEATO," "Abrogate Anti-Communist Act," and "Workers of the World, Unite." [99] Shortly thereafter a Soviet cultural group arrived in Bangkok and several student organizations received invitations to attend the Sixth Moscow Youth Festival. The Soviet cultural team received a warm welcome and many students requested official permission to attend the youth festival in Moscow. The spokesmen of the Sahabhum Party denounced the triumvirate regime because it "has followed America too closely and treats the United States like it is the United Nations." [100]

Ambassador Bishop and some Americans were jolted by the continual upsurge of anti-American sentiment and they felt that Thailand was being rapidly infiltrated by Communists. Yet the reasons for the growing hostility toward the United States and the declining position of the triumvirate regime are not difficult to assess.

The major reason for this unique trend in American-Thai relations was the determined effort by the United States to keep Phibun in power only because he was strongly anti-Communist. By 1957 many Thai wanted the Americans to withdraw their support from the Premier so he and his hated police chief could be removed from power. Mr. Bishop's unswerving support of Phibun symbolized to many Thai the inflexible attitude of the United States in protecting its own militant anti-Communist policies in Southeast Asia with no serious consideration of the impact of these policies on the lives of the local people.

The Democrat leader, Khuang Aphaiwongse, who advocated a pro-Western foreign policy but opposed the unbending American support of Phibun declared: "Bishop's personal backing of Pibul is driving Thailand into the arms of the Communists, just as American support for Chiang Kai-shek drove the Chinese into the arms of Mao Tse-tung . . . If Thailand falls it will be the Americans' fault." [101]

Another factor contributing to anti-American feeling was the extensive military aid provided by the United States to the army and the police. The major impact of this assistance had been to strengthen the government's position in suppressing internal opposition rather than in defending the country against Communism as intended by the Americans. It was therefore natural that the persons who had suffered from this misguided and oversized military program would be the first to appeal for its curtailment or abolition.

A third reason for the growing opposition to the United States was the natural reaction among many Thai political leaders, intellectuals, students, journalists, etc. to the large number of Americans living in the country and the intensive American-sponsored propaganda programs which pervaded the society for several years. After 1955 many of these persons wanted to take an objective look at the other side in the Cold War, not because they were becoming sympathetic to Communism, but because they were curious and wanted to learn something about the Communist nations for themselves.

A final factor contributing to anti-Americanism was the reaction of national pride. As mentioned previously the unusually intimate contacts between the military leaders and American officials gave many Thai the feeling that their government was actually controlled by the United States. This attitude was strengthened by the growing realization that Phibun depended almost entirely on American diplomatic support to maintain his position within the triumvirate regime, and that the United States had a vested interest in the Premier to maintain Thailand's pro-Western foreign policy. The American ambassadors contributed to this resentment by their frequent public appearances with Phibun and their lavish praise of his regime. On several occasions in the past the Thai people had reacted similarly to excessive foreign influence, and by 1957 they again indicated their strong desire to make certain that their government was entirely independent of foreign control.[102]

In spite of this apparent trend in domestic politics, the Americans did not give serious consideration to the reasons behind the declining power of the triumvirate regime or the growing hostility toward the

United States. Instead of making an objective assessment of the emerging opposition forces and possibly modifying their policy, they made a frantic effort to bolster Phibun's deteriorating position and maintain the status quo. The United States suddenly offered the Thai government 300,000,000 baht ($15,000,000) for aid to the economically depressed northeastern provinces. It agreed to assume all the costs of the Thai military forces that had served in Korea, a sum amounting to over 150,000,000 baht ($7,500,000). In July 1957 it accepted more of the costs of the SEATO alliance and reduced the financial obligations of the three Asian members. Due to American prodding the SEATO organization expanded its activities in the non-military fields and granted additional scholarships for the purpose of promoting knowledge of the alliance. The Americans likewise indicated some support for the establishment of a graduate engineering school in Bangkok. They used their powerful influence in the treaty organization to appoint Pote Sarasin, the Thai Ambassador to the United States, as the first Secretary-General of the SEATO secretariat. They hoped the appointment of a Thai to this post would bolster the prestige of the Phibun regime and placate some of the growing hostility towards the United States. Finally, as the opposition to the Premier reached a climax, the World Bank approved a loan of $66,000,000 for the vast Yanhee power and irrigation project in northern Thailand.[103]

Yet these impressive displays of material and moral support by the United States failed to halt the rising opposition to the triumvirate regime. Phibun sought desperately to preserve his own position and reduce the growing power of Sarit by again ordering his ministers to sever their connections with all private commercial organizations. However, by this time the army chief had gained much self-confidence and a large political following. Instead of complying with the Premier's request, he and his aides resigned from the Cabinet with the charge that it was not acting in accord with public opinion. He openly broke with the Seri Manangasila Party and more of his supporters in the Cabinet and the Assembly resigned their positions. He retained his position as Commander-in-Chief of the army and soon became an "advisor" to the Sahabhum Party. His increasing influence forced Phibun to remove Phao as Minister of Interior, as Secretary-General of the Seri Manangasila Party, and finally as Director-General of the police.

Throughout this crisis the military leaders assured the public that there would be no open violence, and Sarit on several occasions promised that he would not stage another coup. However, as the opposition parties sought desperately to overthrow the triumvirate regime and Phibun refused to resign, Sarit seized the government on September 17, 1957 in a bloodless coup with an overwhelming display of military power. The army justified its action with these words: "Owing to the fact that the country is now very disorderly and tends to come close to disaster, the Army is compelled to keep peace and order for the nation's sake. Let all be in peace. Army troops are now taking control of some of the more important objectives."[104] And Sarit himself proclaimed that he had overthrown Phibun and Phao "in the interest of the people."[105] The former legislature was dissolved, a new Assembly of 123 members was appointed, and martial law was declared. An official announcement stated that new elections would be held within ninety days. Phibun was allowed to flee to Cambodia, and Phao was permitted to go into exile in Switzerland. Sarit was appointed by the king as the Military Commander in Bangkok until a new government could be formed. At the same time the army chief declared that he had no intention of assuming power himself.[106]

As in earlier political struggles the final showdown between the military leaders was determined solely by the distribution of military power. Although Phao had appeared aggressive and resourceful and his police force was well equipped with American arms, Sarit held preponderant political power since the army was approximately twice the size of the police and also well equipped with American arms. The army chief held a decided strategic advantage because of the presence of large numbers of army troops in and around Bangkok, while many of the police units were stationed in the provinces. Sarit could have overthrown the triumvirate regime by constitutional means since the opposition parties which supported him were rapidly forming a majority in the Assembly. However, he preferred to remove Phibun and Phao by the use of force to convince them that their political power had definitely come to an end. In spite of their frequent public statements to the contrary, respect for democracy by the two ousted leaders was so low that a constitutional change of government would not have convinced them that they had been permanently displaced from power. Like Pridi they might have been tempted to seek a political comeback by staging a countercoup. A dramatic show of force was therefore much more convincing and it conclusively settled the deep-seated rivalry among the former leaders of the triumvirate regime. In keeping with tradition Phibun and Phao were permitted to go into exile and there was no bloodshed. In spite of his shrewd opportunism and his lavish display of military power, Marshal Sarit was probably the leader most Thai people actually favored at the time.

Chapter VI

THE REVIVAL OF BENEVOLENT ABSOLUTISM

The overthrow of the triumvirate regime by Marshal Sarit revealed to a considerable degree the basic weakness of American policy in Thailand. This event indicated that large-scale military aid did not of itself enhance the security and stability of the country. In certain ways it increased its vulnerability to Communist penetration and subversion. The rising discontent toward Phibun and Phao enabled left-wing groups and a few Communists to exploit anti-government and anti-foreign sentiment and bring about the downfall of the unpopular triumvirate regime. Ironically, these leftist elements were forced to throw their support behind the popular army chief who subsequently adhered to a pro-Western foreign policy and suppressed the very groups which had helped bring him to power.

Yet in September 1957 Sarit was still an unknown figure and he had given some indications that he was not sympathetic to American policy. On numerous occasions he had openly stated that Thailand should seek a policy independent of the United States. He had encouraged Thai journalists and assemblymen to visit Communist China. He had opposed certain phases of the American military program, especially the arming and training of the police. He had criticized some parts of the economic aid program, notably the proposed giant Yanhee hydro-electric project in the northern provinces. The Americans had no assurance that he would not orient a new regime towards radical economic and social programs as Castro, for example, has done in Cuba. In the realm of foreign policy, he could have turned to the Soviet Union for military and economic aid to reduce Western influence as done by other military leaders such as Nasser in Egypt and Kassem in Iraq. Also, the army chief was not in good health at the time and he became seriously ill shortly after the overthrow of Phibun and Phao. Had he died or been incapacitated some other figure could have emerged seeking to lead the country in similar adverse directions.

In effect the United States had taken an enormous gamble in attempting to keep the Thai government aligned to the West primarily through the use of large-scale aid to the military and police forces. At stake was an investment of about $300,000,000 in military equipment and a gradually expanding economic base which could have been used against American interests in Southeast Asia had it fallen into unfriendly hands. The efforts of several thousand official and unofficial Americans who had worked conscientiously for almost seven years to assist Thailand's development were also at stake. Much of the aid provided by the American-owned Sea Supply Company to the police was lost when the army leaders dissolved many of the specially-trained police units and transferred their equipment to the army. A considerable amount of American aid had been forfeited to both Phibun and Phao who used this assistance to enhance their personal fortunes as revealed in the extensive travel and luxuries they enjoyed after fleeing the country. Other losses and abuses in the American aid program were likewise uncovered in the aftermath of the coup. Fortunately for the West, Sarit's decision to continue the same foreign policy as the former regime enabled most of these aid programs to remain essentially unchanged.

One of the major consequences of the overthrow of the triumvirate regime was the end of a seven-year period of increasingly intimate relations between the government of the United States and the Premier of Thailand. Phibun's position was unique in that he had been forced to rely largely on American diplomatic support to maintain his role within the internal power elite. With the emergence of a new military leader such as Sarit who had his own internal base of political power, it was almost certain that the influence of the United States on the government thereafter would decline. The army chief did not have any serious rival on the domestic scene, and his personal achievements during the final months of the triumvirate regime had given him a new sense of self-confidence and independence. Thereafter he would be less susceptible than Phibun to follow American counsel and advice.

Yet both countries had much to gain from a more normal relationship. The Thai government could now exercise more independence in making its own policies and pursuing certain of its national interests which did not always coincide with those of the United States. It could also avoid the appearance that it was controlled by a foreign power. The Americans likewise had other objectives in South and Southeast Asia than merely trying to keep Thailand closely aligned with the Western bloc. They could now pursue some of these long-range goals with more freedom of action. Also, the United States could enhance its prestige in the region which had suffered to some extent by its unswerving support of the unpopular triumvirate regime.

More corruption and human degradation caused by the former military leaders was uncovered in the aftermath of the coup. It was soon discovered that Phibun, allegedly a friend of the United States, had purposely encouraged some local newspapers to denounce the United States so that his government could appeal for more American aid on the grounds that it would help to pacify this "anti-American" segment of public opinion. It was likewise revealed that General Phao, another close friend of the United States, was in secret negotiations with Chinese Communists attempting to establish some kind of clandestine trade.[1] It was also discovered that the police chief had been much more ruthless in suppressing his political opponents than formerly assumed. Some of his atrocities rivaled those of the Nazis and the Communists. The graves of Nai Tiang Sirikhand and four unidentified persons were uncovered in Kanburi province, and further investigation revealed that these victims had been strangled to death while being interrogated by the police.[2] Tiang had been a courageous leader in the Free Thai movement during World War II and later served in the National Assembly. Phao claimed that the former Free Thai leader had escaped from Thailand and joined the Communists. The deaths of other victims of the police were also investigated, but the extent of the torture and murder committed by the former police chief will probably never be fully known.

United States Policy: 1957-1961. A modest change was made in American policy shortly after the overthrow of the triumvirate military regime. To some extent this move was due to the death of Secretary of State Dulles and the more active personal role which President Eisenhower played in foreign affairs during his final years in the White House. United States foreign policy assumed a slightly broader outlook and became somewhat more flexible. It revealed a slow awakening to the political, economic, and social problems confronting the people of the non-Western world. It realized in some degree that Communism cannot be fought solely with the use of military power. This trend encouraged many Americans to engage in some overdue soul-searching regarding the genuine "purposes" of their country. In December 1959 President Eisenhower epitomized this situation in his address to the American people just prior to his departure on a tour of Europe, the Middle East, and Asia. He said: "I earnestly make this suggestion, as I start this journey tonight, that you, and those close to you, join with me in a renewed dedication to our moral and spiritual conviction, and in that light re-examine our own record, including our

...nings. May this examination inspire each of us so to think and ...ct, as to hasten our progress toward the goal our fathers estab... which have made America an instrument for good. In this re-de...cation we shall replenish the true source of America's strength, her faith; and flowing from it, her love of liberty, her devotion to justice."[3]

Three months later while touring in Latin America, Mr. Eisenhower expressed similar thoughts in a speech in Santiago, Chile: "And then I have heard it said that the United States supports dictators . . . This is ridiculous. Surely no nation loves liberty more, or more sincerely prays that its benefits and deep human satisfactions may come to all peoples than does the United States . . . We repudiate dictatorship in any form, Right or Left . . . Our role in the United Nations, in the Organization of American States, in two world wars and in Korea stands as a beacon to all who love freedom."[4]

At first this "rededication" of American ideals made only minor changes in United States policy in Thailand. The Eisenhower administration maintained the large-scale military aid program and it continued to view the country as a strong anti-Communist base in Southeast Asia. At times the Americans actually indicated a desire to increase the size of the armed forces. In October 1958 Secretary of Defense McElroy visited the country and stated that the U.S. might provide the Thai military forces with guided missles as it was doing with some of its NATO allies.[5] In January 1960 the Department of Defense denied rumors that the United States was considering the transfer of its military bases from the Philippines to Thailand. Yet at the same time American military planners were considering the establishment of a task force of "atomic-armed paratroopers" in Thailand to strengthen the SEATO alliance.[6]

American economic aid after 1957 was reduced to approximately $24,000,000 annually with the bulk of this assistance used to support the armed forces. By 1960 the total cost of this aid had reached the sum of $216,000,000. Of this amount about $55,000,000 had been devoted to genuine economic and technical development. The total cost of military aid was $283,000,000.[7] Thus about 12 per cent of American foreign aid to Thailand since the beginning of the Cold War had been devoted to economic and social advancement. The portion of aid provided to the non-military programs did much to improve the economic and social standards of the people. By 1961 Thailand had a gross national product of approximately $2,200,000,000 which had increased at an average rate of 5 per cent each year since 1952. The country had one of the strongest currencies in Asia and the per capita income was approaching $100 per year. American technicians had assisted in increasing rice production in the fertile Chao Phya River Valley which provided the government with 50 per cent of its foreign exchange and 30 per cent of its entire revenue. American experts trained many farmers in establishing cooperatives for the distribution of farm machinery and farm credit. Considerable progress was made in improving economic conditions in the northeastern provinces through the development of a growing livestock trade. Improved breeds of poultry, hogs, and cattle from the United States enabled the country to export meat to Hong Kong and Singapore. Through the Development Loan Fund the Americans financed the construction of the giant Yanhee hydroelectric power project in the northern provinces which will eventually produce 560,000 kilowatts and promote the expansion of industry. Similar advancements were made through American assistance in the fields of transportation, communication, public health, and public administration. In addition to the economic assistance provided through bilateral programs, the United States assisted Thailand's economic and social development through the United Nations and the World Bank.

American private enterprise also helped to develop the economy and elevate the standard of living. The continual expansion of American commercial interests contributed to a diversification of the economy and made the country less dependent on its exports of rice and rubber. American business activity included the production and sale of numerous products ranging from Ipana toothpaste to IBM machines. Trade between the two countries continued to expand. American imports consisting primarily of manufactured goods increased from $53,000,000 in 1956 to over $62,000,000 in 1959. The United States purchased 90 percent of Thailand's rubber and most of its tin.[8] In spite of the gradual expansion of this commercial activity, private American capital in Thailand was relatively small. Of a total private foreign investment of $40,000,000 in the country only $7,500,000 was invested by American companies. The bulk of the foreign capital continued to come from the sterling bloc.

A major reason for this low rate of American investment was the uncertainty caused by political instability. In 1959 the *New York Times* reported: "There was no appreciable foreign investment in Thailand during 1958, principally because of political instability."[9] Corruption and nepotism in the government in addition to the problems caused by more extensive public ownership and economic planning discouraged any significant increase in private foreign investment. The Thai government attempted to overcome this reluctance among potential investors and attract more foreign capital. In July 1959 it provided special tax benefits for new investors and facilitated the remittance of profits. It further guaranteed that no foreign interests would be nationalized or subject to competition from government-owned commercial enterprises.

A major factor in the attempt of the United States to accelerate the economic development of Thailand was the influence exerted by Mr. U. Alexis Johnson who replaced Mr. Bishop as ambassador in January 1958. Like his predecessor Mr. Johnson had previously served at various diplomatic posts in the Far East, and just prior to his assignment to Thailand he had served as the United States Ambassador in Czechoslovakia. In this latter post he had negotiated with the Chinese Communists since the Geneva conference in 1955. During his three-year tour in Thailand he publicly defended the large military aid program and the SEATO alliance. Yet to a considerable degree he removed the previous impression of many Thai that the United States was controlling their government. He accomplished this by avoiding excessive involvement in the affairs of the military leaders and concentrating on the important task of promoting the economic and social progress of the country. Ambassador Johnson frequently urged his superiors in Washington to extend additional economic assistance to Thailand much as General Donovan had earlier pushed for larger grants of military aid. Mr. Johnson sought to make the country a "pilot plant" capable of demonstrating to other underdeveloped nations in Asia that private foreign investment could serve as a major impetus to rapid economic growth. On one occasion he stated: "Thailand presents an opportunity for American capital to demonstrate what private enterprise can accomplish in the economic development of a country."[10]. He claimed that the success of private capital in Thailand could enable it to play a role much greater than its size in promoting the economic growth of other underdeveloped countries. He warned that the failure of the free enterprise system would encourage the expansion of state ownership and governmental planning as the most effective method of accelerating economic growth.

In spite of Mr. Johnson's effort to advance the economic development of Thailand through the extensive use of private foreign capital many problems and uncertainties remained. The inequitable tax structure and the large role of the Chinese in the economy would cause a major expansion of private investment to make the rich richer and place even more economic power in alien hands. Relatively little of the additional wealth would reach the farmers and the lower and middle income groups. Also, there was no sign that other nations in the region were imitating this program in Thailand, and countries such as India were achieving a similar rate of economic growth, often with greater internal problems, through extensive government planning. In spite of its more favorable investment incentives the Thai government was not able to increase significantly the number of foreign investors, and it soon turned towards more government economic planning itself.

Ambassador Johnson stated that the failure to attract more American investors to Thailand was due to the lack of confidence caused by political instability since World War II. He consistently claimed that a favorable political climate had been achieved. Yet he did not indicate to potential investors what might happen when Sarit left the political scene. Regardless of his urgent appeals, the political stability of the country remained in jeopardy due to international uncertainties and the continuation of authoritarian military rule.

The United States continued to assist in the expansion of education, and in September 1958 both governments agreed to an extension of the Fulbright scholarship program.[11] From 1950 to 1958 some 306 Thai nationals were able to study at American institutions of higher education at a total cost of 29,000,000 baht or approximately $1,500,000. The modest sum devoted to this program had a significant impact in elevating intellectual and professional standards in the country. Yet it cost the United States about ½ per cent of the funds devoted to military aid. In 1959 some 933 Thai students were studying in the United States under both public and private sponsorship, including 254 students in the humanities and social sciences.[12] In addition to the Fulbright program the United States provided specialized training for 1500 executive and professional people, including more than 300 educators.[13] Approximately 50,000 school teachers benefited from supplementary training sponsored by the United States, and American educational advisers assisted in introducing new teaching methods in Thai schools. In cooperation with the government, the United States developed more extensive vocational training in specialized schools and at the major universities. Additional educational assistance was provided by the Universities of Michigan, Indiana, and Texas, and Wayne State University. By 1961 Thailand had a literacy rate of about 70 per cent which was one of the highest in Asia.

After 1957 the SEATO alliance made a modest but beneficial change by placing greater stress on the non-military aspects of the treaty organization which had been virtually neglected up to this time. This move came about through a growing recognition that the backward economic and social conditions in the region offered an attractive target for Communist penetration and subversion. This shift was made after the death of Mr. Dulles who had adhered to a military defense of Southeast Asia, although the late Secretary of State himself began to favor a modest expansion in the non-military programs of the SEATO organization just prior to his passing. The major turning point in orienting the alliance toward greater emphasis in the economic and social fields came at the fifth Council conference in Wellington, New Zealand in April 1959. Mr. C. Douglas Dillon, Under-Secretary of State for Economic Affairs, substituted for Mr. Dulles at this meeting and played a major role in promoting a broader policy. "The need for economic development," he stated in his address, "is fundamental and would exist irrespective of the Communist menace . . . We must never forget that while the primary purpose of SEATO remains the collective defense of the area, the security we are striving for will have meaning only in so far as we make use of it to work for the improvement of living standards throughout the area." [14]

This attitude pervaded the conference and was strongly emphasized in the final communique:

"The Council members are aware of the opportunities afforded for subversive activities in situations where basic problems of hunger, lack of opportunity and under-development remain unsolved. In these circumstances not only ceaseless vigilance, but also positive measures, are the price of freedom. . . .

"It was recognized that the raising of living standards and the provision of opportunity for advancement are important to the security of the Area. It was agreed that poverty and under-development are problems affecting several countries in the Area and must be dealt with on the broadest possible basis." [15]

Renewed appeals for additional economic assistance from Thailand, Pakistan, and the Philippines caused the SEATO Council at the Wellington conference to activate the Committee of Economic Experts and the Committee on Information, Cultural, Education and Labour Activities. The United States formally agreed to finance a Cholera Research Project and establish a graduate engineering school in Bangkok. Subsequent expansion in these fields caused SEATO to launch a Skilled Labour Project to expand the vocational training facilities in the region. In 1960 a Meterological Communication Project was be-

gun to improve meteorological aviation communication facil
and between the three Asian members. In the cultura
alliance provided more scholarships, research fellowships, lecture programs, and contacts among Asian universities. In an attempt to promote mutual understanding among all nations in South and Southeast Asia, the treaty organization sponsored a Conference of Heads of Universities in Karachi in January 1961, and invited university officials from member nations and non-member nations alike.

The expansion of these non-military activities did not detract from the military planning for the defense of the region. The advances of the Pathet Lao forces in Laos and the sabotage caused by the Viet Cong guerrillas in South Vietnam kept the treaty organization alert to any serious Communist military threat. It sponsored frequent military maneuvers in the treaty area, and in 1958 it gave temporary consideration to the establishment of closer links between SEATO and other Western military alliances. Special seminars on subversion were held in the Philippines and Pakistan.

The expansion of SEATO into non-military programs and activities has undoubtedly been the most important step taken by the alliance to assist the stability and progress of the region. Yet this favorable move raises the vital question of why this cumbersome international organization was ever created. The means for promoting the economic and social development of the three Asian members had been well established in the United Nations, the Colombo Plan, and bilateral aid programs long before the alliance was formed in September 1954. All of the non-military projects sponsored by SEATO could have been accomplished just as well through these channels. One reason for this broadened activity has been to cloak the essential military purpose of the treaty with programs designed to make it more palatable to both the member and non-member nations in Asia. However, in the military field SEATO has consistently failed to cope with the complex security problems in the region and it has placed the Americans in a serious dilemma. On one hand the United States has provided the only significant military power to the alliance. Yet until the spring of 1962 it had been prevented from taking firm and decisive action by the opposition of the British and the French. On the other hand the Americans have a strong moral and diplomatic commitment to defend the security of the three Asian members. However, the enormous diversity in the national interests of the eight member nations, five of which are located outside of the region, has made strong concerted action impossible.

After 1957 the number of official and non-official Americans living in Thailand and the scope of their activity remained essentially the same as before. Ambassador Johnson's role in stressing private capitalism has already been discussed. Thailand continued to be visited by many prominent Americans, including numerous high-ranking officials. Most of these visitors again stressed the probability of a military invasion from Communist China and the important role Thailand was playing in the defense of the free world. Some restraint was evident in less effusive praise of the military leaders and fewer references to Thailand as a "democratic" country.

The United States also continued to be visited by important Thai officials. Marshal Sarit came to Washington in January 1958 as a guest of President Eisenhower to undergo medical treatment at the Walter Reed Hospital. After a difficult operation for cirrhosis of the liver which may have saved his life, the army chief convalesced in Florida for almost six months. He also held talks with the president and other high-level officials in Washington during which he appealed for more aid.[16] He returned to Bangkok in June 1958 to bolster the government and later completed his medical treatment in Great Britain. As later events vividly illustrated, Sarit was greatly impressed with the economic prosperity and social standards he saw in the West. Much like King Chulalongkorn and Pridi Phanomyong who were earlier influenced by their observations of Western material progress and brought modern advances to their country, the army chief likewise returned to Thailand with a passionate desire to accelerate its economic and social progress. He also sought to promote these reforms "from above" and used his dominant political power to force modern innovations on many of his less ambitious countrymen.

Other notable visitors to the United States included twelve members of the Assembly who toured several American cities and held brief consultations with high-ranking government officials, including Mr. Dulles. The Secretary of State used this occasion to warn the Thai legislators of the imminent Communist threat to their country. He declared that the fall of Quemoy and Matsu to the Chinese Communists would enable them to conquer Formosa, Hong Kong, and all of Southeast Asia.[17] He did not elaborate as to how the Peking regime would achieve this amazing military feat. Shortly thereafter Kukrit Pramoj toured the United States as a guest of the Department of State. The popular journalist assured the Americans that the recent trend toward a military dictatorship in his country did not mean the end of constitutional government. At an interview in Chicago he declared: "I am sure that democracy will be the only form of government suitable for us in Thailand, but democracy requires maturity . . . We are an old people, but democratic forms are new to us."[18] In October 1959 Sarit's deputy, General Thanom Kittikachorn, toured military installations in the United States and held consultations with officials in the Department of State and the Department of Defense.

Perhaps the most memorable tour ever made to the United States by guests from Thailand was the visit of King Phumiphon and Queen Sirikit in June—July 1960. The sincerity and modesty of the young monarch combined with the beauty and charm of the queen made a deep impression on Americans, and the royal couple did much to promote a greater understanding of the problems of their country. During his visit the king reminded Americans that he had been born in Cambridge, Massachusetts while his father was studying medicine at the Harvard Medical School. On his arrival in Washington he stated: "I was born here in this country, so I can say the United States is half my motherland."[19] President Eisenhower welcomed the royal visitors by refering to the "perfect" friendship between the United States and Thailand. The king presented the President with his nation's highest award, the Most Illustrious Order of the Royal House of Chakkri, which was the first time this honor had ever been conferred on a non-royal chief of state. At the White House President Eisenhower conferred the Legion of Merit on the king. While visiting in Washington, King Phumiphon addressed a joint session of Congress in which he appealed for even closer relations between the two countries. Referring to their common devotion to "freedom", he stressed the desire of his people to assume the major burden for their own progress and development: "Although the Americans and the Thai live on opposite sides of the globe, yet there is one thing common to them. It is the love of freedom. (Applause.) Indeed, the word "Thai" actually means free. . . . American assistance is to enable the Thai to achieve their objectives through their own efforts. I need hardly say that this concept has our complete endorsement. Indeed, there is a precept of the Lord Buddha which says: 'Thou are thine own refuge.' We are grateful for American aid; but we intend one day to do without it."[20]

President Eisenhower and the king issued a joint communique reemphasizing the American commitment to defend Thailand and promote its economic and social development. The royal couple was later welcomed to New York City in a colorful ticker-tape parade, and the musically-gifted monarch held a jam session with one of his favorite Americans, Benny Goodman.

The successful visit of the king and queen revealed to a considerable degree the distorted impression of Thailand that most Americans have obtained from their contacts with Thai visitors in the United States. With few exceptions these people have been the most distinguished officials in the service of their country. Most of these dignitaries have been educated in the West. This is true of King Phumiphon, Prince Wan, Pote Sarasin, Thanad Khoman, Seni and Kukrit Pramoj, and many others. The impression of Thailand obtained from these educated and gifted men has been that of a progressive and dynamic country filled with charming people who are rapidly adopting Western technology, customs, and forms of government. Yet very few Americans in the United States have had any significant contact with the persons who have actually exercised political power in Thailand. These men have not been Western-educated or influenced by Western social values, and their visits to the United States have been relatively unimpressive. While Phibun, Phao, and Sarit were well received during their brief tours in the United States, they did not make the same deep impression on Americans as more sophisticated Thai officials such as King Phumiphon, Prince Wan, or Pote Sarasin. During Sarit's six-month convalescence in the United States in 1958 he had limited contact with American officials and no significant exposure to the American public.

Yet many Americans continued to praise the military leaders after Sarit assumed direct control of the government in October 1958. When receiving the new Thai ambassador in June 1959 President Eisenhower stated: "The historic friendship which has developed between Thailand and the United States forms a lasting foundation for our common endeavors to preserve freedom and security in Southeast Asia and the world at large." [21] In a personal letter to Sarit, Secretary of State Dulles reiterated his fear of Communism and praised the army chief for his devotion to the cause of the "free world." "In following developments in your country," he declared, "I have especially noted your forthright public statements reaffirming Thailand's alignment with the free world and its support of the Southeast Asia Treaty Organization, as well as the independence of Thailand against the insidious threat of Communist infiltration and subversion . . . I am confident that by maintaining such steadfastness of purpose and faithfulness to our ideals, we of the free world will hasten the coming of the day when we shall be relieved of the heavy burden of defense and devote our energies and resources to the building of a better life for all." [22]

The Draper Report of 1960 urged the continuation of the military and economic aid programs in the underdeveloped countries much as they had been since 1950. This widely-publicized report was issued by a committee of distinguished private citizens appointed by President Eisenhower to conduct an "independent, objective non-partisan analysis of the military aspects of our Mutual Security Program" and particularly to appraise "the relative emphasis which would be given to military and economic programs." [23] This committee submitted the questionable conclusion that "from the standpoint of U.S. interests it saw no competitive relationship between military and economic assistance, and did not consider that the Military Assistance Program (MAP) is too great in relation to the economic and development program." [24] The report unfortunately did not elaborate on the adverse effect of the military programs from the standpoint of the people living in the countries receiving these excessive quantities of military aid.

Other Americans voiced similar support of American policy in Thailand. Former Ambassador Stanton continued to be an active apologist for the military leaders and their stanch anti-Communist policies. In an article entitled "Communist Pressures in Thailand" in the February 1960 edition of *Current History* he cited each possible Communist threat to the country and praised the government for its harsh suppression of all persons suspected as pro-Communist. Ironically, Mr. Stanton stated that the internal Communist threat was "not so great," "at a low point," and in "a quiscent period." [25] Unfortunately the former ambassador never explained why he entertained such a great fear of Communism in a country where the Communist threat was relatively small. Another American observer likewise praised the army chief: "Sarit has, I am happy to say, surprised me. My cynicism of six months ago has been gradually replaced by growing encouragement. Sarit's actions and plans, if fulfilled, will prove beneficial to Thailand." [26]

In spite of this vocal support, more Americans after 1957 joined in the growing volume of criticism toward the military leaders and their authoritarian rule. In a somewhat sarcastic article just after the September 1957 coup, the *New York Times* correspondent, C. L. Sulzberger, referred to General Phao as "a sort of local Beria" and "a superlative crook" who had engaged in extensive corrupt practices and double-crossed the SEATO alliance by negotiating secretly with the Chinese Communists. [27] Mr. Sulzberger stated that diplomats in Thailand had assured him that Sarit "is a relatively clean scoundrel" who is not considered "too corrupt." He cited the large sources of Sarit's income from public and private commercial enterprises and declared that the army chief was supported by six generals who were fighting among themselves over the "rackets" formerly operated by Phao. The article concluded with the following caveat: "Nobody should be foolish enough to attempt prediction of the future in this happy-go-lucky country whose policy seems strongly behind us. But dishonesty is certainly not the best policy."[28] This article was reprinted in the local press and aroused a bitter comment from Sarit who claimed that it was "twisted." Premier Pote Sarasin charged that Sulzberger's article had "damaged Thai-American relations more than anything that has been published anywhere."[29] And the Thai ambassador in the United States, Thanad Khoman, labeled these remarks as "the foulest attack," "pure slander," and "character assassination and insults against a nation which has done nothing to deserve such a treatment."[30]

This bitter reaction again revealed the extreme sensitivity of the Thai leaders to any adverse comments about their government, especially criticism emanating from the Americans whom they had traditionally considered to be their closest friends. This incident also indicated the vast gulf between Americans and Thai regarding principles of modern democratic government such as freedom of the press. A sizeable segment of the Thai press, including a newspaper owned by Sarit, had been denouncing the United States for over two years with many charges which were grossly exaggerated or outright false. While American officials in Thailand privately regretted this practice, they made no attempt to protest the publication of these articles or get involved in a fruitless exchange of denunciations. Yet one article appearing in an American newspaper criticizing the Thai government and containing many statements which were obviously true served to arouse the wrath and censure of even the most enlightened leaders. Had Mr. Sulzberger been a Thai journalist he would probably have found himself in prison.

Similar criticism of Thailand continued in the United States. Another *New York Times* correspondent, Bernard Kalb, declared in October 1958, after Sarit had abolished the legislature and formally assumed direct control of the government, that the reason for this drastic action was not any serious anxiety regarding internal Communists. Instead it was due to the desire of the army chief to remove any opposition which had "the potential of growing into a constitutionally based threat to the marshal's clique."[31] Shortly thereafter *Life* magazine published an editorial entitled "Afro-Asian Dictators" which stressed the need for the

United States to reduce its eloquent praise of dictators in the non-Western world and encourage some progress toward constitutional democracy.

"Toward the new dictators as a class", the *Life* editorial declared, "the U.S. should offer the tolerant distaste we have learned toward Latin American dictators, coupled with a readiness to side with the people as soon as their true voice can be heard. But in addition, we can insist that no government can be absolutely sovereign as they seem to imagine. The democratic ideal imposes natural limits on all government: limits on what it can do to its own people, limits on how it can behave toward other governments. This principle of limitation, which takes the form of law and respect for law, is the best guidance we can offer those who wish democracy to succeed." [32]

Americans living in Thailand likewise opposed the continual domination of the government by military leaders and voiced their support for a policy which would encourage the expanding middle class to emerge and play an increasing role in political affairs. One observer optimistically stated: "The growing Thai middle class and steady social and economic progress may enable the bourgeois democratic forces to get the jump on both the generals and Communists, and establish a stable system in a way similar to Mexico's emergence from militarist plundering." [33]

By 1960 more Americans were becoming increasingly aware of the revolutionary changes taking place among the people in the non-Western world and their growing demands for an end to the hunger, disease, and illiteracy which had plagued their progress for many centuries. This realization gradually aroused stronger demands for a more realistic policy in meeting the rising aspirations of these impoverished people. In spite of the doubtful conclusions in the Draper Report and official support for non-Communist dictators, an increasing number of Americans urged a reduction in military aid to these authoritarian regimes and a corresponding expansion of economic and social assistance.

The Interim Governments. Marshal Sarit did not immediately assume direct control of the government after overthrowing the triumvirate regime. Instead he installed two interim Cabinets, one led by Pote Sarasin and the other headed by Lt. General Thanom Kittikachorn. At no time, however, was the army chief certain that he intended to remain permanently in the political background.

Pote Sarasin was selected as Provisional Premier because he was not affiliated with any political party and he was in good favor with Sarit, the king, and the United States. He had served for five years as the Thai ambassador in Washington, and just two weeks prior to the ouster of Phibun and Phao he had been appointed as the Secretary-General of the SEATO alliance. His appointment as Provisional Premier thereby mollified American fears regarding the left-wing support behind Sarit and it helped reassure public opinion during another political transition. During Pote's ninety-day tenure he continued the policies of the former triumvirate regime. He defended Thailand's close relationship with the United States and its membership in SEATO. In spite of much criticism from the local press he refused to consider the recognition of Communist China or the adoption of a neutral foreign policy. At the same time he attempted to reverse the impression created by Phibun that the United States was controlling the government. On one occasion he declared that Thailand "is not following the footsteps of America. It upholds international law and principles of the United Nations."[34] Pote's difficult task was made somewhat easier as the army imposed martial law, banned all political meetings, abolished the "Hyde Park" debating centers, and closed six opposition newspapers. Yet the left-wing groups which had been encouraged by their success in the overthrow of the triumvirate regime continued to agitate for popular support. Much of the press advocated a neutral foreign policy and supported the opposition candidates campaigning in the forthcoming election.

The major task confronting Pote's interim government was holding new elections. Some nineteen political parties entered the campaign with 813 candidates seeking the 160 elected seats in the Assembly. The election was considered to be primarily a contest between the Left and Right with both sides making confident predictions of large gains in the national legislature. The balloting held on December 15, 1957 was judged to be "orderly and fair" by all parties.[35] The low turnout at the polls (13 per cent) was largely due to the fact that many people had become disillusioned after the fraudulent voting in the previous February election and many persons felt their vote would have no effect on the formation of a new government. Yet the balloting was fairly heavy in Bangkok, Chiengmai, Ubol and other provinces containing large numbers of educated people. The election results probably indicated with considerable accuracy the opinions of politically conscious Thai. The results were as follows:[36] Independents—61 seats, Sahabhum Party—45 seats, Democrat Party—39 seats, Socialists—15 seats.

The election vividly revealed that the leftists who had created much furor during the campaign actually enjoyed little popular appeal. They failed to win a single seat in Bangkok where they had the support of the press, and they even made a poor showing in the northeastern provinces which had usually been a source of left-wing voting strength. Their representation in the Assembly declined from twenty-two to fifteen seats. The election further showed that the bulk of the people were essentially conservative and almost totally unaffected by socialist propaganda or political action. The fear among many Americans that Thailand was drifting toward Communism or neutralism was groundless. The voting results likewise indicated that Sarit had much popular support for his recent action in ousting Phibun and Phao and at the same time maintaining close relations with the United States. "Marshal Sarit," one observer declared, "can now claim that he has won popular backing in clean elections; and the Americans can assure themselves that neutralist and socialist opinions have not yet, after all, got a very strong hold in Siam." [37] However, the leftists still had a good organization, and the uncertainty surrounding the army chief's health and his desire for political leadership encouraged many of these groups to prepare for a new bid for power.

Shortly after the election Sarit discarded his tacit disinterest in politics and formed a new National Socialist Party (Chartsangkhom) which sought to combine pro-government groups and military officers into a unified bloc. He also appointed General Thanom Kittikachorn as Premier in the new government. Thanom continued to hold the post of Minister of Defense. General Prapart Charusathien, another of Sarit's army aides, was appointed as Deputy Prime Minister and held the powerful position of Minister of Interior. When Sarit left for medical treatment in the United States he appealed to his new political party to give its loyal support to the government headed by General Thanom.

Yet the progress and unity of the Thanom government was hampered from the outset. The new Premier publicly admitted that he had no experience in politics or foreign affairs and he accepted his position only because it was "a call to duty." All important political leaders agreed that Sarit's deputy was not qualified for the demanding job of Premier and they generally assumed that his appointment would only be temporary. Thanom attempted to mollify criticism of his government by adhering to a middle-road policy that offered something to almost everyone. He described his domestic policy as "mild socialism" and stated that "we are going neither left nor right." [38] He also declared that Thailand would follow an "independent" foreign policy in close cooperation with the Western powers and the SEATO alliance.

The Thanom government faced other serious problems. The National Socialist Party was plagued with factionalism among the diverse groups within its ranks. The national economy declined due to a bad rice crop, lower exports, and reduced prices for rubber and tin.[39] The opposition parties launched bitter attacks against the government. Rumors were rife that Thailand was being infiltrated by Communist agents, that Phibun and Phao were planning an anti-government plot, and that General Prapart was organizing a group to seize control of the government. In nearby Laos a coalition Cabinet was formed which included several pro-Communists. Cambodia recognized Communist China while it was involved in a bitter dispute with Thailand over the possession of an ancient temple on the Thai-Cambodia border.

However, the major threat to the stability of this interim government was the same threat that had plagued the political progress of the country since 1947, namely the factionalism and rivalry within the ruling military elite. Few of the disputes within the military leadership were publicized during this time, but it is certain that Thanom's position, and possibly that of Sarit, was most seriously jeopardized by the ambitious and intriguing General Prapart. The powerful Minister of Interior purposely sabotaged Thanom's efforts to negotiate a settlement of the border dispute with Cambodia, and he continually plotted to capitalize on the problems confronting the government. Prapart was supported by several hundred junior army officers who wanted important official positions and a larger share of the graft. It was very likely that he would have seized power if Sarit had not been warned of this situation and promptly returned to Bangkok.

The army chief returned from the United States in June 1958 after receiving reports of serious threats to the Thanom government. During a brief visit he reorganized the Cabinet and again sought to unify the various factions within the ruling National Socialist Party. He informed his followers that Thailand needed a stable anti-Communist government to convince the Americans that it deserved more aid. At the same time he promised that he would not assume direct control of the government himself and rule as a dictator.

Yet before leaving for further medical treatment in Great Britain, Sarit voiced his disapproval of the existing constitution and stated that it should be amended "to give greater stability to governments."[40] He declared that the Thai political system was similar to that in the Fourth Republic in France which gave excessive power to the legislature. He claimed that the executive should have greater freedom in administering the country and the opposition should not be permitted to launch a general debate of the government's policy. He indicated considerable displeasure with the politicians who moved from party to party. He claimed that general elections were expensive and should not be held often. He likewise denounced the press as irresponsible.

One of the reasons for the increased political activity which Sarit criticized was the formation of more highly developed economic and social groups. Many of these groups emerged from the economic and educational advances promoted by the United States. By 1958 they wanted some role in making the policies of the government. A United Thai Federation was established in Bangkok which represented forty-two labor unions and more than 4000 workers.[41] This organization sought a revision of the labor laws to improve protection of workers, and it began to develop contacts with the major political parties. Simultaneously the Businessman's Association of Thailand was organized to represent the business community. In June 1958 the salt farmers in many rural provinces formally requested the government to protect their interests from the increasing competition of cheap salt imported from Hong Kong and Japan. The students of Chulalongkorn University and Thammasat University met to form a National Union of Students and they petitioned the government for a reduction in tuition fees and more classroom space.[42]

In spite of this healthy political trend the military leaders denounced these emerging groups and the elected representatives in the Assembly. The refusal of the legislature, which represented many of these new economic and social groups, to act as a rubber-stamp body became increasingly irritating to the army officers in the government. After almost seven years of undisputed control, they strongly resented any serious opposition to their authoritarian rule. One of their major fears was the emergence of other organized groups which might threaten their monopoly of political power. This clash again illustrated the conflict in values between military officers who were allegedly concerned with the stability and security of their nation and politicians who sought to reconcile and compromise the diverse interests of numerous competing groups. The military leaders had the obvious advantage in this struggle since they controlled the armed forces and claimed that they alone knew what was good for the country. They bitterly attacked the opportunism and corruption of the politicians while they conveniently overlooked the opportunism and corruption within their own ranks. In spite of the conclusions cited in the Draper Report and the praises of Thai national unity by official Americans, this political struggle again revealed the antithetical nature of the military and non-military aid programs sponsored by the United States.

Also, the harsh criticism of the Assembly made by Sarit and his aides revealed their lack of experience and understanding of the legitimate role of a legislature in a genuine democratic system. There was much evidence to justify their analogy between the political party systems in Thailand and France. Both countries have had many political parties and some elected representatives have moved from party to party to enhance their power and fortune. This practice has hampered the efficiency of the legislative bodies in both countries. However, the legislature in the Fourth Republic of France was entirely elected while the Assembly in Thailand contained 123 members who were appointed by the government. These appointed representatives gave the government a sizeable majority in the Assembly at all times in spite of the factionalism within the pro-government bloc. At no time were the opposition parties able to defeat a bill presented by the executive. The closest vote on any bill throughout this period was the 94-68 vote on the move by the opposition parties to repeal the unpopular Anti-Communist Act.

In spite of its many deficiencies the Assembly served an important role in training the politicians and people in the difficult art of constitutional democracy. It provided an outlet for criticism of the government and enabled the Cabinet ministers to obtain some understanding of the problems of the people. While the large number of appointed members made the legislature an undemocratic body, they provided an element of certainty to the policies of the government and served an important stabilizing role during this difficult transitional period. In the meantime the elected representatives were able to build a political organization and gain experience in parliamentary procedure. In time the Assembly might have improved its efficiency and stature and gradually assumed the role of a bona fide legislature. Yet after nine months the uncertainty experienced by the Thanom government combined with the desire of many military leaders for greater wealth and power caused them to abolish this important training device in constitutional democracy and turn to a new form of absolute rule.

The Beginning of Benevolent Absolutism. On October 19, 1958, Sarit suddenly returned to Bangkok and met with the leaders of the Thanom government. The reports which emerged from this meeting indicated that the military leaders were planning to establish a more stable political system. Two days later the army chief ordered his troops to occupy strategic positions in the capital while he announced that he was taking direct control of the government himself. He declared martial law, abolished the 1952 constitution, dissolved the Assembly, and banned all political parties. He also affirmed the establishment of a new Revolutionary Party which would temporarily rule the country from the army headquarters in Bangkok. He further stated that he would serve as the leader of this party which was composed of army, navy, air force, police, and civilian officials who were acting "in the name of the people." [43] As before, the people remained passive during another bloodless "coup."

The reasons for the direct assumption of power by Sarit were the familiar claims that the nation was threatened by the Communists and "the ever-increasing tension both within and outside the country." [44] The new regime declared that all "anti-stability forces such as Communist subversives have to be dealt with drastically." [45] The Revolutionary Party pledged that it would not make any changes in existing political institutions "except where necessary for the safety of the nation." [46] It likewise stated that all government officials would soon receive instructions in new "political ideals." The new official party declared that it would seek the following objectives: "It will uphold the interests of the people in accordance with the United Nations Charter, will maintain freedom of the country, respect rights under the Declaration of Human Rights, and protect the nation, religion and the monarchy." [47]

Military spokesmen explained that Sarit's action was not a coup since it had been taken with the complete agreement of General Thanom and the members of his government. Instead it was a move "against the National Assembly." [48] They also announced that a Constituent Assembly would be formed to draft a new constitution and serve as a legislature. They made no statement regarding new elections.

As army troops occupied important buildings, the police made a sweeping arrest of opposition Assemblymen, newspaper editors, writers, labor leaders, teachers, students, and businessmen who were accused of being Communist suspects. A total of 134 persons were arrested during the first few days after the coup, including Thep Jotinuchit, Klaew Norapati, and other opposition politicians who had visited Communist China. Meetings of more than five persons for political purposes were forbidden. Twelve newspapers were closed including the *Bangkok World* edited by Darrell Berrigan, an American journalist who had lived in the country since the end of World War II. The Revolutionary Party announced that all persons arrested under the Anti-Communist Act would be held without recourse to the civil courts and would be tried by a military court. No action was taken by Sarit against General Prapart and his junior military aides who had been a major threat to the stability of the Thanom government.

American influence on Sarit was evident from the moment he returned to Bangkok. During his talks with Thanom and the members of his government the army chief stressed the need to maintain a stable government and intensify the suppression of local Communists to "ensure continued American trust, confidence, and aid."[49] And the day after the coup he assured Ambassador Johnson that there would be no change in Thailand's foreign policy due to the recent "revolution." The general reaction among many Americans to Sarit's assumption of power was favorable. The only apparent concern of the United States was the promise by the new regime to continue a pro-Western foreign policy. When informed of this action a State Department official declared: "We are gratified to hear that."[50] Sarit, he added, was considered "most definitely favorable to the United States." A deeper concern for the army chief's new political role was further revealed when surgeons were sent from the Walter Reed Hospital to Thailand to perform additional surgery to assure the complete recovery of his health. Thanad Khoman, the Thai Ambassador to the United States who returned to Bangkok shortly after the coup, stated that the American press realized that "Marshal Sarit has saved Thailand from becoming a people's democracy."[51]

Only a few Americans, primarily newspaper correspondents, publicly criticized Sarit's action, charging that his seizure of the government had been motivated more by his desire to eliminate internal opposition than by any serious anxiety over Communist subversion. The remarks of the *New York Times* correspondent, Bernard Kalb, regarding this incident have already been cited.

Darrell Berrigan writing in *The Reporter* likewise commented: "It was surprising that the Communist threat should have been chosen as the principle object of the revolution . . . None of those arrested seemed formidable enough to justify the movement of the three armed forces and the police and the declaration of martial law."[52] Regarding the army chief's attitude toward the previous constitutional system Berrigan added: "He[Sarit] was sick of the National Assembly's interference with his government's attempts to govern, so he abolished it. He was sick of the politicians, both in the opposition and in his own party, so he abolished political parties. He was sick of unlicensed, irresponsible press attacks, so he cracked down on the press. He was sick of the constitution that permitted these to exist as they did—so he scrapped it."[53]

The Christian Science Monitor correspondent, Denis Warner, stated: "In general, therefore, Thailand emerges stronger from the coup. But the very system sows the seeds of its own destruction. Though this has been a coup within a coup, it certainly hasn't been the coup to end all coups."[54]

Sarit's action in abolishing even the trappings of parliamentary government indicated the vast distance the political system had moved from previous attempts to establish some form of constitutional democracy. While the army chief and his aides claimed that they were protecting the country from Communism, they were also motivated by the fear that under the provisions of the 1952 constitution the appointed representatives in the Assembly would be eliminated in 1962. This development would threaten their dominant power. Just before the coup a military spokesman voiced this fear of a fully elected legislature by stating, "it will be the politicians playing politics."[55] Instead of permitting this proposed change to take place, the militarists insisted that they alone had the responsibility of maintaining a stable government and conducting public affairs. Their promise to protect human rights was almost certainly made to placate foreign and local opinion as seldom in recent Thai history have human rights been so flagrantly violated when persons suspected of the slightest opposition to the government were arrested without recourse to the civil courts. In spite of this reversal, there was no internal political force capable of opposing the strong suppressive action of the new military regime. The vast material and diplomatic support provided to the military leaders by the United States helped to prevent the emergence of any competing groups who might check the trend toward absolute political rule and lead the country back to a more modern form of government.

The Interim Constitution. In preparing the legal basis for a new government the Revolutionary Party appointed a fifteen-member committee composed of military officers and experienced elder statesmen to draft an interim constitution. In forming this committee the military regime announced that it was selecting "persons who have knowledge and ability, are experts in various fields, are respected and do not have to depend on political popularity."[56] In a Constitution Day address Sarit indicated that for the first time since 1932 the Thai constitution would not include Western democratic values or institutions but instead would be drafted to meet the current needs of the Thai people. "It should be further admitted," he declared, "that Western democracy is not such a system of government as could be adopted and put into operation immediately by all countries regardless of the state of economic and political progress. As far as Thailand is concerned, it is high time we utilized the lessons we have learned from the past practice of democracy in adapting our democratic system to suit local needs and conditions . . . The garb of democracy was weighing down Thailand, whose ills were too serious to be cured by a pallative. Consequently the Revolutionary Party had to seize power to check the expansion of the activities of the Communists and overhaul the machinery of government."[57]

The Revolutionary Party also announced that the interim constitution would "embody economy principles to the greatest extent possible" to facilitate "short-and-long range economic projects, all of which will be of a permanent nature to ensure continuity of operation."[58] When a few critics remarked that the government was moving toward a military dictatorship Sarit declared: "Some may say this seizure of power is a reactionary step. We admit that it is. But our aim is to step back a pace in order to advance many more."[59]

On January 28, 1959 an interim constitution was promulgated which the Revolutionary Party claimed was based on the principle of the separation of powers and certain elements from the constitutions of the Fifth French Republic, the United Arab Republic, and Pakistan. This constitution consisted of twenty brief articles which in effect established a legal basis for an absolute rule. The titular role of the king remained the same as before and a 240-member Constituent Assembly was to be appointed to draft a permanent constitution and act concurrently as the National Assembly. Whenever a draft of the permanent constitution was completed it would require the approval of three-fourths of the total membership of this legislative body. A Council of Ministers was again established which was responsible for the administration of the country. However, the Premier (now formally called the Prime Minister) and the Ministers were "excluded from membership of the National Assembly."[60] They could attend the sessions of the National

Assembly and express their opinions but they had no right to vote. The king (in practice the Prime Minister) was given the prerogative to remove the Ministers from their posts, and until the Council of Ministers was formed "the Leader of the Revolutionary Party shall discharge the duties of the Council of Ministers and the Prime Minister." The essence of the new constitution was contained in Article 17: "During the enforcement of the present Constitution wherever the Prime Minister deems appropriate for the purpose of repressing or suppressing actions whether of internal or external origin which jeopardize the national security or the Throne or subvert or threaten law and order, the Prime Minister, by resolution of the Council of Ministers, is empowered to issue orders or take steps accordingly. Such orders or steps shall be considered legal."

Since the Council of Ministers was completely responsible to the Prime Minister, this provision actually concentrated unlimited legal and political power in Sarit. This article was almost identical to The Enabling Act which Hitler obtained from the Reichstag in March 1933.[61]

The judicial branch was briefly described in Article 19 which stated: "Judges are independent in conducting trials and giving judgments in accordance with the law." In cases where no specific provisions in the interim constitution were applicable the courts were to be guided by "Thai constitutional practices."

The interim constitution was the seventh constitution promulgated since the overthrow of the absolute monarchy in 1932 and as before its major purpose was to protect a recent change in the distribution of political power and provide a facade of legality for the victorious party. However, it oriented the political system much further to the right than any previous constitution and it failed to provide any channel for popular checks on executive power. For the first time since the briefly used provisional constitution of 1932 the legislature was entirely appointed, and its main function was to rubber-stamp the legislation submitted by the government. The claim of the Revolutionary Party that the innovation of the separation of powers was similar to that used in the West was almost certainly made to mollify local opinion and gain foreign approval. There was no actual resemblance to constitutional practices in any Western democracy. The strengthening of the executive and the weakening of the legislature went far beyond the changes made in the constitution of the Fifth Republic in France where the legislative body continued to be elected and retained some checks on the President. The new constitution in Thailand transferred all legal and political power to the executive and actually destroyed the legitimate law-making function of the legislature. The principle of the separation of powers has been used in Western nations to prevent the establishment of an executive or legislative dictatorship; in Thailand this principle was used to legalize a dictatorship. If any legislature in the West has any resemblance to the Constituent Assembly in Thailand, it is most probably the Cortes in Spain.

Shortly after the promulgation of the interim constitution the Revolutionary Party appointed the Constituent Assembly which consisted almost entirely of high-ranking military officers who were personally loyal to Sarit. Several members were chosen from the professional, business, and academic fields, and even a few former opposition leaders were selected, including Khuang Aphaiwongse, Seni and Kukrit Pramoj, Thamrong Nawasawat, and Vorakan Bancha. These persons were obviously chosen to give the appearance of a "broad" representation in the Constituent Assembly. An indication of the overshadowing role of Sarit and the profound decline in the prestige of these former political figures was revealed in their innocuous remarks at the first meeting of the Assembly. Thamrong, a former liberal Premier, meekly declared: "I shall do my best for the country."[62] Vorakan Bancha, a former protege of Phibun, likewise stated: "I am happy to have been royally appointed and I shall do what I can."[63] In spite of these window-dressing appointments, the military officers constituted an absolute majority in this legislative body.

As expected Sarit was unanimously elected by the Constituent Assembly to assume the post of Prime Minister. The ruling headquarters of the Revolutionary Party was dissolved, but the country remained under martial law. Within a few days the army chief announced the appointment of a "deeds" Cabinet composed largely of talented young men who had achieved notable success in various specialized fields. The new government included General Thanom as Deputy Prime Minister and Minister of Defense, and General Prapart as Minister of Interior. Prince Wan Waithayakon was relieved of his position as Minister of Foreign Affairs and as the Thai representative to the United Nations. He was made a Deputy Prime Minister. To maintain good relations with the Americans, Sarit followed a custom which had been used by the Thai government since World War II. He appointed Thanad Khoman, the Thai Ambassador to the United States, as the Minister of Foreign Affairs. Ironically, only one military officer was included in the Cabinet in addition to Sarit, Thanom, and Prapart, and the civilians in the new regime were widely recognized as outstanding authorities in their respective fields. Many observers judged the new government as the most competent in Thai history. Sarit gave his ministers much independence and seldom held Cabinet meetings claiming that these experts already knew their responsibilities. At the same time the army chief made all major policy decisions and kept the Cabinet responsible to himself. One minister stated: "The Cabinet won't hesitate to express its views, although the determining voice is Sarit's."[64]

The Achievements and Failures of the Sarit Government. During his five years as Premier, Marshal Sarit consistently sought popular support for his government and used his dominant position to bring many material advances to the people. Just after the coup he declared: "Anyone can launch a revolution, but the snag about it is that, once a revolution is staged, how to win public approval." In an attempt to win wide popular appeal the Revolutionary Party promptly sought to reduce the rising cost of living. The new regime lowered the cost of electricity in Bangkok and the adjoining city of Thonburi, and it promised the people that they would soon receive free water. It also placed a price freeze on staple foods, and reduced school fees and bus fares. This action had an immediate impact in relieving the economic pressure on middle and lower income groups and did much to win widespread support for the new regime.

Sarit supplemented this initial action with numerous reforms which accelerated the economic progress of the country. His obsession with the need for rapid economic development on which he justified his absolute rule was revealed in an address he delivered before the Economic Advisory Committee shortly after taking over the government. "The national economy," he declared, "is beset with difficulties, it is, therefore, time that something is done to save the beloved country from this plight and lead it on the path of welfare and prosperity . . . As the supreme desire of the Revolutionary Party is to strain every nerve to achieve welfare and prosperity for the nation, it cannot brook anything lying athwart the path of progress. All obstacles and impediments have, therefore, to be swept away."[65]

Thereafter the army chief sought to reduce corruption in the government by imposing severe penalties ranging from five years imprisonment to the death sentence. He reorganized the budget procedure and established a commission of experts to revise the tax structure and improve the method of tax collection. After voicing his admiration for the rapid economic progress achieved under India's Five Year Plans, he formed an Economic Development Planning Board to draft

Thailand's first long-range economic plan. This Board prepared a Three Year Plan and a Six Year Plan, the latter beginning in October 1961 with the objective of raising the per capita income from 2 to 3 per cent each year. These plans were also designed to diversify the economy so the country would be less dependent on rice and rubber exports and more self-sufficient in manufactured goods. In June 1963 he created a new Ministry of National Development designed to coordinate national level investment and development plans.[66]

In an attempt to attract private foreign capital Sarit abolished all monopolies of government and private corporations. He banned all goods produced in Communist China. The government promoted tourism in an effort to obtain more foreign exchange. One of the most promising signs from the economic reforms was the increasing number of Thai entering the field of industry and commerce which had been traditionally dominated by the Chinese. This trend combined with intermarriage between the Thai and Chinese should bring the business community into a more active political role. In time this expanding entreprenurial class may become an important force behind the effort to establish a constitutional system.

Sarit also used his absolute power to promote numerous social reforms. The national educational system was overhauled and the government extended compulsory education from four to seven years. Vocational training was expanded and a university was established in Chiengmai, the first institution of higher education constructed outside Bangkok. For the first time in Thai history the Ministry of Education received the largest appropriation of any ministry in the government, including the Ministries of Interior and Defense. City planners in Bangkok established a zoning plan and traffic control was improved. The police evicted squatters and street hawkers from public property and the Department of Public Welfare cleared the streets of beggars, lepers, and prostitutes. The government launched a slum clearance program and modern housing projects were constructed in the suburbs surrounding Bangkok. The army chief outlawed opium dens and restricted gambling. He ordered a clean-up campaign in all cities and provided better roads, water, and sanitation. At times he drove through the streets of the capital to observe the progress of his efforts and he personally reprimanded officials who did not follow his orders.

The major shortcoming of Sarit's absolute rule was his failure to promote a stable political system. While many of his economic and social reforms strengthened the prerequisites for constitutional rule, he did not establish any legal framework to check arbitrary executive action. He provided no protection to civil liberties nor suitable channels for some popular participation in public affairs. He prevented competing groups from achieving influence and power. Much like the absolute monarchs, he maintained an unlimited personal rule and held the life and death of the people in his own hands. And at times he used his absolute power to eliminate persons who seemed to threaten the welfare of the nation.

After several serious fires were caused in Bangkok by Chinese arsonists, Sarit personally conducted a brief investigation of these incidents and ordered five suspects to be promptly shot. These executions were held in public to serve as an example and discourage further crimes of this kind. After the first Chinese, Lim Song, was executed the army chief publicly announced: "Whether this act is appropriate or inappropriate I would not consider. I alone take all blame for this act, if there is any wrong."[67] Some foreign observers believed that these executions would arouse a hostile public reaction in a Buddhist country which had long abhorred capital punishment. Yet there was no apparent popular discontent caused by these unprecedented acts. Shortly thereafter Sarit further justified this harsh action by claiming that these fires had been caused by the Communists who were "all out to subvert, sabotage, and cause general unrest and disorder."[68] In spite of this claim, these fires were almost certainly started by agents of debt-ridden Chinese merchants who sought relief by destroying their buildings and collecting their fire insurance, a practice used with some success by similar unscrupulous persons for many years. Yet the army chief used these incidents to instill a deeper fear and submissiveness in the people and to justify his policy that ruthless measures were necessary to protect the country from Communism.

Sarit's action against the Chinese arsonists was generally popular with the Thai public because of the traditional animosity toward this alien class. Yet he soon resorted to similar measures to eliminate suspected Thai nationals as well. In July 1959 Supachai Srisati, the Thai leader of an allegedly pro-Communist group, was executed without a trial by the army chief's personal order.[69] In addition to these summary executions he imposed a rigid censorship of the press and his police officers raided bookstores in search of Communist literature. One uncooperative newspaper had its presses smashed. Trade organizations were abolished because "they engaged in activities which are at variance with stated objectives and hazardous to public peace."[70] Labor unions were banned and the Ministry of Interior assumed the responsibility for regulating wages and working conditions. The police imprisoned many persons on charges of "hooliganism" and anyone suspected of the slightest pro-Communist sympathy was subject to immediate arrest. Intermittent reports of plots against the government (usually attributed to followers of Phibun) and attempts to assassinate high-ranking officials (usually attributed to the Communists) served to intensify the suppression of individual freedom. Sarit warned potential criminals and Communists of harsh punishment under his sweeping powers provided in Article 17 of the interim constitution, and his government announced that "no further mercy will be shown." [71]

The Political Philosophy of the Sarit Government. The political philosophy of the Sarit government was perhaps most vividly explained by Thanad Khoman, the Western-educated Minister of Foreign Affairs and one of the leading spokesmen of the regime. In 1959 he declared: [72]

"We now find ourselves at the crossroads, we must look hard into ourselves, we must know where we are, what we want and what we can do . . . it is of no avail to try to ape those who, after all, are different from us in many respects. The fundamental cause [of unstable governments in the past], for many of us, lies in the sudden transplantation of alien institutions on to our soil without careful preparation and more particularly without proper regard to the circumstances which prevail in our homeland, the nature and characteristics of our own people, in a word the genius of our race, with the result that their functioning has been haphazard and even chaotic. . . .

"How can representative government function if those who are elected to represent the people in the National Assembly forget the interest of the country as a whole and pursue only their selfish gains. More particularly, how can the electorate hope to choose representatives worthy of their trust if it is hardly able to distinguish between promises of an election campaign and the genuine determination to carry out a national program and to uphold political ideals . . .

"If we look at our national history, we can very well see that this country works better and prospers under an authority, not a tyrannical authority, but a unifying authority around which all elements of the nation can rally. On the contrary, the dark pages of our history show that whenever such an authority is lacking and dispersal elements had their play, the nation was plunged into one disaster after another. We are confident at the same time because of the store of democratic faith in our traditions that such an authority will not trespass its proper limits, and if it does, it will do so at its risk and peril. This nation with its long history of freedom has never tolerated for long that its inherent right and freedom are trampled upon, either from within or without. The popular reactions, had in the past, been rather swift and there is no indication that the Thai nation has ever changed in this respect."

Thanad's statement was very similar to the political philosophy proclaimed by the spokesmen of the absolute monarchy after the Western impact began in the nineteenth century. In brief it maintains that an absolute political rule is best for Thailand if it is benevolent and brings material progress to the country. Any attempt by individuals or groups, labeled by the Foreign Minister as "dispersal elements", to seek their own interests is considered to be harmful to the nation as a whole, and only a strong government (supported by the armed forces) is capable of upholding "political ideals." The traditional concept of the Thai people as one unified and harmonious family has been revived, and the various economic and social groups which have evolved from the adoption of modern technology are being coerced to support "a national program" as dictated by the ruling regime.

There is much truth in Thanad's claim that the previous attempts to transplant certain Western political values and institutions into the stratified and hierarchical culture in Thailand were premature. It is also evident that the Thai people in their present status as a transitional society will require strong leadership for many years. The endeavor of the present leaders to look at their own political traditions as a basis from which to develop as a modern nation is a good sign. It should have been done many years ago. The leaders of the past went too far in attempting to imitate certain political institutions and practices of the West.

Yet the Sarit regime overlooked the modest but important political progress which the people had achieved after 1932. It neglected the growing aspirations of many modern-educated Thai for some form of democratic rule. It ignored the increasing attempts of economic and social groups to pursue their interests through some form of constitutional government. During the period from 1932 until 1958 an increasing number of Thai were gradually becoming politically conscious and gaining some experience in parliamentary procedure, political party organization, and free elections even though these "alien institutions" were often badly abused. It is doubtful that the democratic ideas accepted by the growing middle class were any longer Western or "alien". It is doubtful that large numbers of Thai wanted to go back to the rigid and narrow authoritarian political tradition of the past.

And Thanad's charge that the country has been plunged into national disaster only when "dispersal elements have their play" is false. Numerous disasters have befallen Thailand when it was ruled by a strong "unifying authority" which the Foreign Minister so eloquently extolled. In the sixteenth and eighteenth centuries the Burmese twice defeated the Thai and sacked their country when it was ruled by absolute monarchs. During the nineteenth century under the absolute rule of King Chulalongkorn a sizeable portion of Thai territory was lost to the British and the French and the nation narrowly escaped becoming a European colony. In 1941 under Phibun's military dictatorship Thailand was overrun by the Japanese and occupied for four years. Since the reestablishment of authoritarian rule in 1951 the political progress of the country has been plagued primarily by the personal feuds between the military leaders. Thus a major threat to the nation's security and progress has not come from the "dispersal elements" among the newly-emerging economic and social groups or from the elected representatives in the National Assembly. Instead a serious divisive force has been the rapacity and rivalry within the military elites who have dominated the political life of the country most of the time since 1932.

The Sarit government also overestimated "the store of democratic faith" which Thanad claimed has been historically vested in the Thai political tradition. While Thailand fortunately maintained its national independence for many centuries, it has never been a country in which individual political freedom has been respected or preserved. The proud claim of the Thai that the name of their country means "land of the free" really means freedom from foreign domination, not individual freedom of the people. The Thai for many centuries accepted with resignation the burdens imposed by their rulers as matters over which they had no control, and at the time of the Western impact in the nineteenth century approximately one-third of the people were slaves. Until the twentieth century there is no record in the nation's history of a "popular reaction" forcing the rulers to rectify injustices imposed on their subjects. In recent times there have been only two instances in which a small minority has attempted to remove the injustices of an arbitrary government, namely the 1932 coup led by Pridi and the People's Party which abolished the absolute monarchy, and the demonstrations led by Chulalongkorn University students in 1957 protesting the rigged elections of the Phibun regime. The leaders of these minorities in both incidents were influenced by Western, not Thai, political ideas.

To the members of the Sarit government the term "democracy" actually meant benevolent absolute rule moderated to some extent by the ideals of Buddhism and the paternalism of the ancient Thai kings. These men did not interpret democracy as a limited form of government which includes some participation by the people in public affairs. In spite of the promulgation of an interim constitution and frequent claims that Thailand was still a "free" nation, they made no serious attempt to define the "proper limits" which were to restrain the "unifying authority" of the country. The Constituent Assembly met periodically to approve legislation proposed by the government and to draft a permanent constitution. Progress on the latter was slow and halting. In August 1963 it was announced that the new constitution would contain some democratic features, including freedom of speech, separation of powers, and a bicameral legislature.[73] Yet Sarit refused to promulgate the constitution claiming that the people were not yet ready for democracy. The only limits on his government were self-imposed by the army chief himself and the members of his regime.

The claim of this government that it was preparing the country for some form of democratic rule raised the vital question: how are the people ever to achieve the necessary experience in constitutional democracy unless they are given some opportunity to become familiar with the values and institutions of a modern parliamentary system? The Sarit regime actually reversed the intermittent progress made towards this goal by its predecessors. The civilian and military leaders of the 1932 coup maintained an oligarchical rule but they provided a transitional period of ten years to prepare the people for a completely democratic government. Even during the authoritarian triumvirate regime the half-elected, half-appointed legislature at least could go through the motions of parliamentary procedure and offer some criticism of the government. While the leaders from 1932 to 1957 failed to conduct many of their affairs in a democratic manner, they voiced their aspirations for a democracy and promised the people that they were moving gradually towards this goal. And while Sarit and members of his government accused the elected representatives in the Assembly of putting the interests of their political party ahead of the nation, they continued many corrupt practices themselves and showed that they were not above the pursuit of their own selfish gains. Some of this official corruption became more devious and subtle than before, but much of it was open and obvious to the people. The only two television stations in the country were owned by the army and the police. Only military officers could obtain credit from the government to purchase television sets on an easy installment plan. Many Americans wondered how the Thai government could justify its appeals for larger grants of foreign aid when it could afford the luxury of two television stations which were enjoyed primarily by wealthy people and military officers. Also, the government reserved the best land along Friendship Highway for army generals who built elaborate villas and collected high rents. This modern highway was constructed by American aid to strengthen the military defenses in the northeastern provinces and assist the economic development of this backward region. Sarit himself engaged in extensive money-making operations. Just after his death it was discovered that he had amassed a fortune; one estimate put it as high as $137,000,000.

Thai Foreign Affairs. A vital factor discouraging political reforms in Thailand has been the deep fear of the military leaders regarding the security of the country. The Communist threat in Laos and nearby countries in Southeast Asia was frequently cited by Sarit as justification for the continuation of his absolute rule. In his 1959 Constitution Day address he declared that the people could not have constitutional government until they had achieved "national discipline."[74] He added that he would not tolerate "political freedom" or "human rights" as long as they might jeopardize national security.

The Communist threat has continued to be an important problem for American policy in Southeast Asia and it has intermittently strained relations between the two countries. As the United States moved gradually toward a broader policy in the non-Western world by cooperating more closely with neutralist nations and placing less stress on military alliances, it caused considerable disillusionment within the Thai government. The refusal of the United States to increase significantly its military and economic aid programs resulted in considerable frustration among high-level officials. After almost ten years of strong support from the United States, they felt that their anti-Communist policies had given them a special claim on American aid. Sarit voiced this attitude in 1958 when he accused the United States of giving more assistance to neutral nations than to "staunch SEATO allies like Thailand."[75] The following year the Thai government requested the United States to provide an additional $60,000,000 in economic aid and sufficient military assistance to increase the armed forces by 15,000 men. When the Americans failed to take immediate action on this request the Acting Premier, General Thanom, declared: "Some neighboring countries in Southeast Asia which are less close to the United States than Thailand seem to receive much more aid from the United States than our country."[76]

One of the most vocal critics within the Thai government of the broadened American policy has been Thanad Khoman. Since 1959 the temperamental Foreign Minister has frequently exhibited extreme bitterness at the United States for providing large-scale assistance to neutralist nations without meeting the demands of its military allies. In 1960 he went so far as to offer his resignation to Sarit in his anger over an agreement negotiated between the United States and India for the sale of surplus food. The Thai government at the time was attempting to resume the sale of rice to India, and he claimed that the American-Indian agreement caused the price of Thai rice to decline more than 50 per cent. While the army chief refused to accept his resignation, the irate Foreign Minister threatened to make an "agonizing reappraisal" of Thailand's membership in SEATO and close relations with the United States."[77]

Actually Thailand had not exported rice to India for over eight years, and it previously lost this market due to its own corrupt trade practices and the self-sufficiency of India in food production. The decline in the price of Thai rice in 1960 was caused by increasing competition from other rice-producing nations such as Burma and South Vietnam rather than the agreement between the United States and India. Yet this incident gave Thanad a good opportunity to display his ire at the Americans.

Another prominent Thai official who has voiced criticism of American policy in Southeast Asia has been General Prapart. Attempts by the United States to promote a neutral government in Laos and placate the mercurial Prince Sihanouk in Cambodia have caused the powerful Minister of Interior to advocate a neutral foreign policy. In 1961 he upheld a "Thai-ist policy . . . based on Thai history, Thai culture, Thai interests."[78] He further described it as a policy "not pro-West, . . . not pro-Communist, . . . also not neutralist." Yet Prapart's criticism of United States policy has been based partly on his desire to pose as a strong leader and compete with the more favorable position of General Thanom. The shrewd Minister of Interior has attempted to use the international tension surrounding Thailand and the uncertainties of American policy in the region to bolster his own political power.

Nevertheless, these statements by Thanad and Prapart reveal a genuine fear by the Thai leaders that they may lose their favored status with the United States in obtaining military and economic aid.

A much more serious and justifiable concern within the Thai government has been caused by the failure of the United States to cope effectively with the pro-Communist Pathet Lao rebels in Laos. Throughout 1960 the Thai leaders became deeply worried about Communist infiltration in the northeastern provinces which are inhabited largely by Laotian-speaking Thai who have long felt neglected by the central government and occasionally exhibited separatist tendencies. The vacillating policies of the United States in attempting to halt this potential threat became increasingly frustrating. In October 1960 the Americans reluctantly but openly supported Prince Souvanna Phouma, the neutralist Premier in Laos, who advocated the recognition of the Soviet Union and Communist China and sought to include Pathet Lao leaders in his Cabinet. The Thai government strongly opposed this move and advocated a "tough" policy toward the Laotian neutralists, including intervention by SEATO military forces if necessary. When the United States took contrary action the Thai Foreign Minister declared: "Feelings are growing very strong here than we are treated less favorably than those not committed in the cold war . . . Events in Laos during the last week opened our eyes to the situation—made us think of the future, think of what would happen if Thailand should be threatened."[79]

The misguided attempt of the Eisenhower administration to establish a pro-Western government in Laos by providing clandestine military aid to the right-wing General Phoumi Nosavan while maintaining official relations with Souvanna Phouma both pleased and confused the Thai leaders. The failure of this short-sighted venture and the continual inability of the SEATO alliance to prevent further advances by the pro-Communist rebels in Laos aroused increasing disillusionment with the United States.

For a time the growing concern of the Thai government with the ineffective action of the United States caused it to veer closer toward a neutral foreign policy and seek closer relations with the Soviet Union. In November 1960 it signed an agreement with the Russians to establish "commercial, technical, scientific and cultural relations."[80] The following month the army chief held frequent talks with the Soviet ambassador regarding economic aid for the Six Year Plan. He declared that these moves did not alter his policy of cooperating with the West, but he wanted to promote closer trade and cultural relations with the Soviet Union. However, by the end of 1960 as the Pathet Lao forces still advanced and American policy continued to flounder, the Thai leaders became intensely despondent. "If," Sarit pessimistically declared, "the situation in Laos or elsewhere develops to the point where it is obvious that it will inevitably become a danger to the nation, I shall have to fight in defense of it; and in fighting against such Communist danger, I hope to receive the assistance and co-operation of friendly nations of the free world, because fighting against the Communists is a fight for the welfare of the whole free world. . . . However, even if we have to fight alone without help from anyone, it is something that we have to do even if the country is plunged into danger and we die in the end."[81]

The Kennedy Administration. The victory of Senator John F. Kennedy in the 1960 presidential election augured well for a more realistic and effective foreign policy by the United States. Upon entering the White House the new president made certain changes which promised to improve the conditions for peace and progress in many parts of the world. Some of these changes were long overdue. He reduced the dependence of American military power on heavy bombers and nuclear weapons, and strengthened the capability of the United States armed forces to deal more effectively with the contingency of limited war. He expanded anti-guerrilla warfare training at Fort Bragg, North Carolina, and he appointed General Maxwell Taylor as his adviser in military affairs. He stated his desire to concentrate American foreign aid in those underdeveloped countries making adequate reforms so the benefits of progress could be shared by more of the people.

The New Frontier also placed increasing emphasis on the need to promote democratic institutions in the developing nations. When announcing the purpose of this new approach to foreign aid, President Kennedy declared: "Our unfulfilled task is to demonstrate to the entire world that man's unsatisfied aspiration for economic progress and social justice can best be achieved by free men working within a framework of democratic institutions . . ."[82] Other favorable moves by the young president were the attempt to reduce military aid and increase economic aid, to assist the underdeveloped countries on an individual rather than a collective basis, and to make long-term commitments which could enhance the economic and social progress of these people. The general policy of the new administration in promoting the development of these countries was clearly enunciated by President Kennedy in a major speech before Congress on May 25, 1961:

"The great battleground for the defense and expansion of freedom today is the whole southern half of the globe—Asia, Latin America, Africa, and the Middle East—the lands of the rising peoples. Their revolution is the greatest in human history. They seek an end to injustice, tyranny, and exploitation. More than an end, they seek a beginning. And theirs is a revolution which we would support regardless of the cold war and regardless of which political or economic route they should choose to freedom . . . We would be badly mistaken to consider their problems in military terms alone. For no amount of arms and armies can help stabilize those governments which are unable or unwilling to achieve social and economic reform and development. Military pacts cannot help nations whose social injustice and economic chaos invite insurgency and penetration and subversion . . . this [military] program, like economic assistance, needs a new emphasis. It cannot be extended without regard to the social, political, and military reforms essential to internal respect and stability. The equipment and training provided must be tailored to legitimate local needs and to our own foreign and military policies, not to our supply of military stocks or a local leader's desire for military display."[83]

In spite of these good intentions and well-founded policy proposals, the Kennedy administration made no significant modifications in the military-oriented policy in Thailand which the United States had maintained since 1950. The obvious reason was the Communist threat in Laos and South Vietnam. The proximity of Thailand to these countries discouraged any significant changes. As the Pathet Lao rebels continued to advance, the United States attempted to deter further aggression through a series of diplomatic and military maneuvers.

In 1961 the United States joined Great Britain in appealing to the Communists for an immediate cease-fire in Laos and the reestablishment of the International Control Commission set up by the Geneva conference in 1954. The Americans finally decided that the only realistic policy was to promote a neutralist government, and they made great diplomatic efforts to establish a coalition Cabinet. After extensive negotiations the three Laotian leaders, Prince Souvanna Phouma, Prince Boun Oum, and Prince Souphanouvong agreed to include eight neutralist ministers, four pro-Western ministers, and four pro-Communist ministers in the government. However, they continued to disagree over the control of the Ministries of Defense and Interior. This diplomatic and political maneuvering was strongly opposed by the Sarit regime which assumed that a coalition government in Laos would place the country under permanent Communist control and thereby expose Thailand to a serious threat.

The Kennedy administration supplemented this effort with additional diplomatic action to convince the non-Communist nations in Southeast Asia of its determination to keep the region from falling into hostile hands. In March 1961 Secretary of State Dean Rusk attended the seventh SEATO Council conference in Bangkok to reassure the Asian members, especially Thailand and the Philippines, of American concern regarding the Communist threat in Southeast Asia. In his opening address Mr. Rusk declared: "We cannot imagine the survival of our own free institutions if areas of the world distant from our own shores are to be subjugated by force or penetration."[84] The American delegation sought a "tough" resolution which would authorize the SEATO powers to intervene in Laos with military forces if necessary. This move was strongly supported by the Thai and Filipino delegations. The French, however, opposed foreign intervention of any kind and succeeded in obtaining a mild resolution which stated that the alliance could "take whatever action may be appropriate in the circumstances." In spite of the appearance of unity and cordiality at this conference, the United States was disappointed with this equivocal resolution although it was reluctant itself to intervene directly in Laos. Nevertheless, the Americans privately warned the Soviet Union in stronger terms that they would not permit further Communist aggression in Southeast Asia. The United States also sought the assistance of India in urging the Soviet leaders to restrain the Pathet Lao rebels. The SEATO conference did encourage an agreement by the Soviet Union that it would seek a cease-fire between the belligerent forces in Laos. Yet this move failed to calm the fears of the Thai government who continued to hold the United States responsible for preventing any further Communist encroachments near its border.

A second major attempt by the Kennedy administration to bolster the morale of the non-Communist nations in Southeast Asia was to send Vice-President Lyndon B. Johnson on a tour of the region in May 1961. The primary purpose of this mission was to assure South Vietnam and Thailand of American determination to protect them from Communist aggression. It was expected that the Vice-President would press these authoritarian governments to make some political reforms in an attempt to gain more popular support from their own people and reduce the influence of Communist propaganda. It was also suggested that American foreign aid be provided to these autocratic regimes on a quid pro quo basis for adequate reforms. Just prior to Mr. Johnson's departure President Kennedy voiced this attitude of his administration: "We can assist these (threatened) countries by our assistance . . . against outright military invasion. We can assist them through economic assistance to improve the life of their people (and) through defense support . . . against internal guerrillas . . . But in the final analysis —and we cannot do it for them—they have to organize the political and social life of their countries in such a way that they maintain the support of their people. There is a limit beyond which our efforts cannot go."[85]

In spite of these intentions Mr. Johnson appeared to do little more on his tour than promise each of these anti-Communist governments more military and economic assistance. In Saigon the Vice-President offered President Ngo Dinh Diem more military equipment so he could add 20,000 men to his army in addition to more economic aid. In Bangkok Mr. Johnson promised Marshal Sarit that the Americans would not "sit still" and watch Southeast Asia become the victim of Communist aggression. In a television broadcast in Bangkok he likewise declared: "Nothing is more important to the United States than the integrity of your great country."[86] He promised the Thai government that the United States would increase military and economic aid. On his return to Washington the Vice-President recommended that the United States provide an additional $100,000,000 for military and economic assistance to these two countries.

In February 1962 Robert F. Kennedy arrived in Bangkok for a one-day visit on the last part of his round-the-world tour. On his arrival the Attorney General declared that the United States "is dedicated to the security of Thailand."[87] The president's brother conferred with Sarit on the Communist threat in Laos and delivered a personal message from the chief executive.

In the spring of 1962 the Thai government became increasingly disillusioned with these diplomatic moves by the Kennedy administration. While the Thai leaders continued to appear outwardly cordial they became inwardly resentful of the failure of the United States to take effective action in preventing further Communist incursions near their border. As the political future of Laos continued to be in doubt they moved closer toward neutralism. Thanad Khoman again voiced his displeasure at the United States for its failure to give consistent support to Thai policies. When the American delegation at the Geneva conference refused to support his proposals regarding the Laotian dispute he angrily declared: "That country [the United States] instead supported and spread news of the Communist proposals made in the conference . . . We learned from the Geneva conference that the country which claimed to be our great friend likes if foes better than its friends."[88] The growing doubts within Thailand regarding the determination of the United States to defend the region against Communism intensified this sense of despair.

The Thai government soon withdrew further from its previous unequivocal anti-Communist policies. When the United States took a neutral position in the dispute between France and Tunisia in a special session of the United Nations General Assembly in July 1961, Thailand voted with the Afro-Asian bloc in censuring the French. For many years Thailand had almost consistently voted with the Western powers in similar disputes with the neutralist bloc in the United Nations. Further disillusionment with the SEATO alliance caused Thailand to join Malaya and the Philippines in forming the Association of Southeast Asia (ASA) in August 1961 to promote closer economic, social, and cultural relations within the region. While this association had little effect in advancing economic and social progress in Southeast Asia, it again enabled Thailand (and the Philippines) to illustrate their displeasure with the policy of the United States. After joining this association the Thai government continued to talk of the possibility of accepting Soviet economic aid.

This growing frustration with American policy was reversed in some degree by two events in the spring of 1962 which have been important milestones in the relations between the two countries. In March 1962 Thanad Khoman came to the United States to voice the concern of his government over the deteriorating situation in Laos. After a week of negotiations the Thai Foreign Minister and Secretary of State Rusk issued a joint statement which clarified the American commitment to defend Thailand. This agreement made a significant change in the interpretation of the SEATO alliance which was long overdue. The United States agreed to defend Thailand against Communist aggression without waiting for the "prior agreement" of the other members of the treaty organization.[89] Unanimity was thereby no longer required to take action in the defense of the treaty area, and disinterested members such as France could no longer block cooperative measures. The obligation to defend the security of the member nations was defined as "individual as well as collective." Secretary Rusk further promised that the United States would continue its assistance to the Thai armed forces, and future deliveries of military equipment would be accelerated.

This move achieved an immediate and enthusiastic response in Thailand. The growing doubt concerning American policy was partially erased. Sarit appeared before a television audience in Bangkok and stressed the nation's close relations with the United States: "A true friend who is determined to help us, who worries over our happiness such as the United States cannot be found easily . . . If and when our country is invaded it will not stand alone but will definitely receive help from the United States."[90]

Shortly thereafter it was announced that American military advisers were training the Thai army in guerrilla warfare. W. Averell Harriman, the Assistant Secretary of State for Far Eastern Affairs, left for Bangkok to discuss the "implementation" of the agreement to defend Thailand from Communist aggression. And once again the Americans were telling the Thai something they had been hearing for over twelve years, namely that their country was the next Communist target in Southeast Asia.

The second event which brought the two countries closer together was President Kennedy's order in May 1962 to send 4800 American troops to Thailand to reassure the government and bolster the diplomatic effort to establish a neutralist regime in Laos. The official communique stated that American military forces were sent to Thailand "to help insure the territorial integrity of this peaceful country."[91] The American troops were landed at the request of the Sarit government. Token forces were also sent by Great Britain, Australia, and New Zealand. This action appeared to halt further advances by the Pathet Lao forces, and shortly thereafter the three Laotian princes finally agreed on the composition of a government. The Thai leaders were likewise encouraged by the attempt of the Kennedy administration to obtain $50,000,000 from Congress for military aid to Thailand for fiscal year 1963.

Despite these moves by the United States, the Sarit regime continued to show its displeasure over other aspects of American policy in Southeast Asia. Thai officials complained when the International Court of Justice awarded the disputed temple, Khao Phra Viharn, to Cambodia. The Cambodian case had been argued before the Court by former Secretary of State Dean Acheson who was also a confidant of the Kennedy administration. The Thai leaders were also displeased when the President ordered the withdrawal of American troops from Thailand in August 1962, although the United States established a permanent military headquarters in Bangkok to facilitate the return of these military forces if such action became necessary in the future. Relations between the two countries again became strained when the United States provided additional military aid to Cambodia. A visit to Bangkok by General Maxwell Taylor failed to ameliorate Thai criticism of this action. It was at this time that General Prapart upheld a "Thai-ist" policy which would lead the country back to its traditional neutralism.[92] This declaration was combined with an announcement that Thailand had concluded a trade agreement with the Soviet Union. Yet the confusion regarding the genuine orientation of Thai foreign policy continued as American and Thai troops joined in the northern provinces for military maneuvers and the United States announced that it was providing "faster and better" tanks to the Thai army.

The expanding military commitments by the United States did nothing to ameliorate the militant suppression of alleged opponents of the Sarit regime. The Thai police regularly announced sweeping arrests of Communist suspects in the provincial areas, usually in the northeast. When this action did not suffice the army chief again used his firing squads to discourage opposition to the government. In June 1961 he ordered the execution of Krong Chunadwongs and Thongpan Suthiwongs for their participation in an alleged Communist plot in northeastern Thailand.[93] In some degree the execution of these two men symbolized Sarit's contempt for representative government as they had both served as elected representatives in the National Assembly. Both men were executed in their native towns to serve as examples to other would-be opponents of the ruling regime. In May 1962 Sarit ordered his firing squads to execute Ruam Wongphand for his role in a Communist plot in central Thailand. The police issued a confession allegedly made by Ruam just prior to his execution in which he blamed the Chinese for spreading Communism in the country. It is very likely that Sarit took this harsh action to instill a greater fear and submissiveness in the people and to impress the Americans again with the need for more military and economic aid to prevent "Communist" subversion.

Yet by 1962 Sarit himself realized that Communism could not be stopped solely by mass arrests, firing squads, or threats of brutal punishment. The depressed living conditions in many rural areas, especially the northeastern provinces, were recognized as a major cause of discontent and opposition to the central government. His regime accordingly announced the launching of the Northeast Development Program in which $300,000,000 would be spent during the next five years to improve the economic and social conditions in the region.[94] The new plan was admittedly designed to win the loyalty of the Laotian-speaking people in the northeastern provinces before any serious attempts were made to subvert them by pro-Communist agitators operating from near-by Laos. After ignoring these provinces for centuries the central government declared that this program was to "bring the Government to the people, and the people to the Government." For the first time in history large numbers of top-level officials made personal visits to rural areas and learned of their problems by direct observation. Provincial leaders were brought to Bangkok to take training in human relations, the responsibilities of leadership, and Communist tactics and propaganda.

The Americans voiced their strong support for this new program and offered to finance a portion of the plan. The World Bank also supported a large-scale economic development program in northeastern Thailand. The government promoted new projects to develop urgently needed water resources in the region. It sought to reduce the cultivation of rice which requires much water and increase the production of foodstuffs more suitable for this semi-arid land. American and Thai officials hoped that within a few years these programs would enable the people in the northeastern provinces to experience some prosperity and higher standards of living. They also hoped that this effort would prevent the spread of Communism in this strategic part of the country.

An important factor in maintaining good relations between the United States and Thailand after 1961 was the effective diplomatic role of Mr. Kenneth T. Young, Jr. who replaced Mr. Johnson as ambassador. In the opinion of many Americans and Thai, Mr. Young was the most effective United States Ambassador since World War II. He was very ably assisted by his wife, Patricia. He maintained cordial relations with the Thai leaders and at the same time made a determined effort to have better contacts with potentially important groups outside official circles. He made frequent tours to the provinces where he talked with townspeople and peasants. He voiced his concern about the depressed living conditions in the northeastern provinces and promised American assistance in promoting better agricultural techniques for these underprivileged people. He actively supported the efforts of the Sarit regime to broaden its contacts with the rural people. When the Thai government brought village leaders to Bangkok for leadership training, Mr. Young invited many of them to the United States Embassy for personal talks. He also stressed the need for better education in Thailand. He was the first American ambassador to give active and consistent support to the Fulbright Foundation which has continued to send scores of promising students to the United States for higher education.

Mr. Young resigned in the fall of 1963 due to poor health. He was replaced by Mr. Graham Martin, another career diplomat and former deputy coordinator of the Alliance for Progress. Americans and Thai alike hoped the new ambassador would continue the excellent role played by his predecessor.

New Political Leadership. As if by destiny, the United States and Thailand changed political leadership at the same time. President Kennedy was assassinated on November 22, 1963 in Dallas, Texas. Field Marshal Sarit died two weeks later at a hospital in Bangkok. Mr. Kennedy was the first American president to be assassinated since the murder of President William McKinley in 1901. Sarit was the first Thai leader since King Vajiravudh to die while exercising political power.

Vice President Lyndon Johnson took over as the new chief executive in the United States. He immediately announced that he would continue the policies of his predecessor and uphold American treaty obligations "from Berlin to Vietnam." General Thanom Kittikachorn was appointed by King Phumiphon as the new Premier in Thailand. He promptly declared that he would follow Sarit's policies "in every detail, both external and internal."

Since entering the White House, President Johnson has upheld the basic policy of containing Communist aggression in spite of the reduced tension between the United States and the Soviet Union and the growing splits within the Communist bloc. He has made no changes in American policy in Southeast Asia. The new president has maintained a cautious policy seeking to stabilize the precarious military and political situation in Laos, and he has continued a firm commitment to the anti-Communist government in South Vietnam. He has pursued the same policy of friendly mutual cooperation in Thailand. He sent the condolences of the American people to King Phumiphon on the death of Marshal Sarit and expressed his hope for the continuation of good relations in the future. Mr. Johnson is the first President of the United States who has actually visited Southeast Asia and his brief tour in this strategic region may help him in formulating effective policies in the future.

In spite of his insistence to uphold the policies of the late President Kennedy, Mr. Johnson has made minor modifications in the conduct of American foreign policy which may alter its substance in the future. Perhaps most significant has been the expanding role of the Secretary of Defense, Mr. Robert McNamara, and the increasing influence of McGeorge Bundy, the Special Assistant to the President on the White House Staff. Both of these men tend to favor a "hard" policy in dealing with the Communist and neutralist nations and they have stressed the use of military power in supporting American commitments throughout the world. The role of Secretary of State Dean Rusk has intermittently declined. Mr. Roger Hilsman, who served for a brief time as Assistant Secretary of State for Far Eastern Affairs and favored a more flexible policy in Asia, resigned shortly after Mr. Johnson came to the White House. Mr. Hilsman was replaced by McGeorge Bundy's older brother, William Bundy, who has a long background in the Department of Defense and the Central Intelligence Agency. Under these men American policy in Asia may possibly witness a partial return to the military-oriented approach of the late John Foster Dulles, although more consideration will probably be given to political, economic, and social factors within the region. This trend should augur well for future relations between the United States and Thailand since the Thai government will almost certainly be dominated by military officers for many years to come.

The biggest problem confronting the Johnson administration in the field of foreign policy will be the need to obtain adequate financial and legislative support from Congress. The sharp reduction in foreign aid in 1963 from $4 billion to $3 billion, and the indication that many Senators and Congressmen will press for greater reductions in the future will hamper the efforts of the United States to deal effectively with the Communist threat in Southeast Asia.

The future leadership and policies of the Thai government are much more uncertain than in the Johnson administration in the United States. The position of Thanom as Premier will cause considerable anxiety for some time and it is still too soon to determine whether he will continue as the head of the government. His role has been strengthened by the order of succession established by Sarit in which the late army chief clearly designated him as his successor. Thanom has the advantage of having served as Premier for almost one year just prior to Sarit's assumption of power in 1958. He has therefore some experience in administering the government and he is fairly well known inside and outside the country. He has retained the members of Sarit's Cabinet and he has added the venerable and popular Pote Sarasin to fill the important post of Minister of National Development. Thanom is well liked by the people and enjoys a reputation for honesty and selflessness. He has the active support of King Phumiphon who appointed him to the rank of Field Marshal of the Royal Thai Army, Admiral of the Thai Fleet, and Marshal of the Royal Thai Air Force.[96] Thanom is popular with American and other foreign officials in Thailand and he is noted for his strong anti-Communist policies. The Americans also favor his heavy emphasis on the economic and social development of the country. During the short time he has been in office his government has attempted to mediate the dispute beween Indonesia and Malaysia, an action which favors United States interests in Southeast Asia.

Thanom's biggest weakness has been his personality which is not as powerful or aggressive as that of Sarit. The decision-making process within the ruling elite is therefore broadening and other members of the government may pose as competitors to the new Premier. One of his chief contenders is General Prapart whose political ambitions are well known. The powerful Minister of Interior has a large and aggressive following within the armed forces and the civilian bureaucracy. Many of Prapart's military aides want important posts in the government and more of the fruits of political power. The Minister of Interior, however, has several serious shortcomings. He lost considerable prestige within the ruling elite when Sarit intermittently reprimanded him for his excessive ambitions. He is not popular with large segments of the public and many foreign officials. In the opinion of some observers Prapart's seizure of power would bring about some return to the ruthless and rapacious rule of General Phao.

Another possible contender of Thanom is General Chitti Nawisathien, the Chief of Staff of the Thai Army and Deputy Minister of Agriculture. Chitti heads a faction within the military which got few important posts and few financial rewards from the Sarit regime after 1958. Some persons within this faction want a larger share of the power and wealth controlled by the new government. Other top-ranking officers within the armed forces may also become prominent contenders for the office of Premier.

In all probability the foreign policy of the new government will remain generally aligned with the West in the future. Should General Prapart seize power it is possible that Thailand might again veer toward some form of neutralism, although the shrewd Minister of Interior has probably used his appeals for a "Thai-ist" foreign policy more to enhance his own political stature than to indicate the direction he would lead the country in foreign affairs. Thanom and the other military leaders will almost certainly maintain the pro-Western policy of the past. The Thai leaders have become increasingly disillusioned with neutralism after watching the unpromising experiment with a neutral government in nearby Laos. In their opinion Laos can be written off as a total loss to the Communists, and their fears have increased as Communist infiltration continues in the northeastern provinces. In spite of intermittent strains and disputes with the Americans, they will probably retain close relations with the United States.

Chapter VII

CONCLUSION

The major conclusion of this study is that the United States has done much to enhance the national security of Thailand. American technical assistance has also been an important impetus to the impressive economic development of the country. American educational programs have promoted higher intellectual and professional standards. At the same time the heavy emphasis on military aid has contributed to the present imbalance in the Thai political system by helping the military leaders enhance their status as the dominant political group. The United States did not create the conditions which have enabled the military to monopolize the government since 1951. Many of these conditions are deeply embedded in Thai culture and have been shaped by the forces of history. They existed long before the United States became the major foreign influence in the country. Yet the well-intentioned American policy of building Thailand into a powerful anti-Communist base in Southeast Asia has entrenched the military leaders deeper in political and economic affairs than they would be without American aid. Military assistance from the United States combined with a narrow militant anti-Communism have been important factors discouraging an active loyal opposition.

While the Thai military leaders have promoted many excellent advances in building an economic and social infrastructure, they face many problems in their endeavor to stabilize the country and assist its long-run development. One of the major limitations is their inability to represent the diverse interest groups which are emerging from the gradual expansion of modern technology.[1] They cannot make rational and realistic decisions on the complex technical and social problems which the country will face as it moves into more advanced stages of economic growth. They cannot adequately understand or meet the needs of the pluralistic ethnic and religious groups in the country. Nor can they stop the fermentation of liberal and progressive ideas among educated people.

Although political opposition to the military leaders is latent and unorganized, it will almost certainly increase as the process of modernization continues. A study among university students conducted by Dr. Edgar A. Schuler of Wayne State University and Dr. Vibul Thammavit of Thammasat University has revealed that in spite of the long period of military rule the overwhelming majority of students favor some form of representative government.[2] This group indicated that its opposition to dictatorships was stronger than its opposition to Communism, Capitalism, or Imperialism. Authoritarian military rule has likewise been opposed by many businessmen, labor union leaders, journalists, school teachers, intellectuals, and other groups. Thus a need exists to reduce in some degree the gap between the government and the people. This task must be accomplished primarily by the Thai themselves. There are enormous limits on what the United States can do to assist in this endeavor. Yet there are some things it should do.

American policy in Thailand should be part of an over-all strategy designed to promote the security and progress of the country and the surrounding nations. A basic step in this direction is to undertake an objective and realistic assessment of both the international and domestic factors which affect the stability of the countries in this important region. Perhaps in no other area in the world is an accurate assessment of the strengths and weaknesses more sorely needed than in Southeast Asia. No other region has suffered more severely from erratic and unfounded predictions concerning the threat of Communism. For many years some Americans and Thai have claimed that the Communist threat is receding in Southeast Asia and the non-Communist countries are making good progress in providing for their security and the economic and social advancement of their people. Comments reflecting this opinion by both Thai and American spokesmen have been cited throughout this study. On the other hand alarmist predictions of an impending Communist attack have been consistently repeated, usually by military officers. When leading the French military forces against the Viet Minh in the early 1950's the late General de Lattre predicted that the victory of the Communists in this region would enable them to march unopposed to the Suez Canal. For many years the dominoe theory claimed that the loss of any portion of Southeast Asia to the Communists would portend the total collapse of the entire area. At a meeting of the SEATO military advisers in 1961 one Western official pessimistically stated: "It looks as if the whole region is cracking at the seams."[3]

These divergent assessments indicate that a new and fresh look is overdue. For too long has the Communist threat been exaggerated to justify larger expenditures for military power. While the United States could do enormous harm by underestimating the problems in this region, it could also do great harm by overestimating them.

A first task in developing a policy toward any country in Southeast Asia is to assess as accurately as possible the potential threat emanating from Communist China. It has been the assumption that the Chinese Communists have both the intention and capability to overrun this region that has motivated the large-scale military aid programs sponsored by the United States in Thailand, Pakistan, Laos, and South Vietnam. There are some factors which justify this assumption. The Chinese Communists have an army of approximately 3,000,000 men and an air force of 2500 planes, half of which are Soviet-made jets. The rapid advances of Red Chinese troops through the mountain passes in northern India in the fall of 1962 revealed that the Peking regime possesses considerable military power. China has a gigantic population of approximately 650,000,000 people which is increasing at the rate of 12,000,000 people each year. The country has considerable deposits of coal, iron ore, tungsten, and other minerals which in time may assist its development as a respectable industrial and military power.

At the same time there are many significant weaknesses within Communist China which may militate against any rapid development of national power and a policy of overt military expansion. Communist China has no navy of any consequence. This factor will prevent it from launching any sizeable seaborne attacks against the nearby islands or adjoining seacoasts in Southeast Asia. The lack of adequate transportation and communication facilities in southern China which would be an important factor in a successful invasion of Southeast Asia has already been cited.[4] The failure of the "great leap forward" which was clearly revealed in 1962 will probably discourage the Peking regime from undertaking any major military adventure in the near future. Virtually all Soviet economic and technical assistance has been withdrawn from China, and trade between the two Communist powers is decreasing. The Chinese Communists are almost completely dependent on the Soviet Union for the vitally important product of oil. The expanding ideological split and diplomatic estrangement between Moscow and Peking may also be a limiting force when the Chinese Communist leaders are directly confronted with American military power in Asia.

Another restraining factor has been the consistent failure of the Peking leaders to produce sufficient food for the burgeoning population. The bad crops between 1958 and 1962 forced them to use their precious foreign exchange to buy wheat from Australia and Canada.

This move has almost certainly delayed any significant industrial development for at least several years. As the population continues to expand it may actually decrease rather than increase the opportunity for industrial growth and the capacity for Chinese aggression in Southeast Asia. One noted American strategist has declared: "The vision of hordes of Chinese streaming into 'grey areas' (such as Southeast Asia) is unrealistic."[5]

Many American and Thai spokesmen cited in this study have indicated the desire of Communist China to seize the "rice bowl" of Southeast Asia to provide it with the food it needs for its rapidly expanding population. Yet the Chinese Communists must produce between 150,000,000 and 190,000,000 tons of food per year to provide each of its 650,000,000 people with a minimum diet of approximately 600 pounds. If Communist China were able to obtain the total surplus of the three major rice-producing countries, Burma, Thailand, and South Vietnam, it would gain only 3,000,000 to 4,000,000 tons of food each year. This additional rice would provide food for the Chinese for approximately one week and actually do little to solve their vital agricultural problem for very long. The rice surplus of Thailand would last the Chinese about three days. It is highly doubtful that the Peking regime would seek this temporary gain and thereby start a major war which might jeopardize its control of the mainland.

The expansionist tendencies of Communist China also require greater study and consideration. The general assumption among most Western spokesmen since the capture of the mainland by the Chinese Communists is that they intend to expand their control until they dominate all of Asia. There is some justification for this fear. The Chinese were an aggressive people early in their history and they gradually extended their control to the southern provinces of modern China. The Communist ideology as understood by the present leaders in Peking is certainly an important factor promoting an aggressive foreign policy. The intervention of the Chinese Communists in the Korean conflict and the military assistance provided to the Communist rebels in Vietnam and Laos likewise indicate the possibility of long-range expansionist aims. A similar tendency was revealed in the attacks on northern India in 1962.

Yet the Chinese Communists in the long run may become more Chinese than Communist. Their national interest may take precedence over their ideology as it has among the Russian Communists. An important Chinese policy for many centuries prior to the Western impact was to surround the country with buffer states rather than satellites to prevent the exposure of its borders to any hostile foreign power. This policy was primarily defensive rather than offensive. The Chinese relied largely on the influence of their "superior" civilization to maintain their dominant position in Asia rather than undertake any reckless adventure of military aggression. It is possible that the intervention of the Chinese Communists in Korea, Vietnam, Laos, and India has been a revival of this historical policy to protect China's borders rather than an attempt to expand their political control by military force. The policy of the Peking regime to delineate its borders with Burma, Pakistan, and Outer Mongolia may also indicate a desire to reduce the possibility of border conflicts in the future. The only irredentist policy clearly articulated by the Chinese Communists has been their claim to Formosa which may be a policy to remove the potential threat of the Chinese Nationalists rather than to acquire additional territory.

In the event of a major military conflagration in Asia, Communist China is one of the most vulnerable countries in the area to air and naval attack. While China will always be an extremely difficult nation to defeat and occupy militarily, it would be relatively easy to destroy its modest industrial potential and limit its offensive military power. The major industrial installations are concentrated in a few cities, largely in Manchuria and North China. The only significant supply of external assistance comes via the Trans-Siberian railroad from the Soviet Union. An overt military invasion of Southeast Asia would promptly arouse retaliatory attacks by American air and naval forces which could quickly cripple these vulnerable industrial and transportation installations. In the event of a major war the United States would almost certainly assist the Chinese Nationalists to attempt an invasion of the mainland which would probably divert a sizeable portion of the Chinese Communist military forces from any planned invasion of Southeast Asia. It is also doubtful that Communist China would launch an unpredictable venture without the wholehearted support of the Soviet leaders which would probably not be forthcoming considering the capacity of the United States to take retaliatory action against the Soviet Union.

It is extremely difficult to predict how these power relationships will be altered if and when the Chinese Communists develop their own nuclear capacity. The psychological effect of this potentially dangerous development on surrounding countries will undoubtedly intensify the fear of overt aggression and raise appeals for stronger efforts by the United States to deter Communist nuclear attacks. However, a similar condition has existed in Western Europe since 1950 where the nuclear capacity of the United States has served as a major deterrent to Soviet aggression in the small surrounding countries. Nuclear weapons in the hands of the Chinese Communists would be effective as an aggressive weapon only if they could obliterate the entire retaliatory capacity of the United States which is most unlikely. These same weapons might be used by the Chinese Communists to attempt nuclear blackmail in the region, but this policy would probably not achieve significant results in light of the enormous retaliatory capabilities of the United States.

Military Strategy. Although overt military aggression by Communist China in Southeast Asia would be a highly irrational move, the United States should be prepared to cope with such a contingency. Defense for aggression of this kind could be best achieved by increasing the military capacity of the United States, especially by augmenting the number and mobility of trained anti-guerrilla forces at nearby bases such as Okinawa and the Philippines. The additional expense for this expanded military power could be met by decreasing the size of the American-supported military forces in some countries of the region such as Thailand and Pakistan. These indigenous armies would be of marginal value in the event of large-scale aggression, and they command little respect from the Chinese Communist leaders whose major fear is American, not Asian, military power. These oversized military forces have hampered the progress of these countries, and the enormous expenditures for weapons could have been much more effectively used in advancing their economic development. The significant political, economic, and social progress achieved in Japan and the Philippines since World War II has shown the advantages of placing the primary responsibility for the defense of these countries under American instead of indigenous leadership. The authoritarian regimes in Thailand and other recipients of American military aid in Asia have likewise revealed the adverse effect of placing excessive quantities of arms in local hands.

If Communist China assumes a more belligerent policy toward the small countries of Southeast Asia, the United States should scrap the cumbersome SEATO alliance and sign a bilateral defense pact with Thailand similar to its military treaties with South Korea, Japan, Formosa, and the Philippines. This move would give the Americans and the Thai greater freedom of action in maintaining a vigilant defense country and it would reduce the adverse influence of France in the region. It would enable the British, the Australians, and the New Zealanders to concentrate on their mounting defense problems in Malaysia. It would recognize the uselessness of Pakistan in this unique treaty organization and permit President Ayub Khan more freedom of action in his quest for a position more independent of the Western powers. The security of the Philippines would continue to be covered by its bilateral defense pact with the United States.

A stronger commitment by the United States to defend Thailand might encourage the Thai leaders to relax their excessive fear of the Communist threat and devote more effort to the vital task of reducing the gap between the government and the people. In other non-Communist countries in Asia ruled by authoritarian regimes as least some attempt has been made to permit a modicum of representative government and win wider popular support. President Ayub Khan in Pakistan has established a program of "Basic Democracies" and issued a new constitution. The government of South Vietnam under Ngo Dinh Diem held periodic elections and maintained an elected National Assembly. The new civilian regime supported by General Khanh is seeking to broaden popular representation in the government. The Chinese Nationalists on Formosa permit some democratic rule at the provincial and local level. In 1963 General Park in South Korea issued a new constitution and ran for office in the general elections. While these democratic features are little more than trappings of genuine constitutional government, they allow some expression of public opinion and in time they may offer an opportunity for internal political groups to expand their influence. They can assist in keeping these groups loyal to the ruling regimes. They can minimize anti-government discontent and susceptibility to Communism.

No steps in this direction have been taken by the military leaders in Thailand. No national elections have been held since December 1957. In spite of notable economic and social advances, the Thai government has made no serious attempt to assist the political modernization of the country.

Military Aid. The military aid provided by the United States to Thailand should be tailored strictly to the needs of internal security. This aid should consist primarily of military equipment and training designed to counter guerrilla warfare. The existing conventional military forces should be gradually converted to provide this limited capability. In all probability this capacity can be obtained with smaller military forces and any surplus military units should be gradually demobilized.

The United States should do what it can to develop a professional military tradition among the rising leadership within the armed forces. In time this achievement may encourage the military leaders to curtail their interference in political and economic affairs and confine their activities to the legitimate role of national defense. This tradition might be promoted in the training provided to Thai military officers who come to the United States by stressing the concept of civilian supremacy.[6] It is very possible that future military leaders may be less inclined toward the traditional authoritarian system than men such as Phao, Sarit, and Prapart who received their military training and spent their early professional years near the time of the absolute monarchy. One sign in this direction was the attempted coup in October 1948 led by a group of sixty high-ranking army officers who wanted to remove the Coup Group from interference in politics. Although this attempt failed there are possibly many military officers who support civilian rule. The development of a professional military tradition combined with the emergence of sophisticated economic and social groups will be a vital step in the political progress of the country.

Also, the United States should exercise greater control over the military equipment it has provided to the Thai armed forces. One of the greatest weaknesses of American policy since 1950 has been the complete failure to protest to the military leaders when they have used American arms in the local struggle for power rather than confining their use to the intended purpose of defending the country from Communist aggression. American officials have stood by silently and at times admiringly as the military leaders have used American weapons to assert their political power and convert the country into one of the most authoritarian political systems in non-Communist Asia. Never has any American official cited Article I, Paragraph 2 of the 1950 military agreement which requires the Thai government to use American equipment "for the purposes for which such assistance is furnished." Yet within a few months after the first shipment of military aid arrived, the military leaders plunged the armed forces into an intensified internecine struggle in which American weapons were extensively used. The failure of the United States to make any protest regarding the abuses of its military assistance has undoubtedly encouraged the military leaders to intensify their rivalry and suppression which has led eventually to the revival of political absolutism. While it is too late for Americans to rectify these blunders of the past, it is not too late to insist that future military aid be used as a protection against Communist aggression and infiltration and not as a weapon in the internal political struggle.

Economic Aid. The United States should increase its economic aid in a form which raises the living standards of a majority of the Thai people. The excessive quantity of economic assistance in the form of "defense support" which has merely supported the oversized armed forces should be reduced. This aid has also been abused by Thai military officers and it has provided them with a large source of personal income. An increase in genuine economic assistance should be modest and gradual to minimize inflationary forces. In assisting sensitive political regions such as the northeastern provinces the United States might provide more economic aid through the United Nations and less aid through bilateral programs. The United Nations is greatly respected in Thailand and assistance provided through its specialized agencies may minimize criticism of American aid as an instrument in the present international struggle. At the same time this aid can do much to raise the living standards of these people.

The United States should also provide more economic aid in the form of loans rather than grants. Some changes in this direction have already encouraged the Thai government to exhibit greater self-reliance and initiative in promoting the economic development of the country. The increasing assistance channeled through the World Bank and the Development Loan Fund since 1957 has been an excellent move and should be continued. And in promoting economic progress the Americans should not exaggerate the advantages of a free enterprise system. While capitalism is an enlightened and vital force in the United States and Western Europe, its use in Thailand at the present time will not lead to an equitable and just distribution of the new wealth that will come from economic advancement. As in the past it will merely increase instead of decrease the economic and social gap between the wealthy and the lower income groups. For many years some form of government planning and control will be necessary for the rapid economic development of the country as in other underdeveloped nations of the non-Western world. As the Thai economy begins to mature in the future the role of government in economic affairs can be gradually reduced and the country will probably find its place among the mixed economies of the world.

Finally, if Thailand wishes to accept economic aid from the Soviet

Union as its leaders have often threatened, the United States should not attempt to prevent this move by offering to increase its own foreign aid. A modest Soviet economic program in Thailand, as in other countries in South and Southeast Asia, would not jeopardize the security of the country and it would probably bring limited economic progress. In time such a program would almost certainly convince the Thai leaders that Soviet aid is not the panacea to their economic ills as they often seem to assume.

Educational Assistance. The United States should increase considerably its educational program, both in providing the means for more Thai students to study at American institutions of higher learning and in supporting better educational facilities within the country. The educational program has been the least expensive of all American-sponsored activities in Thailand, and yet it has been one of the most effective channels imparting an understanding of the values and institutions required for a more modern form of government. It has been almost entirely through Western-influenced students and intellectuals that opposition to authoritarian rule and advances toward constitutionalism have come. The spread of educational opportunity in time will help to fill the psychological and political vacuum which was created by the sudden overthrow of the absolute monarchy and has been temporarily filled by the military leaders.

Continual stress on education will eventually develop a political maturity which should enable constitutional democracy to evolve from the initiative of the people themselves. This is the only way this advanced form of government will ever be permanently achieved. Perhaps within the next decade or two the spread of Western political and social values through better education will make a military dictatorship as outmoded as the absolute monarchy was in 1932. "Military control of government in Thailand," according to Dr. Vella, "has become a fact, but it has not become a popularly accepted ideal. Ultimately, democratic progress in Thailand depends on the creation of the conditions for democracy from below rather than the imposition of democratic forms from above. And these conditions—popular education, literacy, and political awareness—are slowly and silently developing in Thailand."[7]

Political Reforms. Unlike military aid, economic aid, and educational assistance over which the United States can exercise some discretion and control, political reforms in Thailand will have to come almost entirely from the initiative of the people themselves. A major reason for the limited political advances since 1932 has been the apathy and indifference of the people to public affairs. Yet conditions are changing, and by persuasion and example the United States can exert a modest and indirect influence on the emerging middle class groups who desire modern political reform. Through every appropriate channel the Americans should stress the fact that the military aid which has enhanced national security and the economic and educational programs which have raised material and intellectual standards must eventually be supplemented by political modernization that can satisfy the rising demand for more individual freedom and self-respect.

Actually, a gesture toward promoting a more stable political system was taken in the 1959 interim constitution which provided for the separation of executive and legislative powers. Had Sarit provided for a genuinely representative legislature this move could have been beneficial for future political advances. One of the major weaknesses of the quasi-democratic system from 1932 until 1958 was the adoption of the parliamentary system as used in Great Britain and France and the continual responsibility of the executive to the legislature. This system is ill-suited for most underdeveloped countries and its use has been one reason democracy has often failed in these fledgling nations. A presidential system is usually much better for these countries when they are ready for some form of constitutional government as it can establish an executive elected for a fixed term by the people of the entire nation. This executive together with a legislature composed of representatives elected by the constituent parts of the country can enact the laws for the nation. Sufficient checks can be provided for each branch of the government to preserve the constitutional framework with the balance of power favoring the executive. This arrangement can provide the strong but limited leadership these new nations require. Several countries in Asia, including Pakistan and South Korea, have already moved in this direction. The Philippines have had a stable constitutional system of this kind since 1946.

A major step in establishing this system in Thailand would be to provide for a legislature either fully elected or partially elected but in some way representative of the people. As mentioned previously, the legislature even when not fully elective is a vital training ground for the eventual establishment of a genuine constitutional system. At an appropriate time the Americans might urge the Thai government to call general elections and permit the establishment of such a legislature. In spite of the serious security problems in nearby Laos and South

Vietnam, these elections could serve a useful purpose.

Whenever an elected legislature is convened Americans should speak out more forcefully in support of the important role of the legislators regardless of their initial inefficiencies and shortcomings. One of the major mistakes of the past has been the practice of Americans to concentrate their support only on executive and administrative officials and praise their contributions to the country while neglecting the struggling but important efforts of the members of the National Assembly. In the future greater emphasis should be placed on elevating the stature of the elected representatives. One method of achieving this goal would be to promote closer contacts between American officials and members of the Assembly. It would also be helpful to promote more visits to the United States and Western Europe by both pro-government and opposition representatives where they can observe reasonably effective constitutional systems in actual operation. In closer contacts with these elected members, Americans might remind them of their important contribution to the preservation of democratic institutions. It is only by elevating the prestige of these representatives that they can eventually gain the experience, self-confidence, and sense of responsibility which will be required to make the national legislature an effective institution.

Whenever the civil courts are restored in Thailand, the United States should follow the same practice by stressing the vital role of the judiciary in maintaining constitutional government and individual freedom. Thai judges, like Thai legislators, should be invited frequently to the United States and they should be encouraged to maintain closer relations with the judicial profession in democratic countries. American law schools could perhaps assist in this important endeavor by offering more scholarships to Thai students.

Americans can also promote political reforms by strengthening the private economic and social groups in the country. American businessmen, assisted perhaps by the United States Chamber of Commerce, might form closer relations with business groups in Thailand and enhance their role in formulating the economic policies of the government. American labor leaders, assisted perhaps by the international division of the AFL-CIO, may in the future be in a position to promote a mature labor union movement. The United States might also be able to train future labor leaders in the techniques of responsible and democratic union leadership as was done during the American occupation of Japan and at the American-sponsored Labor Education Center at the University of the Philippines. Similar contacts might be established between American agricultural organizations, press associations, and professional groups and their counterparts in Thailand. Commercial, labor, and agricultural components of the United Nations might also be encouraged to arouse and strengthen responsible interest groups. United Nations offices in these various fields are already established in Bangkok.

Finally Americans might do what they can to encourage King Phumiphon to speak out more forcefully for the establishment of a constitutional form of government. The king has already indicated his desire to see a democratic system established, and as cited in this study he has at times placed modest restraints on the military leaders. As he gets older and more experienced he might be encouraged to intensify these efforts. Occasional visits by the king to the United States might perhaps strengthen his personal role in maintaining good relations between the two countries and in exerting greater political influence. The visit of the king and queen to the United States in 1960 was eminently successful and should be repeated periodically. The king's unique background, including his birth in Boston and the education of his father at Harvard University, might be emphasized and used to encourage urgently needed political reforms in his own country. Within the next few years some American university, probably Harvard University, might offer a scholarship to the Crown Prince so he can receive his advanced education in the United States and continue this unique family tradition. The king might also assist the political development of his country by following the example of the Shah of Iran in his recent efforts to push political and economic reforms. These and other actions may enable the highly respected Thai monarch to contribute to the eventual establishment of a Democratic government.

Western Ideology. A final policy recommendation is to propose that the United States revive its historic mission of promoting an understanding of Western ideology in Thailand and other countries in the non-Western world. As pointed out by Arnold Toynbee in his monumental *The Study of History* the elan of Western civilization is becoming the dominant force in every region of the modern world. Western ideas are causing a mental fermentation in most underdeveloped countries and creating a dissatisfaction with the traditional political and social systems. This emerging force is the major impetus behind the increasing demand for change to a better life. The growing discontent and rising aspirations in these regions have often been mistaken by Western observers as Communist-inspired. Actually these eruptions have been caused by the impact of Western values. Unscrupulous but astute Communists have recognized the enormous revolutionary force behind these Western-inspired movements and exploited them for their own gains. The Communist-captured revolution in Castro's Cuba is a recent example. Obviously the United States cannct rely exclusively on its ideology to advance its foreign policy objectives. Military and economic power combined with diplomatic influence are more immediate forces in the present state of international politics. However, the vital role of Western ideology must be recognized and strengthened. These ideals must have some influence on the application of physical power. Their neglect can lead to serious reversals. Even the iron hand of an autocrat such as Bismarck was guided in some degree by such "intangibles."

A policy of promoting Western ideology does not mean that the entire Western civilization is inherently superior to all other civilizations. Many elements in Western culture are undesirable and should be discarded; many elements in non-Western cultures are very valuable and should be strengthened. In the long run the entire world should profit from an eclectic process of taking the best in both Western and non-Western cultures and blending them for the common advancement of mankind. Yet the vital and revolutionary element of Western civilization based on the inherent dignity of the individual human being has universal significance and is gradually spreading to every region of the world. Throughout much of their history the American people have served as important disseminators of this revolutionary ideology. By example and personal contact Americans have encouraged the development of individual freedom and its concomitant form of government, constitutional democracy, in many countries in Europe and Asia. The United States has also served as an example to democratic movements in Latin America. While some of these countries have failed to preserve constitutional government they have at least made a beginning in this direction and possibly laid the groundwork for the establishment of democratic institutions in the future.

Since the beginning of the Cold War the United States has largely neglected its historic role of promoting democracy and greater respect for human freedom because of its excessive fear of Communism. While great efforts obviously must be made to contain Communist expansion, this is not the only task confronting the American people. A policy of anti-Communism if pushed too far may lead to a form of tyranny which is almost as degrading as living under Communist rule. Since 1948 an overzealous anti-Communist policy has frequently placed the United States on the losing side in the clash between traditional and modern groups in the underdeveloped countries of the non-Western world. It has caused the Americans to support the traditionalists in suppressing the genuine revolutionary forces which have been aroused by the impact of Western ideas and will certainly emerge victorious in the long run.

The basic values of Western ideology have been familiar to many people in Thailand for several decades. These ideas include freedom, equality, progress, popular sovereignty, and respect for law. Yet since 1932 the military leaders with few exceptions have applied these values primarily to the nation, not to individuals. They have minimized the opportunity for an effective opposition by promoting higher living standards for a favored minority of the people. However, they have suppressed their opponents and retarded the political modernization of the country. And they have permitted a wide and dangerous gap to develop between themselves and the people.

In spite of intermittent strains in the relations between the United States and Thailand, both countries have much to gain from continual cooperation and accommodation in the future. The economic and social progress of Thailand depends heavily on American public and private assistance. As long as Communism is a threat to Southeast Asia, the Thai government and people will need the military and diplomatic support of the United States. The American defense of this strategic region in turn can gain enormously from a stable political base in Thailand. Other non-Communist countries in the region can likewise benefit from a wise and realistic policy between the two countries. As the leaders and people of both nations consider the uncertainties of the future they might well reflect on the concluding words of John Stuart Mill in his essay *On Liberty*:

"The worth of a State, in the long run, is the worth of the individuals composing it; and a State which postpones the interests of their mental expansion and elevation to a little more of administrative skill, or of that semblance of it which practice gives, in the details of business; a State which dwarfs its men, in order that they may be more docile instruments in its hands even for beneficial purposes—will find that with small men no great thing can really be accomplished; and that the perfection of machinery to which it has sacrificed everything will in the end avail it nothing, for want of the vital power which, in order that the machine might work more smoothly, it has preferred to banish."

REFERENCES

CHAPTER I

1. Walter F. Vella, *The Impact of the West on Government in Thailand* (Berkeley and Los Angeles: University of California Press, 1955), p. 317-20.

2. Sir John Bowring, *The Kingdom and People of Siam* (London: Parker and Sons, 1857), Vol. I., p. 291.

3. Somchai Anuman Rajadhon, "Early Siam—U.S. Relations," *Saranom Magazine* (May, 1955), p. 61.

4. George B. McFarland (ed.), *Historical Sketch of Protestant Missions in Siam* 1828-1928 (Bangkok: The Bangkok Times Press, 1928), p. 6.

5. Anna Leonowens, *The English Governess at the Siamese Court* (London: Arthur Barker, Ltd., 1870), p. 45.

6. Cited in Kenneth E. Wells, *History of Protestant Work in Thailand* 1828-1958 (Bangkok: Church of Christ in Thailand, 1958), p. 61.

7. Tyler Dennett, *Americans in Eastern Asia* (New York: The Macmillan Company, 1922), p. 348. For a detailed account of the Harris mission in Siam see also *Mongkut, The King of Siam,* Abbot L. Moffat (Ithaca: Cornell University Press, 1961), pp. 62-87.

8. John Russell Young, *Around the World with General Grant* (New York: The American News Company, 1879,) Vol. II, p. 247.

9. *Ibid.,* p. 246.

10. Francis B. Sayre, "The Passing of Extraterritoriality in Siam," *American Council,* Institute of Pacific Relations, 1928, p. 4.

11. Eldon R. James, "Yale and Harvard in Siam," *The Harvard Graduates' Magazine,* (June, 1926), pp. 525-28.

12. *Siam General and Medical Features* (Bangkok: The Bangkok Times Press, 1930), p. 11.

13. Sayre, *op. cit.,* pp. 10-2.

14. Victor Heiser, *An American Doctor's Odyssey* (New York: W.W. Norton and Company Inc., 1936), p. 482.

15. Andrew A. Freeman, "A Tabloid in Bangkok," *Asia* (August, 1930), p. 555.

16. Personal interview with Don Garden, April, 1959.

17. Virginia Thompson, *Thailand The New Siam* (New York: The Macmillan Co., 1941), p. 205.

18. Andrew A. Freeman, "His Majesty King Prajadhipok of Siam," *Asia* (May, 1931), p. 277.

19. Vella, *op. cit.,* p. 341.

20. D. G. E. Hall, *A History of South-east Asia* (London:Macmillan & Co. Ltd., 1955), p. 676.

21. Carl Crow, *He Opened The Door of Japan* (New York and London: Harper and Brothers, 1939), p. 69.

22. O. Frankfurter, "King Mongkut," *The Siam Society Fiftieth Anniversary Commerative Publication,* Vol. I (1954), p. 12.

23. Vella, *op cit.*, p. 357, citing *The Government of Siam* (Bangkok: The Bangkok Times Press, 1926), p. 9.

24. Horace G. Q. Wales, *Years of Blindness* (New York: Thomas Y. Crowell, 1943), p. 271.

25. W. D. Reeve, *Public Administration in Siam,* (London: Institute of International Affairs, 1951), p. 25.

26. Vella, *op. cit.*, p. 352, citing P. Schweisguth, *Etude sur la literature siamoise* (Paris: Imprimerie Nationale, 1951), p. 324.

27. Norman B. Hannah, "Power and Politics in Constitutional Thailand," (unpublished Doctoral dissertation, University of Minnesota, Minneapolis, 1958), pp. 13-4.

28. St. Clair McKelway, "Siam Tries a People's Party," *Asia* (November, 1932), p. 555.

29. Some members of the royal family who were favorably inclined toward the new regime were permitted to serve as advisors and diplomatic officials for the government.

30. Hall, *op. cit.*, p. 679. Phibun's name is also spelled Pibul or Pibun in some English language sources.

31. Rupert Emerson, et al., *Government and Nationalism in Southeast Asia* (New York: Institute of Pacific Affairs, 1942), pp. 121-2.

32. Sir Josiah Crosby, "The Failure of Constitutional Government in Siam," *The Asiatic Review* (October, 1943), p. 416.

33. Vella, *op. cit.*, p. 382.

34. Lily Abegg, "Thailand—Old and New," *The XXth Century* (October, 1941), p. 41.

35. Six political prisoners had been sentenced to death for their participation in the abortive royalist counterrevolt in October, 1933. All of these sentences were later commuted.

36. John Coast, *Some Aspects of Siamese Politics* (New York: Institute of Pacific Relations, 1953), p. 16.

37. Department of State, "A Brief Survey of Siamese Relations with the United States," Office of Intelligence and Research (November 1, 1945), pp. 3-4.

38. Pridi assumed the position as Regent for the absent boy-king just prior to the outbreak of the war.

39. Personal interview with M. R. Seni Pramoj, June, 1956. For a thorough and objective survey of official relations between the United States and Thailand during World War II see James V. Martin, Jr., "Thai-American Relations in World War II," *The Journal of Asian Studies,* (August, 1963), pp. 451-67. This article is based on official files in the Department of State.

40. Personal interview with Kharb Kunjara, June, 1956.

41. Nai Samrej, "That Thailand May Be Free," *Asia,* (February, 1945), p. 94.

42. The British government recognized the declaration of war and throughout the duration considered itself in a state of war with Thailand.

43. Personal interview with Dr. Landon, December, 1959. Dr. Landon had served as a Presbyterian missionary in Thailand for ten years prior to his appointment in the Department of State. Throughout the war he served as the leading American adviser on Thailand to the United States government.

44. Corey Ford and Alastair MacBain, *Cloak and Dagger* (New York: Random House, 1945), pp. 180-2.

45. Stewart Alsop and Thomas Braden, *Sub Rosa The O.S.S. and American Espionage* (New York: Reynal and Hitchcock, 1946), p. 112.

46. *Ibid.*, p. 103.

47. Nicol Smith and Blake Clark, *Into Siam Underground Kingdom* (New York and Indianapolis: The Bobbs-Merrill Company, 1945), p. 189.

48. Vella, *op. cit.*, p. 387.

CHAPTER II

1. Sir Josiah Crosby, "Observations on a Post-War Settlement in Southeast Asia," *International Affairs*, (July, 1944), p. 362.

2. Sir Josiah Crosby, "The Failure of Constitutional Government in Siam," *The Asiatic Review*, (October, 1943), p. 420.

3. *Ibid.*

4. Alec Peterson, "Britain and Siam: The Latest Phase," *Pacific Affairs*, (December, 1946), p. 364.

5. Kenneth P. Landon, "Thailand," *The Annals of the American Academy of Political and Social Science*, (March, 1943), p. 118.

6. *New York Times*, September 15, 1945.

7. *Ibid.*, April 19, 1947. 8. *Ibid.*, December 12, 1945.

9. John Coast, *Some Aspects of Siamese Politics* (New York: Institute of Pacific Relations, 1953), p. 30.

10. Stewart Alsop and Thomas Braden, *Sub Rosa The O.S.S. and American Espionage* (New York: Reynal and Hitchcock, 1946), pp. 99-100.

11. Virginia Thompson, "Governmental Instability in Siam," *Far Eastern Survey*, (August 25, 1948), pp. 186-7.

12. "Siam Heads Off Communism," *The Economist*, (February, 1955).

13. Personal interview with Dr. Kenneth Landon, December, 1959.

14. Coast, *op. cit.*, p. 33.

15. Chun Prabha, "Siam's Democratic King," *Asia*, (March, 1946), p. 117.

16. Coast, *op. cit.*, p. 34.

17. Shortly after the death of Ananda a new Regency Council appointed the deceased king's younger brother, Phumiphon Aduldet, as the new monarch. Phumiphon had been born in Cambridge, Massachusetts while his father was studying medicine at Harvard University. He had attended school in Switzerland with his brother, and shortly after Ananda's death he returned to Europe to resume his studies.

18. *New York Times*, June 7, 1946. 19. Thompson, *loc. cit.*

20. Alexander MacDonald, *Bangkok Editor* (New York: Macmillan Company, 1949), p. 149.

21. Thompson, *op. cit.*, p. 188. 22. Coast, *op. cit.*, p. 40.

23. Introduction to the 1947 Provisional Constitution. 24. *Ibid.*

25. *The Bangkok Post*, November 10, 1947.

26. *New York Times*, November 10, 1947. 27. *Ibid.*

28. *Ibid.*, November 11, 1947.

29. Edwin F. Stanton, *Brief Authority* (New York: Harper and Brothers, 1956), p. 209.
30. MacDonald, *op. cit.*, pp. 163-4.
31. *New York Times*, November 23, 1947. 32. Coast, *op. cit.*, p. 44.
33. *Ibid.* 34. Coast, *op. cit.*, p. 46. 35. MacDonald, *op. cit.*, p. 175.
36. *New York Times*, April 12, 1948.
37. H. C. K. Woddis, "Siam: Cockpit of Anglo-American Interests," *Eastern World*, (January, 1949).

CHAPTER III

1. *U.S. Department of State Bulletin*, August 22, 1949.
2. Personal interview with Prayad Buranasiri, Technical Adviser to the Under Secretary, Ministry of Finance. In 1949 Prayad participated in the negotiations with the SCAP authorities in Japan.
3. *New York Times*, February 13, 1950. 4. *Ibid.*
5. *The Bangkok Post*, February 20, 1950.
6. *New York Times*, August 31, 1949.
7. Richard Coughlin, "The Status of the Chinese Minority in Thailand," *Pacific Affairs* (December, 1952), pp. 380-2.
8. Andrew Roth, "Siam: Tranquillity and Sudden Death," *The Nation* (October 1949).
9. Alexander MacDonald, *Bangkok Editor* (New York: Macmillan Co., 1949), p. 222.
10. John Coast, *Some Aspects of Siamese Politics* (New York: Institute of Pacific Relations, 1953), p. 53.
11. MacDonald, *op. cit.*, p. 220. 12. Coast, *op. cit.*, p. 48.
13. *The Bangkok Post*, June 5, 1950.
14. Hermit, "Education and Democracy," *Standard* (December 9, 1950).
15. Coast, *op. cit.*, p. 54. 16. MacDonald, *op. cit.*, pp. 217-8.
17. *The Bangkok Post*, June 4, 1949. 18. Coast, *op. cit.*, p. 53.
19. *New York Times*, July 23, 1950.
20. *U.S. Department of State Bulletin*, August 14, 1950.
21. *The Bangkok Post*, July 4, 1951.
22. Edwin F. Stanton, *Brief Authority* (New York: Harper & Brothers, 1956), p. 254.
23. *The Bangkok Post*, September 19, 1950.
24. *United Nations Bulletin*, November 15, 1950.
25. Stanton, *op. cit.*, p. 256.
26. *U.S. Department of State Bulletin*, October 30, 1950.
27. Stanton, *op. cit.*, p. 256. 28. *The Bangkok Post*, January 24, 1951.
29. Edwin F. Stanton, "A Century of Friendship," *Standard* (August 14, 1949).
30. Harold H. Martin, "They Love Us in Siam," *Saturday Evening Post* (April 24, 1948), p. 34.
31. *The Bangkok Post*, January, 1950—January, 1952 passim.
32. *Ibid.* 33. Stanton, *Brief Authority*, p. 275
34. *The Bangkok Post*, December 19, 1952. 35. *Ibid.*, July 4, 1951.

36. Virginia Thompson and Richard Adloff, *The Left Wing in Southeast Asia* (New York: William Sloane Associates, 1950) p. 52. Similar conclusions regarding the small Communist movement in Thailand have been made by David Wilson in *Marxism in Southeast Asia,* edited by Frank Trager, (Stanford: Stanford University Press, 1959) and by J. H. Brimmell, *Communism in South East Asia*: *A Political Analysis* (London: Oxford University Press, 1959).

37. *Ibid.*, p. 59. 38. Mac Donald, *op. cit.*, p. 205.

39. *The Bangkok Post,* June 30, 1950.

40. *Ibid.*, December 30, 1950 and October 8, 1951. One baht is approximately equivalent to five cents (U.S.).

41. S. Y. Lee, "A Critical Review of Thailand's Foreign Trade After the War," *Far Eastern Economic Review* (March 31, 1955), p. 389.

42. *The Bangkok Post,* November 28, 1950. 43. *Ibid.*, June 30, 1951.

44. *Time,* July 9, 1951. 45. *The Bangkok Post,* July 3, 1951.

46. Coast, *op. cit.*, p. 57. 47. *New York Times,* July 5, 1951.

48. *The Bangkok Post,* November 30, 1951.

49. *New York Times,* December 2, 1951.

50. *The Bangkok Post,* November 30, 1951.

51. *Ibid.*, December 12, 1951. 52. *Ibid.*, December 7, 1951.

53. Personal interviews with faculty members and students at Chulalongkorn University and Thammasat University. Similar assessments were received in discussions with Thai businessmen, school teachers, journalists, provincial administrative officials, and peasants.

54. Amry Vandenbosch, "Thailand, The Test Case," *The Virginia Quarterly Review* (January, 1951), p. 35.

55. *Thailand–U.S. Technical and Economic Cooperation* 1951-1956, International Cooperation Administration, May, 1956, p. ii.

CHAPTER IV

1. *New York Times,* February 2, 1953. 2. *Ibid.*, January 21, 1953.

3. *Ibid.*, February 2, 1953. 4. *Ibid.*, January 28, 1953.

5. *Ibid.*, January 13, 1954. 6. *Ibid.*

7. John Foster Dulles, "Policy for Security and Peace," *Foreign Affairs* (April, 1954), pp. 363-4.

8. *New York Times,* May 4, 1953.

9. Edwin F. Stanton, "Spotlight on Thailand," *Foreign Affairs* (October, 1954), pp. 78-9.

10. *The Bangkok Post,* July 30, 1954. 11. *Time,* August 9, 1954.

12. *New York Times,* December 26, 1953.

13. Personal interview with a Thai student who visited Sibsongpanna in Yunnan province by land routes on his return from the Moscow Youth Festival in 1957. For a detailed description of the Thai people in Yunnan province see *Lu*: *Khon Thai Nai Prathed Cin* (*Lu*: *Thai People in China*), Bunchuay Sisawad, (Bangkok: Nainoi Chuacedton, 1955) (In Thai).

14. *The Bangkok Post,* January 26, 1954.

15. *U.S. Department of State Bulletin,* July 26, 1954.

16. *New York Times,* July 16, 1954.

17. *Thailand-U.S. Technical and Economic Cooperation* 1951-1956, International Cooperation Administration, (May, 1956), p. ii.

18. *Newsweek*, July 26, 1954. 19. *The Bangkok Post*, July 2, 1954.

20. *Ibid.*, March 15, 1954. 21. *Ibid.*, January 26, 1954.

22. Major General William J. Donovan, "Our Stake in Thailand," *Fortune* (July, 1955), p. 94.

23. *The Bangkok Post*, August 8, 1952.

24. Stanton, *op. cit.*, p. 83. 25. *Ibid.*, p. 85.

26. Personal interview with the United States Vice-Consul, United States Embassy, Bangkok, June 1956.

27. *The Bangkok Post*, January 1952–June 1955, passim.

28. *Ibid.*, April 20, 1953. 29. *Ibid.*, June 22, 1955.

30. *Ibid.*, May 19, 1953. 31. *Ibid.*, December 21, 1954.

32. *New York Times*, April 7, 1954. 33. *Ibid.*, July 15, 1954.

34. *Ibid.*, September 6, 1954.

35. *The Bangkok Conference of the Manila Pact Powers*, Department of State Publication 5909 (U.S. Government Printing Office: Washington, 1955), p. 15.

36. *Ibid.*, pp. 26-28. 37. *The Bangkok Post*, June 1, 1953.

38. *Ibid.*, March 30, 1953. 39. *Ibid.*, April 23, 1954.

40. *Ibid.*, December 18, 1951. 41. *Ibid.*, December 28, 1951.

42. Prince Chula Chakrabonse, "Siam's Anti-Communist Role," *Standard*, May 22, 1954.

43. Edwin F. Stanton, *Brief Authority* (New York: Harper and Brothers, 1956), p. 270.

44. *The Bangkok Post*, March 25, 1952.

45. American-educated Pote Sarasin who was also popular with the Americans was selected to replace Prince Wan as the new Thai Ambassador to the United States.

46. *The Bangkok Post*, May 1949-December 1952, passim.

47. *Ibid.*, February 28, 1952. 48. *Ibid.*, November 11, 1952.

49. *Ibid.*, November 13, 1952. 50. *Ibid.*, November 20, 1952.

51. *Ibid.*, December 13, 1952. 52. *Ibid.*, December 27, 1952.

53. *Ibid.*, February 28, 1952.

54. Rupert Emerson, *Representative Government in Southeast Asia* (Harvard University Press: Cambridge, Massachusetts, 1955), p. 148.

55. *The Bangkok Post*, September 4, 1952. 56. *Ibid.*, November 12, 1953.

57. Personal interview with Thep Jotinuchit, June, 1956.

58. *The Bangkok Post*, January 23, 1954. 59. *Ibid.*

60. Personal interview with Klaew Norapati, June, 1956.

61. *The Bangkok Post*, September 17, 1954.

62. *Ibid.*, July 12, 1952. 63. *Ibid.*, January 18, 1952.

64. James Macgregor, "The Tragedy of Thailand," *The Progressive* (November, 1954), p. 13.

65. *Ibid.*

66. Virginia Thompson, "Thailand: Nationalism and Prosperity," *Current History* (August, 1952), p. 97.

67. Macgregor, *op. cit.*, p. 16.

CHAPTER V

1. *New York Times,* July 25, 1955. 2. *Ibid.,* April 21, 1955.

3. Statement by U.S. Ambassador Max W. Bishop at his press conference, March 3, 1956.

4. *The Bangkok Post,* August 10, 1955; September 15, 1956; May 31, 1957.

5. *Ibid.,* March 14, 1956. 6. *Ibid.,* July 30, 1956.

7. *New York Times,* March 9, 1955. 8. *Ibid.*

9. *The Bangkok Post,* September 16, 1955.

10. *New York Times,* March 17, 1955.

11. *The Bangkok Post,* February 23, 1956.

12. Indicative of Mr. Peurifoy's devotion to duty and his enthusiasm toward the military build-up of Thailand is the fact that his death came in an automobile accident while he was observing maneuvers by Thai police forces in southern Thailand. This tragedy also took the life of his young son.

13. *Ibid.,* January 11, 1955.

14. Personal interview with Police Deputy, Ubol Province, February, 1956.

15. *The Bangkok Post,* December 13, 1955.

16. *New York Times,* June 10, 1957.

17. *The Bangkok Post,* March 4, 1956.

18. Statement by U.S. Ambassador Max W. Bishop, *op. cit.,* p. 5.

19. *The Bangkok Post,* June 2, 1956.

20. *Ibid.,* January 16, 1956. 21. *Ibid.,* January 24, 1956.

22. *Ibid.,* June 1955 to September 1957, passim.

23. *New York Times,* July 9, 1956. 24. *Ibid.*

25. *The Bangkok Post,* January 12, 1956. 26. *Ibid.,* October 18, 1955.

27. *Ibid.,* March 20, 1956. 28. *The Bangkok Post,* April 25, 1955.

29. *New York Times,* April 26, 1955. 30. *Ibid.,* May 4, 1955.

31. *Ibid.* 32. *Ibid.,* May 5, 1955.

33. *The Bangkok Post,* May 5, 1955.

34. *U.S. News and World Report,* May 20, 1955.

35. *New York Times,* May 11, 1955. 36. *Ibid.*

37. The influence of General Donovan in obtaining this distinctive honor for Phibun was revealed when the former ambassador to Thailand presided on behalf of Dr. Grayson Kirk at the meeting where this honorary degree was conferred.

38. *New York Times,* May 3, 1955. 39. *Ibid.*

40. *The Bangkok Post,* May 4, 1955.

41. *New York Times,* May 11, 1955. 42. *Ibid.,* May 18, 1955.

43. *The Bangkok Post,* July 1, 1955. 44. *Ibid.,* October 14, 1955.

45. *Ibid.,* July 8, 1955. 46. *Ibid.,* July 19, 1955.

47. *Ibid.,* August 19, 1955. 48. *Ibid.,* August 24, 1955.

49. "Pibul Imports Democracy," *The Economist* (September 3, 1955).

50. Darrell Berrigan, "Thailand: Pibul Tries Prachathipatai," *The Reporter,* (June 14, 1956), pp. 32-3. "Prachathipatai is the Thai word for "democracy."

51. *The Bangkok Post,* July 1, 1955. 52. *Ibid.,* January 5, 1956.

53. "A New Look in Siam," *The World Today* (December, 1955), pp. 504-5.

54. *The Bangkok Post,* August 19, 1955. 55. *Ibid.,* July 29, 1955.

56. Berrigan, *op. cit.*, p. 30. 57. *The Bangkok Post,* January 3, 1956.
58. *Ibid.*, October 22, 1955. 59. *New York Times,* February 23, 1956.
60. *Ibid.* 61. *The Bangkok Post,* February 22, 1956.
62. *Ibid.*, May 28, 1956. 63. *Ibid.*, November 3, 1955.
64. *Ibid.*, February 4, 1957. 65. *Ibid.*, September 12, 1956.
66. *The Bangkok Post,* October 18, 1955. 67. *Ibid.*, October 5, 1955.
68. *Ibid.*, October 8, 1955. 69. *New York Times,* June 12, 1956.
70. *The Bangkok Post,* March 28, 1957. 71. *Ibid.*
72. *Ibid.*, January 27, 1956. 73. *Ibid.*, June 26, 1956.
74. *Ibid.*, January 6, 1957.

75. David A. Wilson and Herbert P. Phillips, "Elections and Parties in Thailand," *Far Eastern Survey* (August, 1958), p. 116.

76. Albert Pickerell and Daniel E. Moore, "Elections in Thailand," *Far Eastern Survey* (June, 1957), pp. 95-6.

77. *The Bangkok Post,* July 16, 1955.

78. *New York Times,* March 2, 1957.

79. "The Siamese Elections of February 1957," *The World Today,* May, 1957, p. 223.

80. *The Bangkok Post,* February 26, 1957. "Firecards" are illegal ballots already marked in favor of a candidate which are placed in ballot boxes by persons who are not registered in a voting district. "Paratroops" are illegal voters who cast votes in the name of a legally registered voter in a voting district.

81. *Ibid.*, February 27, 1957. 82. *Ibid.*, February 28, 1957.
83. *Ibid.*, March 6, 1957. 84. *New York Times,* March 1, 1957.
85. *Siam Rath Weekly Review,* February 28, 1957.
86. *The Bangkok Post,* March 2, 1957.
87. *New York Times,* March 2, 1957.
88. *Siam Rath Weekly Review,* March 21, 1957.
89. *New York Times,* March 3, 1957. 90. *Ibid.*
91. Pickerell and Moore, *op. cit.*, p. 92.
92. *New York Times,* March 5, 1957. 93. *Ibid.*
94. *The Bangkok Post,* March 4, 1957.
95. *Ibid.*, March 5, 1957, citing SEATO communique.
96. *New York Times,* March 11, 1957.
97. *The Bangkok Post,* March 7, 1957.
98. *New York Times,* June 18, 1957.
99. *The Bangkok Post,* May 2, 1957. 100. *Ibid.*, July 21, 1957.
101. *The Christian Science Monitor,* September 13, 1957.

102. In 1688 the Thai overthrew King Narai for excessively intimate relations with the French and kept Europeans out of their country for almost two centuries. In 1932 King Prajadhipok was overthrown by the Western-influenced People's Party partly because the royalists retained extremely close contacts with ultra-conservative European economic and social interest groups. And during World War II Phibun became extremely unpopular due to his early collaboration with the Japanese. When the Japanese withdrew their support from Phibun in 1944 the Premier was promptly overthrown.

103. *New York Times,* September 13, 1957.
104. *Ibid.*, September 17, 1957. 105. *Ibid.*, September 18, 1957.
106. *The Bangkok Post,* September 20, 1957.

CHAPTER VI

1. *New York Times,* November 6, 1957.
2. *The Bangkok Post,* December 27, 1957.
3. *New York Times,* December 4, 1959.
4. *Ibid.,* March 2, 1960. 5. *Ibid.,* October 22, 1958.
6. *Newsweek,* January 4, 1960.
7. *Economic Assistance and Progress in Thailand,* Address by U. Alexis Johnson, U.S. Ambassador to Thailand, May 11, 1960, Department of State Publication 7017, p. 6.
8. "The Happy Kingdom," *Fortune,* April, 1958, pp. 132-3.
9. *New York Times,* January 13, 1959.
10. *Ibid.,* April 16, 1960. For a detailed assessment of Thailand's economic system and proposals for and against public or private investment see *A Public Development Program for Thailand,* Report of a Mission organized by the International Bank for Reconstruction and Development at the request of the Government of Thailand (Baltimore: The John Hopkins Press, 1959) and "Some Crucial Issues in Thailand's Economic Development," Eliezer B. Ayal, *Pacific Affairs,* Summer 1961, pp. 157-164.
11. *The Bangkok Post,* September 12, 1958.
12. *Open Doors* 1959, Institute of International Education, May, 1959, pp. 42-3.
13. *Fact Sheet: Mutual Security in Action: Thailand,* Department of State Publication 6733, November, 1958.
14. *New York Times,* April 11, 1959.
15. *SEATO: Record of Progress* 1958-59, SEATO Headquarters, Bangkok, Thailand.
16. *The Bangkok Post,* May 8, 1958. 17. *Ibid.,* October 14, 1958.
18. *Chicago Daily News,* December 10, 1958.
19. *U.S. Department of State Bulletin,* July 25, 1960. King Phumiphon is the only reigning monarch in the world born in the United States.
20. *Congressional Record, Proceedings and Debates of the 86th Congress, Second Session,* Vol. 106, June 29, 1960, pp. 13894-5.
21. *New York Times,* June 2, 1959.
22. *The Bangkok Post,* December 23, 1958.
23. *Report to Congress on the Mutual Security Program,* Department of State Publication 6926, January 1960, p. 5.
24. *Ibid.*
25. Edwin F. Stanton, "Communist Pressures in Thailand," *Current History,* February, 1960, pp. 106-7.
26. *New York Times,* April 5, 1959. 27. *Ibid.,* November 6, 1957.
28. *Ibid.* 29. *Ibid.,* November 19, 1957.
30. *Ibid.,* November 30, 1957. 31. *Ibid.,* October 25, 1958.
32. *Life,* December 1, 1958, p. 38. 33. *New York Times,* March 22, 1959.
34. *The Bangkok Post,* September 24, 1961.
35. *Ibid.,* December 16, 1957.
36. *New York Times,* December 28, 1957.
37. "Siam Stays Right," *The Economist,* December 21, 1957.
38. *The Bangkok Post,* January 2, 1958.

39. David A. Wilson and Herbert P. Phillips, "Elections and Parties in Thailand," *Far Eastern Survey* (August, 1958), p. 117.
40. *The Bangkok Post,* July 7, 1958.
41. *Ibid.,* March 18, 1958. 42. *Ibid.,* June 13, 1958.
43. *New York Times,* October 21, 1958.
44. Darrell Berrigan, "Tidying Up in Thailand," *The Reporter* (November 27, 1958), p. 29.
45. *The Bangkok Post,* October 24, 1958.
46. *New York Times,* October 21, 1958.
47. *The Bangkok Post,* October 21, 1958.
48. *New York Times,* October 22, 1958.
49. *The Bangkok Post,* October 20, 1958.
50. *Ibid.,* October 22, 1958. 51. *Ibid.,* October 24, 1958.
52. Berrigan, *loc. cit.* 53. *Ibid.*
54. *The Christian Science Monitor,* October 23, 1958.
55. *The Bangkok Post,* October 20, 1958.
56. *Ibid.,* November 3, 1958. 57. *Ibid.,* December 11, 1958.
58. Berrigan, *loc. cit.* 59. *Ibid.*
60. Article 10.
61. The essence of the Enabling Act declared: "The Fuehrer must have all the rights demanded by him to achieve victory. Therefore—without being bound by existing legal regulations—in his capacity as Leader of the Nation the Fuehrer must be in a position to force, with all the means at his disposal, every German, if necessary . . . to fulfill his duties. In case of violation of these duties the Fuehrer is entitled, regardless of rights, to mete out punishment and remove the offender from his post, rank and position without introducing prescribed procedures." Cited in Alan Bullock, *Hitler A Study in Tyranny* (New York: Bantam Books, Inc., 1958), p. 340.
62. *The Bangkok Post,* February 5, 1959. 63. *Ibid.*
64. *New York Times,* April 5, 1959.
65. *The Bangkok Post,* November 5, 1958.
66. David A. Wilson, "Thailand: A New Leader," *Asian Survey* (February, 1964), p. 712.
67. *The Bangkok Post,* November 7, 1958.
68. *Ibid.,* November 10, 1958. 69. *New York Times,* July 7, 1959.
70. *The Bangkok Post,* January 5, 1959.
71. *Ibid.,* March 23, 1959.
72. *Ibid.,* March 10, 1959, citing Thanad's address to the American Association of Thailand entitled "A New Era for Thailand."
73. *The Christian Science Monitor,* August 12, 1963.
74. *The Bangkok Post,* December 11, 1959.
75. *Ibid.,* July 26, 1958. 76. *New York Times,* April 9, 1959.
77. *Ibid.,* May 13, 1960.
78. David A. Wilson, "Thailand: Old Leaders and New Directions," *Asian Survey* (February, 1963), p. 87 citing *The Bangkok Post,* September 6, 1961.
79. *New York Times,* October 25, 1960. 80. *Ibid.,* November 3, 1960.
81. Darrell Berrigan, "Thailand Is On the Spot," *The Reporter,* January 19, 1961, pp. 30-1.

82. *Newsweek,* March 27, 1961.

83. John F. Kennedy, "Urgent National Needs," Department of State Publication 7204, June 1961, pp. 2-16, passim.

84. *New York Times,* March 27, 1961.

85. *Newsweek,* May 15, 1961.

86. *New York Times,* May 18, 1961.

87. *Ibid.,* February 19, 1962.

88. *Ibid.,* June 10, 1962.

89. *U.S. Department of State Bulletin,* March 26, 1962.

90. *New York Times,* March 11, 1962.

91. *Ibid.,* May 16, 1962.

92. *Ibid.,* September 23, 1962.

93. *Ibid.,* June 3, 1961.

94. *Ibid.,* April 24, 1962.

95. *Ibid.,* January 13, 1964. Thanom also holds the post of Minister of Defense and Supreme Commander and Commander-in-Chief of the Army.

CHAPTER VII

1. Lucian Pye, "Armies in the Process of Political Modernization," Center for International Studies, Massachusetts Institute of Technology, July, 1959.

2. Dr. Edgar A. Schuler and Dr. Vibul Thammavit, *Public Opinion Among Thai Students: A Study of Opinions, Attitudes and Values Held by a Random Sample of Students in Colleges and Universities,* Thailand, 1959, p. 2.

3. *Life,* October 13, 1961, p. 50.

4. An intelligence report in early 1963 revealed that the Chinese Communists are building two roads from southern China to northern Laos. This report has aroused fears in the United States that the Chinese Communists may be preparing to launch military operations against Laos or Thailand. The likelihood of American retaliatory action combined with the long distance from the major industrial centers in China to Southeast Asia and the limited logistical capacity of the Chinese Communists would most probably require any such military operations to be of a limited nature.

5. Henry A. Kissinger, "Military Policy and Defense of the 'Grey Areas,'" *Foreign Affairs,* April 1955, p. 420. See also Alexander Eckstein, "The Limits to Chinese Power," *The New Republic,* January 19, 1963, pp. 15-8, whose major conclusion is that Communist China in the foreseeable future will be capable only of engaging in small scale military operations along its borders.

6. See Charles Windle and T. R. Vallance, "Optimizing Military Assistance Training," *World Politics,* October 1962, pp. 91-107.

7. Walter F. Vella, *The Impact of the West on Government in Thailand* (Berkeley and Los Angeles: University of California Press, 1955), p. 398.

INDEX